Kerry McSweeney is a member of the Department of English at Queen's University.

Four Contemporary Novelists

McGill-Queen's University Press   Scolar Press
Kingston and Montreal   London

Kerry McSweeney

Four Contemporary Novelists
Angus Wilson
Brian Moore
John Fowles
V.S. Naipaul

© McGill-Queen's University Press 1983
ISBN 0-7735-0399-4
Legal deposit 1st quarter 1983
Bibliothèque nationale du Québec

Printed in Canada

First published in Great Britain in 1983 by

SCOLAR PRESS
James Price Publishing Limited
13 Brunswick Centre
London WC1N 1AF

ISBN 0-85967-673-0

Canadian Cataloguing in Publication Data

McSweeney, Kerry, 1941-
Four contemporary novelists

Includes index.
ISBN 0-7735-0399-4

1. English fiction - 20th century - History and
criticism.   2. Fiction - Technique.   3. Realism in
literature.   I. Title.

PR881.M38   823'.91409   C82-094647-8

British Library Cataloguing in Publication Data

McSweeney, Kerry
Four contemporary novelists.
1. English fiction - 20th century -
History and criticism
I. Title
823'.912'09   PR881

ISBN 0-85967-673-0

Contents

For Susanne

Acknowledgments

Several persons read and commented on parts of my book: John Metcalf of Ottawa, John Mills of Simon Fraser University, David Staines of the University of Ottawa, Edward Baugh of the University of the West Indies, and my colleague Colin Norman. I am grateful to David Norton of McGill University and A.C. Hamilton of Queen's University for their counsel, and to Brian Cox of the University of Manchester for the opportunity to write about three of my subjects in the *Critical Quarterly*. Avrom Fleishman of Johns Hopkins University took the time to answer queries, as did Barry N. Olshen of Glendon College, York University, and J.H. Stape of the University of British Columbia. I would also like to thank John Beal of the Queen's University School of Graduate Studies for his encouragement, and the School's Advisory Research Committee for its support. Kathy Goodfriend and Sherril Barr once again cheerfully typed their way through a manuscript of mine. Donna Ketchen helped with the index. Lucy and Kendra McSweeney were helpful in other ways.

Earlier versions of parts of this book appeared in the *Critical Quarterly*, the *Journal of Modern Literature*, and the *Wascana Review*. Their editors have kindly granted permission to reprint. I am also grateful to the following for permission to quote: Faber & Faber and Farrar, Straus & Giroux for the extracts from Philip Larkin's *The Whitsun Weddings* and *High Windows*, Marvell Press for the extract from Larkin's *The Less Deceived*, and Alfred A. Knopf and Faber & Faber for the extract from Wallace Stevens's *Collected Poems*.

This book has been published with the help of a grant from the Canadian Federation for the Humanities, using funds provided by the Social Sciences and Humanities Research Council of Canada. Publication has also been assisted by the Canada Council under its block grant program.

Introduction

The following chapters offer accounts of the fiction of Angus Wilson, Brian Moore, John Fowles, and V.S. Naipaul. I have attempted to chart the development of each writer; identify dominant themes, controlling techniques, and informing sensibility; explain what each has tried to accomplish and compare theory to practice; provide an appropriate context for appreciation and evaluation of all parts of each canon; and make qualitative discriminations. In subject matter, themes, schemata, style, and sensibility each novelist is distinctly different from the others; the contexts within which their work has tended to be discussed are also dissimilar. Most of the critical commentary on Naipaul has been by students of Commonwealth literature. Of the three monographs devoted to Moore's fiction one is in a series on Irish writers, the other two in series on Canadian writers; and one of the best discussions of his work is in a book called *Forces and Themes in Ulster Fiction*. As for Wilson and Fowles: though their novels have attracted a good deal of sophisticated commentary, there has been a tendency, especially on the part of British critics, to see their fiction through the prism of the condition-of-the-contemporary-English-novel question. By bringing these four novelists together I hope to create a less partial and less parochial context within which to analyse and assess their work. If one adopts a sufficiently comprehensive perspective it becomes possible to see some important similarities among the four.

By far the most important resemblance is that in a time of widespread feeling that the form of the realistic novel is exhausted and no longer able to perform its traditional moral functions and of widespread interest in alternative forms (metafiction, fabulation, *anti-romans, ficciones,* comic apocalypses, documentary fiction), Wilson, Moore, Fowles, and Naipaul have remained committed to the representational, communicative, and instructive functions of the novel. Despite the contemporary *crise de roman*, none has had any doubts about the continuing vitality and centrality of the form. Naipaul rejects out of hand the diagnosis of exhaustion: "I don't believe that the world has all been written about. The world is so new."[1] For him, if "the novel as a form no longer carries conviction," the reason is that "experimentation ... has corrupted response; and there is a great confusion in the minds of readers and writers about the purpose of the novel. The novelist, like the painter, no longer recognizes his interpretive function." As a result, "the world we inhabit, which is always new, goes by unexamined, made ordinary by the camera, unmeditated on; and there is no one to awaken the sense of true wonder. That is perhaps a fair definition of the novelist's purpose, in all ages."[2] In describing his intentions as a writer of fiction, Brian Moore has several times invoked Joyce's "wonderful phrase ... 'the celebration of the commonplace'."[3] And he has remarked that "one of the crises of the novel that nobody discusses nowadays" is that writers are "losing sight of that real world in which our parents and relatives still live ... [that] real, ordinary, dull world."[4]

Wilson and Fowles have considered at some length the question of whether the novel is a dead form. In "The Dilemma of the Contemporary Novelist," the former notes that those "who speak rather blithely of the disappearance of the novelist ... are usually anti-humanist in tendency [and] have not any very strong feelings about human individuals as such." The novelist, on the other hand, is "essentially a humanist." Of the threats which appear to menace the novel, Wilson is unconcerned by "the problem of the visual medium." He even believes that film and television are salutary: in supplying popular entertainment they free the serious novelist to get on with his proper task. The emphasis on the factual or documentary novel is a more serious threat. Like Naipaul, who calls the documentary approach "the final dereliction of artistic responsibility,"[5] Wilson insists that the documentary aspect of novels "does not matter at all." A conception of the novel, à la James and Flaubert, as "pure art" is also threatening, for "the element of humanity is essential in the novel," which deals "with human beings and with human emotions; it is a projection of another human being's feelings about the humanity around him." For this reason the novel is "the most hopeful form of communication in the present age. It is a sort of breakdown by corresponding imaginations of the immense isolation that we all feel."[6]

In an article called "Is the Novel Dead?" Fowles opens by asserting that "the novel survives and is going to survive." Like Wilson, he is unconcerned by the competition of film and television: "that we [novelists] have lost the bored-fool part of our audience is not a cultural tragedy, but thoroughly healthy." The "basic question" is whether "as a means of communicating human experience [there are] special functions and capacities of the novel form that no other art can reproduce." Fowles is quite sure there are, though he admits that there are "many traitors in the camp," ranging from the novelists who are "writing film scripts in disguise" to those writing "technical exercises in style or quasi-philosophical theses."

There are, Fowles observes, countless things the novelist can do that no filmmaker can: depict in detail a psychological state of mind; relate present feelings to past ones; use similes and metaphors. In fact, the only boundaries to a novel are words, "man's most flexible and highly developed tool." This recognition leads to Fowles's principal point: that the most important function of the novel lies in "the fundamental uniqueness of the reading experience": that reading is a co-operative activity. A film or a television play "is the tyranny of the maker's imagination upon those of his passive viewers." But in a novel, since "words can only suggest the events and people and moods they describe," the reader must use his own imagination in collaboration with the author's, for "the only meaningful actualization" of a novel "takes place in the reader's mind." To denigrate the novel is to denigrate "something much more essential to human development and vital to human happiness – the right, the power and the need to exercise the individual imagination."[7]

All four novelists are, then, convinced of the continuing vitality of the novel as a unique medium for communicating human experience, and all are committed to its traditional constructive concerns. At the same time, however, the work of each novelist has been affected by various contemporary pressures and by an awareness of what Bernard Bergonzi calls "the essentially problematic nature of fictional form in our time."[8] Take, for example, the question of fictional endings, concerning which Naipaul has observed:

I don't think it is possible any longer for people to write those novels where you could say, "They lived happily ever afterwards," because we no longer have this assurance of the world going on. Societies everywhere have been fractured by all kinds of change: technological, social, political. We can no longer regard the action of a novel as covering a little crisis, a little curve on the graph which will then revert to the nice, flat, straight, ordered life: and I think this is one reason why ... the traditional novel is just no longer possible. It is also one reason why people find it very hard nowadays to read fiction, and why people go back to what they call the old masters. I think there's an element of nostalgia in reading Hardy, and even in reading Dickens or George Eliot. There is narrative there, the slow development of character, and people are longing for this vanished, ordered world.[9]

Fowles's views on the subject of endings are similar. Indeed, Naipaul's observation provides a perfect gloss not only for the notorious dual endings of *The French Lieutenant's Woman* but also for the opening of the last chapter of *The Magus*:

The smallest hope, a bare continuing to exist, is enough for the anti-hero's future; leave him, says our age, leave him where mankind is in its history, at a crossroads, in a dilemma, with all to lose and only more of the same to win; let him survive, but give him no direction, no reward; because we too are waiting, in our solitary rooms where the telephone never rings, waiting for this girl, this truth, this crystal of humanity, this reality lost through imagination, to return; and to say she returns is a lie.

But the maze has no centre. An ending is no more than a point in sequence, a snip of the cutting shears. Benedick kissed Beatrice at last; but ten years later? And Elsinore, that following spring?

So ten more days. But what happened in the following years shall be silence; another mystery.

Brian Moore echoes Naipaul when he says about the termination of his novels: "I try to make fiction as open-ended as life. In other words, I do not try to write nineteenth-century novels ... "[10] And while Angus Wilson's early novels tended to end on an upbeat note (however ironically qualified), his later novels end less conclusively and less positively, one of them with an explicit rejection of the evolutionary optimism of the harvest scene finale of E.M. Forster's *Howards End*.

The reflexive concern with endings is part of a larger aspect of the fiction of all four writers: the inescapable self-consciousness which as contemporary novelists they share, and the consequent effort of each to express and put to positive use this reflexive awareness. Fowles has succinctly diagnosed the condition and placed it in historical perspective:

The so-called "crisis" of the modern novel has to do with its self-consciousness. The fault was always inherent in the form, since it is fundamentally a kind of game, an artifice that allows the writer to play hide-and-seek with the reader. In strict terms a novel is a hypothesis more or less ingeniously and persuasively presented – that is, first cousin to a lie. This uneasy consciousness of lying is why in the great majority of novels the novelist apes reality so assiduously; and is why giving the game away – making the lie, the fictitiousness of the process, explicit in the text – has become such a feature of the contemporary novel. Committed to invention, to people that never existed, to events that never happened, the novelist wants either to sound "true" or to come clean.[11]

In *The French Lieutenant's Woman* Fowles brilliantly exploits the novelist's impulse to both sound "true" and "come clean." So does Angus Wilson in two of his later novels, in which his self-consciousness is channelled into "alienation techniques" designed to disturb the "over-smooth" relationship between the writer and the reader of the traditional novel.[12] V.S.Naipaul has explained that his conception of writing as a "religious act" intimately connected with self-knowledge is rooted in his awareness that:

There's something absurd about the fictional form: it's an artificial activity, made-up people taking part in invented actions. The first thing for the writer to understand is *why* he's setting all these people in motion ... But at quite an early stage writing becomes a religious act, with the discovery and knowledge of oneself, of what one is. This is where, from simply wishing to *be* a writer, one has to discard all one's concepts of "the writer," discard everything one has read. It becomes a solitary occupation, an exercise in self-knowledge. Because these absurd characters who act out artificial stories must come out of a certain moment of resolution – of a mood, a situation, an attitude to the world. There must be a *centre*.[13]

While he has an active dislike of technical experimentation, structural deformation, or any display of authorial self-consciousness, Naipaul has made the creative process – the "slow magic" of writing and its power to repair loss – a central subject of one of his novels and an important theme in two others. Finally, while scrupulous realism and a concern for ordinary humanity were the hallmarks of Brian Moore's early works, two of his later novels have been portraits of the artist with strong autobiographical overtones; another uses a fantastic premise to explore the creative process and the relationship of the artist to his creation and his public.

Of course the self-conscious awareness that novel writing is an artificial activity, the employment of alienating techniques and supra-realistic devices, and the tendency to make the creative process a subject of the novel are hardly peculiar to these four contemporary novelists. What does give them a special affinity is that their various expressive concerns and self-conscious devices have remained subservient to their constructive and communicative concerns; and while they have made the reader-writer contract more complex, they have never undermined its representational basis.

Chapter One

Angus Wilson: Diversity, Depth, and Obsessive Energy

I

One of the most impressive features of Angus Wilson's career as a novelist has been his ability to keep from repeating himself; each of his eight novels has been a fresh, ambitious conception, and he has never hesitated to make heavy demands upon his powers of invention, stylistic fluency, and technical adroitness. This variety and range, however, should not obscure the fact that the informing concerns of Wilson's novels have remained consistent. As a novelist of manners and a social realist Wilson offers in his fiction incisive (sometimes devastating) depictions of various sections of English middle class society in the twentieth century, particularly since the Second World War. But Wilson is not only a Balzacian secretary of English society; as C.B. Cox showed in *The Free Spirit: A Study of Liberal Humanism in the Novels of George Eliot, Henry James, E.M. Forster, Virgina Woolf, Angus Wilson,* he is also a novelist of morals and a prober of the ethical life, in particular of the dilemmas of liberal humanists who are forced to confront the reality of evil without and within. These two representational concerns are complementary and mutually reinforcing; they can be further strengthened (but also qualified, even undermined) by the third informing principle of Wilson's fiction, which may be called expressive. Each of his novels is in some degree energized by Wilson's obsessive sense of the black, cruel, and destructive forces in human life, which he once called his "grand guignol side, ... a great lump of a kind of Dickensianism [which] distinguishes me from that sort of George Eliot writing."[1]

Wilson is not only one of England's foremost contemporary novelists; he is also an exemplary figure whose development as a writer has been representative of some major changes that have taken place in the English novel since the war.[2] Born in 1913, Wilson comes a generation after the great experimental novelists of the early twentieth century; in his first two novels – *Hemlock and After* and *Anglo-Saxon Attitudes* – he consciously set out to bring back into English fiction something of the social breadth of the nineteenth-century novel; as he wrote in 1951, "some elements of social realism must return to the novel if it is going to be reintegrated into modern life."[3] At the same time, Wilson deeply admired the achievement of modernist writers like Henry James and Virginia Woolf in exploring the inner life of their characters. His third novel, *The Middle Age of Mrs Eliot*, was a product of his attempt to combine nineteenth-century *diversity* with modernist *depth*. In later novels like *No Laughing Matter* and *As If by Magic* a *tertium quid* enters the picture: for by the mid-1960s Wilson had come to recognize "the essentially problematic nature of fictional form in our time" and to introduce into his fiction various alienating devices and self-referential features designed to call attention to the fictive nature of the text. At the same time, these *anti-roman* techniques provided Wilson with a fresh channel into which his obsessive emotions could flow; just as his interest in diversity plus depth is related to his ambitions as a socio-moral novelist, his interest in alienating devices is related as much to his grand guignol side as it is to the contemporary fictional climate.

In addition to his novels, Wilson has written a good deal of critical commentary since he began his literary career in the late 1940s. The richness of this body of writing on novels and novelists would be more apparent if the best of his articles, review articles, reviews, introductions, lectures, and interviews were collected in a volume that could stand between his biographical-critical studies of Zola (1952), Dickens (1970), and Kipling (1978) on the one hand and *The Wild Garden or Speaking of Writing* (1963), his critical study of his own life and early work, on the other. In addition to its intrinsic value, this material throws a good deal of light on Wilson's novels and I have not hesitated to make use of it in the following examination of the interrelationship of social, moral, and expressive concerns in each of the novels, and of the major techniques and formal devices used to present them. It is the interpenetration of these concerns that gives Wilson's canon much of its complexity and richness, and that must be regarded as the principal gauge of his achievement as a novelist.

II

Wilson's first two books were collections of short stories. *The Wrong Set* (1949) and *Such Darling Dodos* (1950) brought him immediate critical recognition: Edmund Wilson, for example, spoke of their author as the successor to Evelyn Waugh; and V.S. Naipaul was to observe that the "conventions and modes of English speech [had] never been better dissected."[4] In his next book, *Hemlock and After* (1952) Wilson successfully made on his first attempt the often difficult transition from short story writer to novelist. Rich to the point of congestion – there are twenty-five characters packed into its 250 pages – *Hemlock and After* is an ambitious attempt on Wilson's part to do justice to each of his social, moral, and expressive concerns as a novelist.

Set in 1951, the novel depicts pockets of post-war English society with the same caustic brilliance, pitiless detachment, and eye and ear for telling detail that made his early stories so impressive. Wilson is particularly hard on the affluent business and professional commuters to London who form the *soi-disant* gentry of Vardon, the Home Counties' town in which most of the novel takes place. Their neo-conservative, authoritarian views are epitomized by James Sands, a barrister with no interest in "understanding humanity. Indeed, the whole appeal of the law ... lay in his belief in justice. If people were too weak or too stupid to cope with life as it was, they had to be taught." This set is contrasted with older characters of liberal disposition whose roots are in the 1920s and 1930s. Chief among them is Bernard Sands (the father of James), a distinguished novelist in his late fifties, who as the novel opens seems remarkably successful in both public and private life. On the one hand he has at last brought to fruition his scheme for the establishment at Vardon Hall of a government-sponsored home for young creative writers; on the other his autumnal indulgence of long-suppressed homosexual tastes has, so he thinks, involved no compromises with his exacting humanist ideals. Sands's efforts on behalf of Vardon Hall bring him into contact with representatives of the civil service and the cultural establishment; his "divergence from sexual orthodoxy" introduces the reader to the gay world of London, in particular the "golden spiv group" of young adventurers who exist "in a state of moral anaemia" on the "homosexual borderland between respectability and *loucherie*." In the novel's principal set piece, the comedy-of-manners account of the disastrous opening day ceremonies at Vardon Hall, representatives of these and other social enclaves are brought into collision.

The central subject of *Hemlock and After* is the moral quandaries of Bernard Sands, the prototype of the Wilsonian baffled liberal humanist. Sands believes in tolerance, compassion, intelligence, the dignity and freedom of the individual, and the primacy of personal relationships. Like E.M. Forster, he has devoted his energies as a writer and an enlightened member of society to upholding these values. The particular dilemmas that press upon him are equally common to liberal humanists. They concern the proper exercise of authority, purity of motive, "the dual nature of all human action," and the problem of evil. In the novel there are four foci of external evil: Hubert Rose, whose sexual compulsions necessitate the procuring of young girls; Sherman Winter, a vicious homosexual who is trying to entice into his web Terence Lambert, an ex-lover of Sands; Celia Craddock, whose theatrical charm masks a determination to keep for herself her twenty-one-year-old son, Sands's catamite; and Mrs Curry, an extraordinary procuress. Sands's efforts to confound the machinations of these characters are undermined by his discovery of the evil within himself. At the end of the first of the novel's three parts, while waiting in Leicester Square for a friend's arrival, Sands suddenly experiences an "intense ... violent excitement," "a sadistic excitement," when he sees the hopeless terror on the face of a young man being arrested for soliciting. This discovery brings in its wake the recognition of a hidden affinity between himself and "the saturnine arrogance of Hubert's sneer, or the blond malice of Sherman's 'camp' chatter, or the gracious jealousy of Mrs. Craddock's careful charm, or the enveloping hatred of Mrs. Curry's sweet cooing ... it was not an external picture of concerted enemies that he saw, but the reflection of his own guilt, of his newly discovered hypocrisy, his long-suppressed lusts."

One of the shortcomings of *Hemlock and After* is that the Leicester Square scene is rather too stagy and insufficiently prepared for. Sands is moved too quickly from a time of almost "complete bliss" to the incapacitating shock of recognition that begins his slide towards death. As a result the reader never really becomes convinced of his internal evil or considers it as serious a matter as Sands himself does. Another reason for this failure to convince fully has to do with the conventional limitations of 1952 concerning the degree of sexual explicitness allowable in a novel. One does understand that Sands's interests in comely homosexuals are not simply benevolent and preceptorial; but no attempt is made to depict the physical side of his taste for young male flesh. As a result, the evil and grossness within Sands have to be suggested tangentially (through the malign *frisson* in Leicester Square) or symbolically, as they are through Mrs Curry and Hubert Rose. The "horrible *ménage*" of the former, as Evelyn Waugh saw, "forms a caricature of the secret life of Mr Sands."[5] As fat, suety, and corrupt as he is thin, ironic, and devoted to the higher ethical life, Mrs Curry is Sands's opposite equal. The force of this symbolic linkage is weakened, however, because Mrs Curry is not quite believable in her own right as a character in a realistic novel. She is too untempered a product of Wilson's grand guignol side. The omniscient narrator of *Hemlock and After* knows this perfectly well: one of the first things said of Mrs Curry is that this "elephant figure of animated–cartoon chubbiness before her vulgar, picturesque teacosy cottage was a cinch, of course, for a symbol."[6] There are also difficulties with the presentation of Hubert Rose, Sands's principal antagonist. These have been excellently analysed by Karin Wogatzky, who argues that Wilson's admiration for Dostoevsky led him to the unfeasible attempt to make Rose a symbolic double of Sands and an embodiment of "transcendent evil." But Rose's character and his inner life are insufficiently developed and as an agnostic humanist Wilson is ill equipped to "present demonic evil and deal with it as a metaphysical problem as Dostoevsky does in *The Possessed*."[7]

The closing section of *Hemlock and After* is also imperfect. Just as there is too much of the grand guignol in Mrs Curry and too much of Dostoevsky in Hubert Rose, so there is something too sentimental (and too perfunctory) about what happens after Sands's death. What is drunk after the hemlock tastes faintly of bromide as we are shown how, with the help of his widow, who is too abruptly restored to mental health after a long illness, Bernard Sands's good lives after him: little Elsie Black is saved from Hubert Rose, Terence Lambert from Sherman Winter, Eric Craddock from his mother, and Bernard's sister Isobel from a career she hates; and Mrs Curry's activities are at least temporarily checked. Wilson subsequently came to recognize the imperfections of *Hemlock and After*, pointing out that it was shorter than it should have been (a comment that no one would make about his next six novels) and even claiming that its mixture of diverse "elements and modes [made] it a failure as a novel." Certainly there is some point to the first of these observations: the scale of *Hemlock and After* is not equal to its scope, and there are discontinuities caused by trying to touch so many bases. But on the whole Wilson was surely right to claim for his first novel "an originality and a directness, freshness," and Evelyn Waugh to describe it as "a singularly rich, compact and intricate artifact."[8]

In the six years following the publication of *Hemlock and After*, Wilson published some interesting reflections on the state of English fiction and on his own ambitions as a novelist. "The Future of the English Novel," "Diversity and Depth," and an interview he gave to the *Paris Review* all date from the mid- to late 1950s and have several important features in common.[9] In the first of them Wilson examined "the climate in which English novels are written today." He allowed that "like other literary forms" the novel depended upon "a personal vision and adequate powers of endurance to battle with the formal problems of communicating that vision." But novels, he insisted, differ from other literary forms "in two important respects. They are works of entertainment and, since they express their meaning in terms of characters, they are ultimately social statements." Owing to the great inter-war novelists' "absorption with psychology" and with "indirect presentations of the external world – interior monologue and stream-of-consciousness writing," the "entertainment element of serious novels has begun to disappear; and its absence has undoubtedly impoverished English novels." There were signs of a change for the better, but "the elements of narrative and description," which could do much to make the serious novel competent entertainment, "were still insufficiently utilized." On the other hand, the "essential relationship" between the novelist and his society was confused. The "social context of novels has become a somewhat disreputable theme, not only because of its flavour of easy marxist analysis, but also because social realism has become the refuge of the novelist without vocation." Documentary representations of parts of the social scene have nothing to do with the novelist's "essential relationship" to society. But – at this point Wilson's analysis becomes cryptic and reflexive – while a sense of social reality was important to the novelist, old social orders had changed and a "new ruling class" had come into being. This was "a world which [could not] inform the creations of those of us [authentic novelists?] who were born before it came into being." Those who attempted to use this world for creative inspiration would "fall into documentary."

In the *Paris Review* interview Wilson had a good deal to say about his second novel. *Anglo-Saxon Attitudes* (1956) is the story of the awakening of the conscience of Gerald Middleton, a sixty-year-old professor of me-dieval English history who belatedly attempts to satisfy his suspicions con-cerning the possible perpetration years before of a hoax (the placing of a pagan idol in the East Anglian tomb of a seventh-century bishop) with important consequences for historical scholarship, and to involve himself in the affairs of his wife and children, from whom he has long been es-tranged. With its complex plot rooted in past mystery and in what Mid-dleton calls "complicated webs of muddled human activity" which reach out to involve a wealth of characters from a variety of social strata, *Anglo-Saxon Attitudes* is Wilson's most Dickensian novel. Its title, a phrase from *Through the Looking-Glass*, refers not only to the Anglo-Saxon period, the subject of the researches of Middleton and his colleagues, but also to the complex of attitudes and prejudices that made up the English temperament of the 1950s. In the interview Wilson admitted that he was deliberately trying "to get back to the Dickens tradition." He was attempting "to con-vince the reader that he was seeing society as a whole" and to that end used "a lot of minor characters and subplots ... to suggest the existence of a wider society." In this and other ways his bias was reminiscent less of any of the great modernists than of their Victorian predecessors, for Wilson insisted that the reader "should be unaware of techniques" and the novelist should be "only concerned with exposing the human situation" in a way that will "touch the heart" of the reader.[10]

The social breadth of *Anglo-Saxon Attitudes* is undoubtedly impressive and there can be no question that as superior fictional entertainment this densely populated, dextrously plotted, and descriptively rich work is wholly successful. It is equally clear, however, that success on these levels was only achieved through the suppression of obsessive energy and at the cost of moral and psychological depth. The majority of the *dramatis personae* of

Anglo-Saxon Attitudes, which Wilson was subsequently to describe as "the most 'thought' ... and the least 'felt' " of his (first four) novels,[11] are social and intellectual types particularized by means of techniques related to those of caricature: verbal impersonation (at times approaching mimicry), as with Mrs Salad's cockney chatter; typing gestures, like Professor Clun's cutting "his roll into four equal pieces and [placing] on each of them an equal share of butter"; comic or grotesque exaggeration, for example Mr Cressett, the market gardener with the automatic memory, who is murdered by his daughter; and explanatory captions, like the gloss provided for an incident illustrating the character of Frank Rammage: "the little scene had satisfied the mixture of bullying and masochism that lay on the surface of his strange Dostoevskian philanthropy."

While the Dickensian proliferation of subordinate characters makes for a wealth of social notation which does suggest "the existence of a wider society," these characters do not at the same time possess the richness of psychological implication found in comparably presented characters in Dickens's great novels. In *Little Dorrit*, for instance, to give as examples only the "gallery of neurotics" cited by Wilson himself in his book on Dickens, there are Mrs Clennam, Miss Wade, Fanny Dorrit, Henry Gowan, Mrs Gowan, and Mr Dorrit.[12] In *Anglo-Saxon Attitudes*, on the other hand, the roots of only a very few of the characters reach down into the subsoil of Wilson's obsessive concerns. They include Larrie Rourke and Yves Houdet, who live off their sexual attractiveness and whose cloying surface charms mask an instinctive viciousness, and Dollie Stokesay and Elvira Portway (one a generational variation of the other), both liberated, sensual, vulnerable, and unusual in their direct honesty. But the only character in *Anglo-Saxon Attitudes* who can withstand even momentary comparison with the characters of *Little Dorrit* is the splendidly grotesque figure of Middleton's estranged wife Inge, a monster of emotional dishonesty, vicarious living, and predatory sentimentality – she describes as follows the convalescence of her repellent homosexual son, who despises, but is dependent upon, her: "He is so helpless still, but we are very happy. We have now our first fires with the pine cones that give such a lovely scent. We sit at the window and we watch the brown and yellow leaves falling down. Round and round they go, caught in great gusts of wind. Some people are made sad by it. But Johnnie and I are happy. We know that one day will come spring."

With Middleton, the only character whom Wilson attempts to present in the round, one can again be reminded of *Little Dorrit*, this time of Arthur Clennam. Both men are their novels' central figures, the points at which multiple plot lines converge, and the only characters of whom the reader is allowed extended inside views. The slow process by which both are recalled to life – Clennam to love, Middleton to moral responsibility and a positive acceptance of his loneliness – are their novels' principal thematic hinges. Dickens's difficulty in creating three-dimensional characters is notorious; Clennam is no exception. Wilson is more successful with Middleton. The parallels between his refusals to face the truth in his professional life and in his family life give depth to his characterization; and while his reinvolvement in the world of historical scholarship is successful, the results of his re-entry into the family sphere are more equivocal and more interesting. The stages in Middleton's moral regeneration are, however, rather too visibly engineered to be fully convincing or involving. This mechanical quality is seen most clearly in the long flashback sequence which concludes the first half of the novel. The pettiness and bitchiness of his family's Christmas Day conversations trigger memories that are juxtaposed with the present scene in a way that brings to a head Middleton's decades-long evasions of public and private responsibility. But despite Wilson's adroitness, this contrived expedient cannot shed its resemblances to what Middleton himself calls "such a clumsy stage situation."

In one important particular, however, Dickens's handling of his central character's inner life is clearly superior to Wilson's. In *Little Dorrit*, the central thematic aspects of Clennam's story – the dead hand of the past, the crippling power of money, emotional starvation, seeming versus being, self-imprisonment – are diffused through the novel; they are restated in different ways in the situations of other characters and intensified through a rich network of image and symbol. In *Anglo-Saxon Attitudes*, on the other hand, the moral propositions of Middleton's story are not disseminated throughout the novel. For example, the extended account of a meeting of medievalists near the novel's beginning may be "perhaps the most brilliantly observed scene in all Wilson's writing," but that is all it is.[13] And almost nowhere in *Anglo-Saxon Attitudes* does one find any of what Wilson calls that "diffusion of obsessive emotion ... which is the indefinable personality of the novel itself [and is] derived from the deepest level of its creator," and which accounts for the "magical power" of the great nineteenth-century novelists.[14] For example, the long account near the end of Marie-Hélène's party, which brings together many of the characters, is extraneous to the story of its central character (unlike the comparable scene of the opening of Vardon Hall in *Hemlock and After*). The party scene – its guests "absorbed in their habitual interchange of cultured nullities" – does exemplify the obsessive theme of "the hell of a society that has lost the power of communication" which runs through Wilson's early novels; but neither through analogy nor contrast is this theme effectively related to Middleton's dilemmas.

The notion of the hell of a society suggests a final point of comparison between *Anglo-Saxon Attitudes* and Dickens's novels. In *Little Dorrit*, as John Holloway has argued, distinctive aspects of a character's presentation, the exaggerations and distortions by which he or she is individualized, register the ways in which these figures have been warped by society. In Holloway's phrase, "caricaturing *is* characterization."[15] In the mature Dickens this shaping pressure is constantly felt and its marks are everywhere visible. In *Anglo-Saxon Attitudes* there is little sense of the influence of environment on character and personality. There is a great deal of incisive *social observation*, which is distilled into the depiction of a variety of sharply etched types, but there is very little real *social vision*. From this point of view, even admiration of the social breadth of Wilson's second novel must be qualified.

In "Diversity and Depth," published in 1958, two years after *Anglo-Saxon Attitudes*, Wilson showed a more balanced and considered awareness than he had in the *Paris Review* interview of the need for contemporary novelists to combine nineteenth-century diversity with modernist depth. Jane Austen, William Makepeace Thackeray, George Eliot, and Anthony Trollope could all "command the serious attention of men and women of affairs" in part because they set their characters in a "socially responsible setting," unlike "Chad or Stephen Dedalus or Birkin or Mrs Ramsey [who] for all the brilliant social observation that surrounds them, exist in a sort of intellectual and emotional separateness from responsible society at large." The need for diversity and a socially responsible setting pointed towards the reintroduction of "traditional forms": "the formal frameworks of plot, narrative sub-plot, suspense, or, in some hands, picaresque presentation."

There were, however, dangers inherent in the post-war return to the social novel. Through the work of Anthony Powell, C.P. Snow, and the early Doris Lessing the English novel once again had "a firm structure of contemporary society, an ethic set solidly in contemporary England." But these successes had one serious drawback, "the sacrifice of depth of vision for ... breadth of setting"; for the central characters of these novelists' *romans fleuves* – Powell's Nick Jenkins, Snow's Lewis Eliot, Lessing's Martha Quest – were "inferior in reality and depth" to the central characters of Virginia Woolf. And, Wilson admitted, so were Bernard Sands and Gerald Middleton, the central characters of his own first two novels. Wilson concluded by insisting that the need to combine "depth of vision" with "breadth of setting" was the principal problem for the contemporary English novelist, and that for this reason two things demanded strict attention: consideration of narrative point of view and a re-examination of the internal monologue form.

In the same year as "Diversity and Depth" appeared, Wilson published his third novel, clearly an attempt to resolve the problem posed in his article. *The Middle Age of Mrs Eliot*, the finest of his first three novels, has two central characters, Meg Eliot and her brother David Parker. The other characters (appreciably fewer than in *Anglo-Saxon Attitudes*) are depicted with Wilson's characteristic abundance of social notation and do create the sense of a "socially responsible" middle class setting. But they are never allowed to become objects of attention in their own right. They are present only for what they can tell us or (through comparison or contrast) show us about Meg or David. Even Else Bode, a melancholy version of Inge, who tells David that "The autumn trees will give meaning to your sadness" and Meg that "There is some sadness in this middle May all the same. The first time that young Spring finds himself a little tired and cannot think why it is so," is kept strictly under control. And there is a corresponding change in the narrative point of view. Omniscient narration, "the 'God's eye view' in frequent use among the nineteenth-century novelists I admire,"[16] which Wilson had employed so skilfully in *Hemlock and After* and *Anglo-Saxon Attitudes*, is replaced by a more restricted point of view. Everything in the novel is seen either through the eyes or over the shoulder of Meg or David.

Because of this sharpening of focus, the plot of *The Middle Age of Mrs Eliot* is uncomplicated. Given the initial premise of the violent death of Meg's husband in the novel's first part (he is shot in the airport lounge of an eastern capital while attempting to foil an assassination attempt), the story unfolds naturally and plausibly. And the novel's structure – the contrasts and parallels in the personalities and situations of Meg and David – has a powerful simplicity. Intimate during the genteel poverty of their childhood and adolescence, when they "had obliterated dreary hotel bedrooms and hideous furnished flats" by immersing themselves in nineteenth-century novels, Meg and David have grown apart during the years of her successful marriage to Bill and his equally stable relationship with Gordon Paget. Both husband and friend die during the course of the novel, and brother and sister enter difficult periods of transition. Meg eventually has a breakdown and comes to live with David at Andredaswood, his plant nursery. In the last of the novel's three parts, the loneliness and anxiety of each is gradually mitigated by the renewal of their childhood interdependence.

The strengths of *The Middle Age of Mrs Eliot* are owing to the moral and psychological insight which informs the characters of David and Meg. In the brother, Wilson has studied a syndrome analysed elsewhere in his fiction: the retreat from human involvement to which certain kinds of liberal humanists seem prone. David has determined that if Gordon dies it will be the climax of his own life and that he will never again allow himself to need others. He feels that emotional dependence would sap the inner strength necessary to maintain his stance of non-involvement with the world. Though this self-effacement comes "perilously near to negation," David feels it is the only posture that can keep his ideals intact and allow him "to cross the shapeless tract of human existence with grace and with gentleness." Like most of Wilson's central male characters, David is self-questioning and does wonder whether "his own carefully built up detachment [is] only a self-induced blindness to the Evil that governed the universe." But while he continually meditates on such questions, David can never bring himself to act upon their promptings. At the end of the novel, after his sister leaves Andredaswood, it is clear that David will never again be tempted from his life of sterilized isolation from the world, the only reward of which is depression and unhappy self-consciousness.

David's self-withering is tellingly portrayed, but it is the story of his sister and her troubles that dominates the novel named after her. As she prepares for her round-the-world trip with Bill, Meg makes certain that "the basic necessities of the voyage" are in her hand luggage: *Emma, The Mill on the Floss, The Small House at Allington, The Portrait of a Lady*. A little later she reflects that while the "high spirits" and "high hopes" of Emma Woodhouse, Maggie Tulliver, Lily Dale, and Isobel Archer "were hers exactly," she had been born in a later century and "had avoided their defeats." The principal function of these allusions is to help characterize Meg: her self-satisfied reflections on having avoided the plight of her fictional forbears, for example, is an index of her lack of self-knowledge and a foreshadowing of the *via dolorosa* she will have to walk. And later it is largely through novels and references to them that Meg and David reestablish contact with each other. But with a novelist as aware as Wilson of the tradition of English fiction, it is hard not to feel that these allusions also have an authorial reference. Like *The Middle Age of Mrs Eliot*, each of the nineteenth-century novels Meg takes on her journey offers a full-scale representation of the inner life of a forceful and impulsive central female character, each of whom attempts to impose her own vision on reality but comes to learn some sobering truths about herself and the world. In later novels like *No Laughing Matter* and *As If by Magic*, Wilson uses overt literary allusions to destabilize the reader and to raise questions about the status of the text and the novel's traditional mimetic and communicative functions. But in *The Middle Age of Mrs Eliot* the allusions rather reflect Wilson's abounding confidence (for which one wonders if *sprezzatura* or *chutzpah* is the better word) in his ability to paint a portrait of a contemporary lady, with a socially responsible setting as background, that will rival in moral richness and depth the canvasses of his nineteenth-century predecessors.

In Meg Eliot, Wilson dramatizes the working out of a crisis of personality caused by what Anthony Storr would call a dislocation between the inner world of subjectivity and the outer world of external reality, which "both compels re-examination of fundamentals and ... demands new creative solutions."[17] Though intelligent and perceptive, Meg is a worldly woman whose marital and social success, and whose busyness (including volunteer social work), have kept her at some distance from self-knowledge and from realization of the greyness of the human situation. "She's got such energy to skim over things," Gordon remarks; and David reflects that while "loneliness was the condition of man ... so many lives – Meg's for instance – seemed shaped to hide it."

In the second of the novel's three parts, the widowed Meg is introduced to reality. Not only must she adjust to sharply reduced circumstances and find some means of earning a living; she also has some home truths forced upon her, including her failure to detect a deep-seated unhappiness in her husband (which may have precipitated the intervention that cost him his life) and her unsuitability to be a social worker: for she would charm people's troubles away rather than help them to live with themselves – that is, she would impose on others the pattern of evasion that has characterized her own life. Internal pressures reach the point where Meg feels herself "unknown, a creature without purpose or place" and deprived of the "sense of intimacy she so desperately needed." Eventually she has a complete breakdown.

Meg's downward progress in this section is handled by Wilson with considerable skill. It is true that in one particular – the deployment of Viola, Poll, and Jill, Meg's oldest friends – there is more than a hint of signposting. These friends, whom Meg has come to think of as her "lame ducks," were all introduced early in the novel and the varieties of their reduced circumstances contrasted with Meg's affluent happiness. In the second part, when Meg has herself become widowed and comparatively impecunious, the friends are successively reintroduced, each for the purpose of representing different but equally unwholesome ways of coping with Meg's life situation. Viola tells her to get married again: "A woman needs a setting and a background that only a husband can provide"; Poll recommends a Bohemian life: "there just isn't any place for women of our age and upbringing who haven't any money ... You'll just have to settle for being a slut." Jill's grim advice is to live on memories. But despite their imperfect incorporation into the texture of the novel, these negative exempla, like the fully assimilated counterpoint of David, do help the reader to see that Meg's decision at the end of the novel to leave the security of David's nursery for the world of interesting jobs, superficial social intercourse, getting and spending, is an affirmative and liberating act.

In the third and final part of *The Middle Age of Mrs Eliot* the reader comes to see this even more clearly. As the section opens Meg is returning to health at Andredaswood. But her brother is worried that she has reached only a centre of indifference or "negative sort of calm," that she may "lapse into a feeble, contented dependence" on him, and that her emotional demands will undermine his stoic detachment from life. But as time passes brother and sister are drawn together "in a growingly easeful communion" through their shared past and through books – "their own recreation of a dead world [and] the creations of other worlds by men now dead." (The title of the third section, "Nursery Ins and Outs," has more than one meaning.) Gradually Meg comes to take a more active role in life at Andredaswood as her appetite for new experience begins to return. But she realizes that she still needs the intimate emotional contact and support that only her brother can give. At the same time David's severe self-repressions have begun to weaken; he comes to feel amazed that "he could so completely share his life with anyone ... without feeling invaded or exhausted or swallowed up." Finally he comes to realize "what utter desolation Meg's absence would mean for him."

The nuances and undertones of Meg and David's renewed relationship come to a head in the novel's climactic scene, "a magnificent page," as Frank Kermode has said, in which Wilson "both transcends himself and justifies his claim to belong to a great tradition of moralizing novelists."[18] Brother and sister are spending what will be their last evening together reading – they are at work on a study of the early novel. They exchange some comments as Meg is saying good night; after she has gone David reflects that "this was the happiest evening of his life." But Meg is at the same time deciding – it is the climax of her moral maturation and her return to psychological health – that she must leave Andredaswood. For David's answers to her apparently offhand questions have sparked the recognition (by the reader as well as by Meg) that their evening was in fact characterized by "a sentimental, cosy futility" and that David has lapsed into the condition he had earlier feared Meg would fall, "a feeble, contented dependence" – what the next morning, in announcing her departure, Meg calls "a vegetable ease" and "a self-indulgent apathy" from which she must break free in order to save both herself and David.

One of the best features of *The Middle Age of Mrs Eliot* is that Wilson does not overplay the significance or the profundity of Meg's crisis and its resolution. He assures that the reader will not make too much of her story by gradually moving the point of view away from her. The whole first part of the novel is narrated exclusively from her point of view, but the second part begins by plunging the reader into David's mind, and in the third part Meg is seen strictly from the outside: even the climactic scene with her brother is narrated from his point of view; and her decision to leave Andredaswood is made offstage. On the other hand, while it is excellent that no false depths are plumbed, no factitious victories won, it can be argued that Meg Eliot is not a person of enough complexity or depth, or her crisis sufficiently profound, to justify such full-scale treatment. In saying so there is no need to invoke the intimidating standards of *Emma*, *The Mill on the Floss*, or *The Portrait of a Lady*. One may compare Meg's story to that of Kate Brown in Doris Lessing's 1975 novel, *The Summer before the Dark*. (The novel dates from the later period of Lessing's career, by which time she had come by a path very different from Wilson's to give radical primacy in her fiction to psychological depth.)[19] Meg and Kate, both middle-aged wives of well-to-do professional men, are pleased to reflect on their enlightened and successful marriages. Both unexpectedly find themselves on their own at the same time that they come to realize some unpleasant truths about their marriages and to see the gap between their flattering self-images and the reality of their lives. Both undergo periods of confusion and emotional stress; both eventually recover their balance and return to the world they have left with increased self-understanding and a more objective view of that world. After a point, however, the differences between the two stories become marked. Doris Lessing takes one much further into the psychic life of her central character. Kate undergoes a searing mid-life crisis that forces her to undertake a radical reinterpretation of the meaning of her past life. Meg by comparison only accommodates herself to reduced circumstances and, having "realized how completely identity seemed governed by milieu," comes to equip herself with a new identity card. Lessing forces upon Kate an awareness of sexual politics and of the exploitation of women; at the same time she is brought to a more radical political consciousness through awareness of other kinds of inequality and exploitation. In *The Middle Age of Mrs Eliot*, on the other hand, as in *Anglo-Saxon Attitudes*, social observation and social notation are unaccompanied by an informing social vision.

But having recognized the self-imposed limitations of Wilson's portrait of Meg Eliot, one may once again admire the considerable skills brought to bear on making the story of her (and her brother's) social and psychological readjustments the principal subject of a full-scale novel possessing a controlled diversity and a genuine depth.

III

In 1963 Wilson published *The Wild Garden*, which did for his own fictional canon (then consisting of his three short story collections and four novels, *The Old Men at the Zoo* having been published in 1961) what he had earlier done for Zola and was subsequently to do for Dickens. In the study of Zola, Wilson had argued that what mattered in the work of that great naturalistic novelist, "who notoriously depended upon exact fact for the stimulation of his imagination ... was the nature of his imagination, not the facts that stimulated it."[20] In *The World of Charles Dickens* the similarly complex relationship of social facts and obsessive psychological concerns would be emphasized. In *The Wild Garden*, Wilson attempted an analysis of his own creative processes and of the relationship of the surface of his novels to his own inner depths. One previously hidden theme he discovered was "the dichotomy of the two evils – the hell of a society that has lost the power of communication ... and the hell of the neurotic self-communing,"[21] which, as Wilson showed, runs through his early novels and, as he could not have then known, reappears in *As If by Magic* (1973) in the contrast between Alexandra Grant and Hamo Langmuir. Wilson went on to argue for the primacy of obsessive psychological concerns, of subconscious and hidden motives, in the writing of fiction. His boldest claim, explicitly made in the face of "the paramount importance placed upon the supervening significances of the novel, moral, social and so on by critics and novelists alike today" came in the closing paragraph. There it was said that novels are "moments of vision," that "a novel is an extended metaphor [and] that the metaphor is everything, the extension only the means of expression."[22]

The shift in Wilson's thinking about the novel is so marked as to raise the question of whether the emphasis in *The Wild Garden* on the primacy of obsessive psychological elements is compatible with his insistence during the 1950s on "the paramount importance" of the novel's social and moral functions – a claim which was in fact eloquently restated early in *The Wild*

Garden when "the real challenge and triumph of the novel" was said to be the creation of "that sense of being fully made alive, of disseminating the moral proposition so completely in a mass of living experience that it is never directly sensed as you read but only apprehended at the end as a result of the life you have shared in the book."[23] One explanatory point is that "moments of vision" metaphorically expanded describes a work of fiction from the point of view of its mysterious genesis and emphasizes its expressive function; "disseminating the moral proposition" so as to move the reader deeply describes a work of fiction from the point of view of its communicative function and consequently emphasizes the means through which the author contrives to affect the reader. When it comes to describing the relationship between the novelist's expressive and communicative urges, however, Wilson is not nearly so satisfying as he usually is in his critical prose. In *The Wild Garden* he provides only a sketchy and rather mechanical account (having to do with the struggle of three different levels of imagination) of the stages through which the moment of vision becomes the finished artifact. And in a 1961 article he is comparably vague in speaking of the "three personalities or separate wills [that] exist during the making of a book – the narrator, the craftsman and the residue" (the last being, "I suppose, the source of the book").[24] But whatever the specifics of their interaction, few would deny that expressive and communicative elements do exist synergistically in many novels – including Wilson's own.

Wilson's article on "Evil in the English Novel," first published in 1962-3, also helps to explain the shift in emphasis in his critical thought.[25] As in *The Wild Garden*, his interest is in what lies beyond the boundaries of social breadth and moral depth. Wilson begins by asserting that the contemporary English novel "is becoming provincial, and the novel of manners – strong though it is – is an increasingly restrictive influence." One of the troubles, Wilson says, "is that we are too much concerned with right and wrong, and not enough with evil." He explains that for this reason he has decided to review the development of the novel in England – from *Moll Flanders* and *Clarissa*, through the great nineteenth-century novelists, to Henry James, Virginia Woolf, and Joseph Conrad, and, finally, to Graham Greene, William Golding, and himself – to see "whether evil was ever really there, if it dropped out (and how), and whether we are beginning to bring it back." He ends on a personal note, remarking that "our transcendent sense of evil is being destroyed all the time by our psychological knowledge," and speaking of his sense of "the real evil that I feel abroad in the world today" and of his attempts to introduce such a sense into *Hemlock and After, The Old Men at the Zoo*, and what became *No Laughing Matter*.[26]

"Evil in the English Novel" is one of Wilson's finest pieces of literary criticism, deeply meditated and full of clarifying insights. But when Wilson's argument is considered in relation to his own creative work and to his own vision of life certain questions arise. First, it is one thing to argue that the English novel should break out of its "provincial, encaging shape ... and yet do so without losing the great richness that our social, ethical tradition has given us." But it is quite another thing to say how this is to be done. William Golding, for example, has certainly introduced a sense of "transcendent evil" into his fictions, but, says Wilson, "these books remain great fables rather than novels."[27] And while Graham Greene's *Brighton Rock* (a novel Wilson discusses) flaunts its concern with good and evil as opposed to right and wrong, I would argue that its good/evil theme is to an appreciable degree imposed from without upon its seamy story, and that the novel's wealth of telling sociological and psychological notation offers a too convincing naturalistic explanation of evil, which undermines its claims to transcendent status. As Henry James acutely reflects in his preface to *The Turn of the Screw*: "One had seen, in fiction, some grand form of wrongdoing, or better still of wrong-being, imputed, seen it promised and announced as by the hot breath of the Pit – and then, all lamentably, shrink to the compass of some particular brutality, some particular immorality, some particular infamy portrayed: with the result, alas, of the demonstration's falling sadly short."[28]

Second, for an agnostic writer of liberal-humanist beliefs, which Wilson has often declared himself to be, it is hard to see how evil can, strictly speaking, be considered "transcendent" (the word is used repeatedly in "Evil in the English Novel"); that is, more than the sum of moral obliquity, psychological aberration, the cruelty of stunted natures, or natural catastrophe. Certainly Wilson would not claim for evil the supernatural or metaphysical status it has, say, in the novels of Georges Bernanos. And we have already seen that in his first novel Wilson was unsuccessful in his attempt to make Hubert Rose a Dostoevskian symbol of demonic evil. It would seem to follow that for Wilson "transcendent" indicates degree rather than kind, quantity rather than quality. But if this is so, then his use of "transcendent" is open to the charge of being factitious. As Miranda Gray, the heroine of John Fowles's *The Collector*, comes to realize: "all the evil in the world's made up of little drops. It's silly talking about the unimportance of the little drops. The little drops and the ocean are the same thing."

A third question relates to the source of Wilson's apprehensions of evil. Are they owing to insights of the social and moral novelist scrutinizing the world in which he lives, or are they rather subjective in origin, the projections of the novelist's private obsessions? As Wilson has said of the "strong sadistic impulses which do come out in my books ... how am I to know whether they are mine, or those of the world in which I live?"[29] A final problem is that a sense of transcendent evil would seem to admit of the possibility of some kind of transcendent good, a quality beyond moral probity or right conduct. Wilson has spoken of his belief in a form of grace and tried to dramatize its operation in the story of Sylvia Calvert in *Late Call*. It is clear, however, that this grace has to do with the integration of the personality and is wholly humanistic. In Wilson's novels evil may seem transcendent and pervasive, but the good which opposes it is always immanent, humanistic, and fragile.

The contrast between pervasive evil and fragile good is one of the principal themes of Wilson's fourth novel, *The Old Men at the Zoo*, the first major reflection of his "feeling that the traditional form [of the novel] was inhibiting me from saying all that I wanted to say."[30] The future setting of the novel and its first person narrator, both unique in his canon, are the two major devices utilized by Wilson in his attempt to steer a fictional course that would take him beyond what had come to seem the Scylla and Charybdis of diversity and depth. In the opening scene of *The Old Men at the Zoo*, most of which takes place in the London Zoological Gardens in Regent's Park, the loveliness of a May morning is shattered by the screams of young Filson, a keeper who is being trampled to death by a giraffe, normally among the least ferocious of animals. All save one of those in responsible positions have their own reasons for not wanting this ghastly incident properly investigated and responsibility fixed. The keeper's death consequently remains unexplained, the first in a series of ugly events involving animals which generates a sense of gratuitous evil: the death of the promiscuous Harriet Leacock, killed by her huge Alsatian, whose sexual favours she had been enjoying, the lynx ordered destroyed by her father for purely public relations reasons; Matthew Price, the epicene curator killed by a mob attacking the Zoo; the selected massacre of Zoo animals after London is bombed; the slaughter of badgers by the narrator late in the novel; the chained Russian bear pulled down by hounds, and the American eagle torn to pieces during a period when the Zoo is used for political propaganda; Blanchard-White, whose plans to bring his countrymen "closer to the rich vein of Mediterranean cruelty on which our European legacy so much depends" include a scheme for the pitting of political prisoners against wild beasts as a public spectacle. And all of these incidents are counterpointed by political machinations beyond the world of the Zoo that eventually bring destruction and famine to much of England.

The events described in *The Old Men at the Zoo*, published in 1961, take place in the early 1970s, when it is imagined that hostile relations between England and a federated Europe culminate in a non-nuclear war in which the smaller combatant is easily defeated. Though their pressure is continually felt, however, public events are kept strictly in the background and it would be a mistake to regard the novel as genuinely futuristic or dystopian. As Evelyn Waugh observed:

Old Men at the Zoo is not a novel like *Brave New World* or *1984* in which a warning is offered of the dangers to posterity if existing social tendencies fructify ... Consciously or unconsciously [Wilson] has written a study of 1938-42 ... he required *a* war for his plot and the war he has given us is what many Englishmen feared at the time of Munich ... Mr Wilson has accepted all that body of – as it happened – quite false assumptions and has used it in the machinery of his story. What he is concerned with, and what he so brilliantly portrays, is the working of the machinery on the lives of his characters.[31]

While Waugh's observations are acute, it is also true to say that the imaginative licence made possible by the future setting does provide Wilson with an outlet for his grand guignol side, what Anthony Burgess described as a "world of private nightmare ... far beyond the scope of ordinary fictional plausibility." It is this energy which is responsible for the novel's most striking and original effects, and which led Burgess (who has little interest in traditional realistic fiction) to claim that *The Old Men at the Zoo* was the "best thing that Wilson has ever done."[32] Unfortunately, this imaginative intensity is not evenly distributed. The novel is weakest in the two long opening chapters (which should have been shorter) and the two short closing ones (which should have been longer). In the former, it seems to take Wilson some time to write himself out of the naturalistic mode of his earlier novels: as Waugh pointed out, the novel's longest and least successful scene, the young keeper's funeral in the second chapter, is the one most in Wilson's earlier vein; and in the closing chapters too much happens too quickly and perfunctorily, including the offstage liberation of Britain.

Simon Carter, the novel's narrator, is the Secretary of the London Zoo, a position which he hopes will allow him to combine his exceptional administrative talents with his deep interests as a naturalist (his specialty is badgers). During the course of the novel Carter faithfully serves four different directors, each of whom has his own ideal of the Zoo (just as each is shown to have a different point of view concerning young Filson's death). It is in these figures and their different conceptions of the Zoo, not in the

futuristic background elements per se, that the novel's parabolic sugges-
tiveness concerning the condition of England is found. The contrast between
Leacock and Falcon, the first two directors Carter serves, is particularly
suggestive. The former is an old-fashioned liberal, big on visionary schemes
but inattentive to detail and politically and morally naïve. His ideal of
"limited liberty" for animals in a great natural reserve is partially realized
but soon founders because his optimistic assumptions have failed to take
into account the realities of human nature. His successor, an aging hero
famous for his foreign expeditions, dreams of bringing back "the good old
days" by returning to the *Gemütlichkeit* of the Victorian zoo. A "British
Day" is organized to inaugurate Falcon's extraordinary exercise in nostalgia:
one exhibit features "birds from every corner of the earth that was now or
ever had been British. For, of course, it was only by cheating and taking
in history, that a British Day could cast its net wide enough." But war
begins on the eve of British Day and London and its Zoo are bombed. In
a spectacular nighttime scene, the high point of the novel's dark exuberance,
a now demented Falcon turns on the exhibition's illuminations. As the
bombs fall, firework set pieces spell out "God Save Our Gracious Queen"
while "the British Lion and the Indian Elephant came alive in glorious
sulphurous blue, and demon red and palest amber white." Meanwhile "Home,
Sweet Home" booms out from the loudspeakers, mixing with "the agonizing screams and roars of hippos, rhinos, zebras, apes and trumpeting
elephants," while escaped condors, vultures, and golden eagles circle overhead.

The future setting of the novel is also put to less pyrotechnical uses. The
constantly changing political situation in the country and at the Zoo makes
it possible for Wilson to increase the frequency of crisis situations, multiply
confusions, and sustain a sense of the bizarre and unpredicated. This allows
him to ring some changes on the theme of the dilemmas of liberal humanism, for *The Old Men at the Zoo* may be read as a black farce on the subject
of the impossibility of making enlightened and humane values prevail against
human pride, self-interest, and evil. Simon Carter has the hallmarks of the
Wilsonian liberal humanist (though his heterosexuality is unusual): he is
agnostic, self-questioning, humane, and tolerant, possessing a deep sense
of responsibility and a hypersensitive conscience. He is also something of
a fool. As he rightly reflects, "moments of moral decision play a ludicrously
large role in my life." Sententious, loquacious, pulled programmatically
between desire and duty, relishing opportunities for self-denial and for
reassessing his priorities rather than acting decisively, Carter sometimes
seems to the reader the "figure of fun" he once seems to himself as his good

intentions, like his administrative skills, become increasingly irrelevant and increasingly ineffectual.

Near the end of *The Old Men at the Zoo* Carter recalls one of his favourite axioms: "Whate'er is best administered *is* best." Wilson has said that distrust of the moral universe of C.P. Snow's fiction was an influence on his novel, and it is clear that through Carter he is concerned to explore the bureaucratic personality and its limitations, and again to ponder the proper exercise of authority. In his unswerving devotion to his adminstrative responsibilities at the Zoo (when forced to choose between job and wife, he opts for the former), his passion for organization, his obsession with means, and his Vicar of Bray adaptability to ends, Carter seems both a model bureaucrat and a morally suspect individual, luxuriating in "the warmth I generated in my cocoon of busyness." For example, while he seems initially determined to get to the full truth concerning the circumstances of young Filson's death, he ultimately does nothing and even comes to use his liberal conscience and moral scruples to help rationalize his conduct: "How could I be sure," he lamely reflects, "that my doubt [about the death] was not simply a product of my general mistrust of the declaredly important."

While Carter's personality is of major interest from the point of view of Wilson's critique of administrative man, from the point of view of reader involvement Carter's characterization and voice must ultimately be judged a major shortcoming of *The Old Men at the Zoo*. For Carter's qualities are much too insistently underlined and repetitiously instanced; the scenes with his wife are totally unconvincing; and since he does not really change or develop during the novel he ultimately comes to bore the reader. In addition, while Carter is given a convincing verbal signature, the resources of his voice are limited and ultimately seem an unnatural constriction of his creator's great natural fluency. As Wilson himself has rightly recognized, his "natural aptitude as a novelist is ... for narration rather than for craft."[33] When the former is repressed the result is an intermittent thinness that at times approaches the tedious. That is why the best scenes in the novel, like the nighttime bombing of the Zoo, are those in which Carter's voice and personality are most recessive and the dark exuberance of Wilson's imagination most dominant; and that is why, for all its freshness and all the fine things in it, *The Old Men at the Zoo* must ultimately be regarded as one of its author's less successful novels.

In one important particular, *The Old Men at the Zoo* looks forward to Wilson's next novel. A principal reason for Simon Carter's imbalances – his administrative obsessions and his fruitless introspections – is his failure (psychological rather than moral) to "end the bifurcation of my life" through

bringing together reason and intuition, thought and feeling, duty and pleasure. The emblem of Carter's deeper emotional and intuitive needs are the
shy badgers he longs to spend time observing, which have in the past enabled
him to know life "only though my senses." But circumstances repeatedly
frustrate his attempts to refresh and regenerate himself through sympathetic
participation in natural life. Because one part of his being, the roots of
which lie in the natural and animal world, is denied nourishment, the other
part – the city and adminstrative side – comes to dominate his personality
with consequent impairment of his judgment and sense of values. And late
in the novel, when Carter finally returns to his beloved badger setts, it is
to slaughter, eat, and regurgitate the harmless animals which had once
symbolized his ideal of the integrated personality but which have now
become another emblem of his creator's sense of pervasive evil.

While the importance of recontacting and nourishing the instinctual side
of one's nature is an important theme in *Late Call* (1964), in almost every
other way it and *The Old Men at the Zoo* are so dissimilar as to suggest on
Wilson's part a recoil from the expressionistic concerns of the previous
novel. For with *Late Call* Wilson renews his commitment to social realism
and to exploration of the inner life – to diversity and depth, manners and
morals – through tackling two major new subjects: life in a New Town
and the spiritual regeneration of an unexceptional old woman, whose consciousness is untouched by the liberal-humanist dilemmas that afflict the
central characters of his earlier novels. These subjects are not only made to
fit neatly together: their interpenetration gives *Late Call* a dimension that
makes it more than simply a skilful mixture of social and psychological
modes and a much more satisfying novel than *The Old Men at the Zoo*.

As social and moral concerns once more become dominant, a sense of
pervasive evil necessarily becomes recessive. One suspects it was Wilson's
unhappiness over this trade-off that is responsible for the only feature of
Late Call which seems out of place: the introduction two-thirds of the way
through of a "little humpbacked old woman" of central European background who narrates her life story, the sorrowful peregrinations of which
recall some of the twentieth-century's principal manifestations of evil. This
interpolation is not only out of key thematically with the rest of *Late Call*;
Wilson has even flirted with alienating devices in its presentation. For the
woman tells her story in a "singsong foreign accent," to which Wilson's
talent for mimicry is fully equal, and the discontinuity between serious
tenor and droll vehicle makes for a farcical effect. In addition, as Wilson
subsequently pointed out, the woman's sententious citations of Tolstoy,
Strindberg, and others are all made up. Fortunately very few readers will

notice this last indication of the author's lapse in decorum. For *Late Call* is not about pervasive evil; it is about humanistic good, and for its success everything hinges not on the reader's alienation but on his sympathetic engagement – so firmly established in the novel's opening chapters – with the central character and her crisis of old age.

The family of Harold Calvert, a recent widower in early middle age with three children on the threshold of adult life, is Wilson's reference point for a detailed picture of life in Carshall, a New Town on the edge of the Midlands. Wilson's successful appropriation of this important post-war sociological phenomenon confirms his credentials as a social novelist of impressive range. Indeed, the amount of social notation in *Late Call* sometimes seems to approximate the thoroughness of inventory: there are full accounts of the Calvert family's schmaltzy Christmas card; the menu of a party at their house; the tasteless décor of a neighbour's living room; the flashy appointments at Chen Fu's, the local restaurant; a community performance of *Look Back in Anger*; an evening of bowling at the Town Hall Centre; a civic meeting at which tempers flare over a planning board decision concerning the development of a meadow adjacent to the town; and so on. But the tendency towards the merely documentary is for the most part held in check by the sharpness of Wilson's comic and satiric observation and by his ability to make social notation an index of character, as in the passage in which Harold explains to his mother the workings of his polymathic stove:

"with an autotimer, there's no need to have a sense of timing ... We've relegated instinctual cooking to the lesser breeds without the law. And *they* aren't going to put up with it for long. Now take this meal we're cooking this evening. Of course, it's not a normal meal. I've specially designed it to illustrate all the equipment," he smoothed his moustache with a certain pride. "The goulash in your top oven. And just for this evening – an example of conspicuous waste – an apfelstrudel in your lower oven. Of course, that's really reserved for the big fellows, turkeys and such and for any fiestas. We'll bake there for this little party we're giving for you before Christmas. Then, on the drop-in hob – soup for Dad on the simmerstat, and on the two hob points two veg, also for my conservative-minded parents" – he winked at her – "and then a special treat for Dad whose true blue palate can't take goulash – a half chicken for the grill. Frankly, I shouldn't have pandered to him like this if it hadn't been a very useful way of demonstrating the rotoroaster."

As this passage so drolly illustrates, Harold Calvert is committed to the up-to-date. A headmaster of progressive views, Harold is pillar and epitome of the New Town community. Well-intentioned and abounding in civic virtue, he is at the same time full of an irrepressible, rather vulgar bonhomie and a naïve enthusiasm for material conveniences that leave him no time for self-appraisal or for realizing that others may not share his tastes or values. His personality and attitudes are contrasted with those of his aging parents, who have come to live with their son. The father is Arthur Calvert, a rasping n'er-do-well who was an officer during the First World War, a conflict which ruined his lungs and, in raising him from the ranks, cut him off from his lower middle class origins and made him a socially displaced person. Arthur is one of the finest supporting players in Wilson's novels and his characterization (so different from the caricature of the humpbacked old woman) illustrates one of his creator's strongest suits as a novelist: his feeling for class differences, for the intricacies of social relationships and their comic undertones.

But it is Arthur's wife who is the central character in *Late Call*. Retired from her career as a manager of small hotels, Sylvia Calvert has come with her husband (a reminder in the present time of the novel of the self-abnegating drabness of her adult life) to live in Carshall New Town, an adjustment she finds difficult to make. While Sylvia initially assumes that in her new home there must be some work to get on with, she comes to feel increasingly useless. The kitchen, bristling with appliances she does not understand, seems at one point to be closing in on her; "the black emptiness" of the hills seen from her window becomes more persistently oppressive; and her sense that "the weeks, the years ahead, stretched out in front of her in empty uselessness" eventually intensifies into severe climacteric anxiety. Her son's house comes to seem a prison; she finds self-images in the reviled old mother in Osborne's play, in the "Jewesses she had read of going to the gas chamber," and in the victim of a grisly murder she reads about. Finally, Sylvia's feelings of uselessness harden into an "unappeased loneliness," "a pervasive depression or a nagging ache of anxiety" which lead her out of Carshall New Town and into the surrounding countryside on long, solitary walks.

It is at about this point that the reader of *Late Call* begins to remember its self-contained short story length prologue, which is set in "The Hot Summer of 1911" and describes an interlude in the round of chores of an unnamed ten-year-old daughter of a poor East Anglian farmer. One of Wilson's finest pieces of writing, the prologue begins by introducing the genteel Mrs Longmore and her seven-year-old daughter Myra, who are spending their summer holiday boarding at the farm of the uncouth Tuffield family. One afternoon the unnamed girl goes with Myra on an unauthorized outing into the meadows and woods and begins "to do all the things that she had wanted to do for years, things for which there was never time because there were so many duties in the day." While the spoiled, self-absorbed Myra looks for opportunities to preen and to fantasize, the farm girl is pleased "just to be" and to savour "a sense of happiness not to be lost." She is content to admire the creamy flowerheads of Queen Anne's Lace, while Myra crumbles them into "stardust," of which she announces herself princess while demanding that her companion "scatter the stardust for the Stardust Princess." When the wandering children are found, Myra's mendacity soon restores her to her mother's favour, but the farm girl's day of contentment ends with her being severely beaten by her brutish father and with her mother's malediction: "*You* wanted to be different! Well you're nothin'. Nothin'. And you always will be."

As the story of her increasing unhappiness in Carshall unfolds, it becomes clear that Sylvia Calvert was the young girl in the long-ago summer and that the novel's prologue and the parallels between it and the body of the novel have given the reader a sympathetic understanding of the instinctual and emotional needs that lie beneath the surface of Sylvia's decades of self-effacement, her dislike of physical contact, her dowdiness, television watching, and light novel reading, and that have intensified the "lonely fears" that lead her into the country. Sylvia does dimly sense that her compulsive walks are connected with the desire to find "some shape in life however small" and with a "vague idea of return": "Perhaps to weave all the threads together again she needed to return to the country world of her childhood." For many days the only sign of such a reconnection is the discovery that after many years she still has the knack of snapping the neck of an injured rabbit. But one afternoon her depression and anxiety are brought to a head by a sudden lightning storm. Only when it begins to rain does Sylvia hear the screams of a terrified little girl standing under a solitary oak from which she rescues her. Sylvia holds the small trembling girl to her until old woman and child "seemed to merge into one sodden mass" as a "jagged blinding flash [of lightning] zigzagged across the field and the rotten oak went down in a moment's flame and a long plume of funeral smoke."

This storm scene, in which Sylvia saves the seven-year-old Mandy Egan from death, and in so doing suffers a slight stroke, is the climactic moment in *Late Call*. While it is unquestionably sensational, the scene is less a melodramatic vignette than a symbolic figuring forth of Sylvia's recontacting of her own childhood past, of rediscovering a pulse of feeling and a desire to live that she had felt most strongly during that long-ago day in the hot summer of 1911. It is, so to speak, the moment in *Late Call* when its prologue is fully fused with the body of the novel, when the past lives again in the present. It is also the moment when Sylvia's childhood deprivations, which prefigured the deprivations of her adult life, are fully compensated for – a pattern of loss and gain symbolically accented by the transformation of the seven-year-old Myra Longmore into the seven-year-old Mandy Egan.

The symbolic mode of this scene does ruffle the surface of a novel which otherwise flows in the channels of naturalistic realism – though Wilson excellently manages the modulation back to a realistic mode. For Mandy Egan is no Dickensian prepubescent embodiment of good, and while Sylvia's relations with her and her parents are at first intensely warm and loving, they inevitably wane as family concerns – for her failing husband and over-worked son – come to reassert their priority. But however implausible on the level of realistic fiction, the climactic scene of *Late Call* is fully credible psychologically. Recontacting a living sense of one's childhood or youthful past, and the regenerative, life-giving result, is described, or enacted, over and over again in the literature of the nineteenth and twentieth centuries: in Wordsworth's "Immortality Ode," in Tennyson's *In Memoriam,* in George Eliot's *The Mill on the Floss,* in Arnold's "Thyrsis," at the end of Swinburne's *The Tale of Balen,* in Proust's *A la recherche du temps perdu,* in Robert Frost's "Directive." It is the great Romantic naturalist principle of recompense for loss through being borne back into the past through memory and the medi-ation of the natural world, and thereby gaining, however fleeting the actual moment of imaginative fusion, a sustaining sense of continuity, wholeness, and completion. Of course there are difficulties in convincingly representing such moments within the framework of a realistic novel, and some readers of *Late Call* would doubtless argue that the lightning storm is as contrived and offputting an expedient as the flood at the end of *The Mill on the Floss,* which brings release to Maggy Tulliver through reuniting her with her brother, embodiment of the true life of her past. And of course a major difference between *Late Call* and all of the works cited above is that Sylvia Calvert is not a person of exceptional gifts or exceptional needs. But I would argue that it is in precisely this difference that the premier distinction of Wilson's novel lies: in having so sympathetically and on the whole suc-cessfully dramatized the workings of this restorative process in so ordinary a person.

In the last section of *Late Call* one sees that through recovering a sense of her childhood self and of her vision of being content "just to be," Sylvia Calvert succeeds where Simon Carter had failed: in ending the bifurcation of her life. She finds happiness in her friendship with the Egans, is able to talk without bitterness about her own unhappy childhood, and is surprised at how much she is now able to remember about her early days. And with "her own feelings [to tell] her now so clearly what to do," she is able to accept her husband's death and – in a nice reversal – to help Harold, the rootless New Town booster whose life has not been comparably enriched.

It is in the contrast between Harold and Sylvia that the more explicitly moral dimension of *Late Call* is found. The contrast is most sharply focused in the scene in which the Calvert family goes to church on Easter Sunday and are surprised by the absence of their trendy vicar. His replacement is an elderly Scottish preacher whose subject is Grace and good works:

So we ask for Grace to be given to us, for we'll not get it by shouting or fussing and fretting away our souls. No, not all the charity, the social work, as they call it now, can save your soul alive if there's no soul left to save ... You can go out to meet God's Grace. Go out to mind who you are. Go out, not into the busy clamour of getting and spending, nor even into the soothing clamour of good works. No, go out into the dreadful silence, into the dark nothingness.

Like his neighbours, Harold is appalled by the preacher's "barbaric doctrines" and "all this rubbish about Grace"; but Sylvia is moved by what she has heard and thanks the old man. Of course Wilson means for the reader to transpose the sermon into a humanistic key: Harold is a man without grace but with every sort of good works. The good works are not without value; indeed at the end of the novel Sylvia says that her son is quite right to be proud of Carshall and the egalitarian values it epitomizes. But on the next page we again see that good works are not enough: for Harold's blinkered progressive notions and his underdeveloped emotions, cut him off from the most loving of his children. His initial reaction to the discovery of Ray's homosexuality seems enlightened. He writes the young man urging him to come home and consider "having some decent up-to-date treatment." But when Ray writes that he prefers to stay in London and speaks of his "real hope of making a happy life with Geoffrey," Harold tears up the letter, announces that he no longer wants Ray's name mentioned in his house, and that "I wash my hands of him." Sylvia on the other hand is able to accept her grandson's homosexuality and applaud his positive attitude towards it. It is Sylvia's secular grace – rooted in her cultivation of the instinctual and emotional – that enables her to do this and it is the absence of this quality in Harold and his circle that is the most serious criticism that *Late Call* has to make about life in a New Town.

IV

While Wilson had renewed his commitment to social realism in *Late Call*, he was at the same time beginning to become uneasy over his facility to write "the traditional novel" and the facility of his readers to "gobble it up." The "whole relationship" of writer to reader was "too smooth"; indeed, Wilson had come to feel that their "unthinking happy embrace" was a serious threat to the health of the contemporary novel.[34] As a result of these apprehensions, he had begun to take a more positive attitude towards experimental and *anti-roman* techniques. Wilson's attention was particularly drawn towards alienating devices: "this willed alienation of the reader ... is a technique that we can't afford to do without now. I think we must be prepared to alienate our readers at times so that they shall not go through our books as by rote, feeling comfortable and happy and feeling that they are reading warm, moving books." Wilson has explained that his endeavours "to keep my readers at a distance from my books with parody" began in *Late Call* (with the interpolated life story of the humpbacked old woman) and that much more extensive use of parodic and other alienating devices was made in *No Laughing Matter* (1967): such devices "seemed to me peculiarly necessary in a bourgeois family saga novel where the reader is by custom likely to immerse himself and lose sense of the full meaning of the book."[35] As early as the *Paris Review* interview, Wilson had admitted that "All fiction for me is a kind of magic and trickery – a confidence trick, trying to make people believe something is true that isn't"; but at the same time, as we have seen, he had insisted that the reader should remain "unaware of techniques" so that he could be convinced he was "seeing society as a whole" and so that his heart could be touched.[36] But by the mid-1960s, Wilson had determined (to use John Fowles's terms) both "to sound 'true' " and "to come clean."[37]

No Laughing Matter is Wilson's longest and most complex fiction, and his major achievement as a novelist: the most complete fusion of his interests as a social historian and moralist with his obsessive energies; the richest commingling of these with his natural aptitude for narration, powers of characterization, and stylistic fluency and range, including the gift of "impressionistic mimicry" that he has called his "principal natural asset as a writer."[38] Boldly ambitious in conception, the novel is executed with an energy and inventiveness that begin to flag only towards the end of its almost 500 pages.

One of the major organizing principles of *No Laughing Matter* is panoramic. The story of the public and private careers of the six Matthews children from their Edwardian childhood to the brink of old age in the 1960s is a chronicle of a half century of English upper middle class life and to a degree a microcosmic account of English history in the twentieth century. The novel opens "Before the War" (the First World War), with an account of a Matthews family outing to the Wild West Exhibition in Kensington. Like "The Hot Summer of 1911" prologue to *Late Call*, the scene is given a certain prelapsarian aura: watching a silent movie that stimulates their various fantasies, the "volatile, edged, and edgy family" experience for some minutes "a union of happy, carefree intimacy that it had scarcely known before and was never to know again." The next two sections are set in 1919 (an eventful Saturday night and Sunday in the Matthews' family home at 52 Gillbrook Street, London SW1) and 1925 (during a time of largely egotistic development on the part of the now post-adolescent siblings). But the long sections set in the mid- and late 1930s are the centre of *No Laughing Matter*. At that time the pressure of public events – Stalinism, Nazism, home front fascism – is felt in different ways by each of the six siblings. The principal focus for the impingement of public on private are the Jewish refugees who have fled Hitler's Germany. In a series of encounters with refugees, the liberal, enlightened values of the Matthews children are severely tested and, in the case of two of them, subjected to a withering scrutiny. In these scenes the interests of Wilson the social chronicler and Wilson the anatomist of the moral life come power-fully together. The three comparatively short sections that follow – set in 1946, 1956, and 1967 – round out the family saga side of *No Laughing Matter*. But they are not much more than a series of postscripts and are less important to the novel, and less well done, than the brilliant opening sections – the 30-page "Before the War" and the 130-page "1919."

These sections lay the foundation of the novel's second major organizing principle. As Wilson has himself observed:

No Laughing Matter [is] about the emancipation of a whole generation of people, and they are deeply involved in politics because the Thirties was a very political period. But their emancipation really occurs long before that political time, it occurs in their fight with their parents on all sorts of other matters: for example, the right to have some privacy, the right to have some education. Their parents are totally selfish and, in a sense, what I was brought up to call fascist people: that's to say that they're right-wing anarchists. The children's emancipation later is seen in all sorts of political forms – to do with the Spanish War, to do with Russia, to do with every kind of thing. But it all began with much, much smaller things: the way that it was monstrous that the younger son was made to sleep in the little box-bed, the fact that he was beaten because he wetted his bed, the fact that the letters of the eldest daughter who was having an affair with an older man were read by her father, and the fact that the mother, when she was in a bad temper, should openly insult the middle daughter about the beginning of her menstruation. And other things which are purely personal but which represent the beginning of their emergence as political beings.[39]

The six Matthews children grow up to be different from each other in personality and vocation. Wounded in the First World War, Quentin becomes a radical journalist, an early anti-Stalinist à la Orwell, and finally a Malcolm Muggeridge-type pundit and television personality. Stout, good-natured, latterly blowsy, Gladys becomes a businesswoman and continues her liaison with an older married man. Rupert takes to the stage and begins his ascent of the theatrical ladder. Margaret becomes a fiction writer of the Jane Austen-miniaturist-in-acid sort that the early Wilson was sometimes taken to be. Sukey, her twin, becomes the wife of a schoolmaster, the mother of three sons (Senior, Middleman, and PS), and immerses herself in domesticity. Marcus, the youngest and the only homosexual, becomes a kept man and a complete aesthete – "ageing but still beautiful young man, friend of the Sitwells and Cocteau, part owner of Kandinskys and Braques ... lover of Jack and Ted, occasional sufferer from haemorrhoids, giver of green balls" – before developing a political conscience during the 1930s.

The stories of each sibling are moved forward in alternating short story length scenes or vignettes which are given a certain unity and coherence in the 1930s sections when all six are forced to react to the same public events. But the dominant unifying principle in *No Laughing Matter*, which makes the novel, for all its wealth of heterogeneous episodes, a cogently organized and cohesive work, is that, no matter how varied they may appear on the surface, the adult personalities of the children are rooted in and determined by the shared parental and familial background. *No Laughing Matter* has no epigraph; were one required it would be hard to think of anything better than the first stanza of Philip Larkin's "This Be the Verse":

> They fuck you up, your mum and dad.
> > They may not mean to, but they do.
> They fill you with the faults they had
> > And add some extra, just for you.

William and Clara, the Matthews parents, are splendid characterizations. Both are totally self-centred, promiscuous, mendacious, spoiled, and living beyond their means; both are also appalling parents, alternately neglectful, ingratiating, vampiric, and patronizing. The only mitigating feature of their presentation is that one sees something of how they too have had their personalities shaped by *their* elders. For the second stanza of Larkin's poem is equally apposite to Wilson's novel:

> But they were fucked up in their turn
>> By fools in old-style hats and coats,
> Who half the time were soppy-stern
>> And half at one another's throats.[40]

"Soppy-stern" is particularly appropriate, for what is most incongruous about Granny Matthews ("all sables and black velour hat ... on her lap sits Pom," her pet dog) and Clara's aunt, Miss Rickard ("dressed in a rather mannishly cut grey tweed skirt and coat and a tricorne hat. On her shoulder is perched a green Amazon parrot") is their mixture of high-minded Victorian probity and ruthlessly indulged sentimentality. The latter quality is seen in their treatment of their pets, on whose behalf they insist, on tacit threat of withdrawing their financial support, that Clara and William dispose of their children's harmless kittens.

Even "before the war" it is clear from the content of their rich fantasy lives that each of the Matthews children already possesses in embryo his or her fundamental psychological characteristics. These surface again in "1919" when the children first play The Game, an impromptu theatrical in which each sibling impersonates a different adult member of their family or household (except for Quentin who does Mr Justice Scales). The Game is born of the children's "need to relieve their pent-up shame, distress, and anger in histrionics, to heal their hurts with mimicry's homeopathic sting, and no doubt as well to indulge some sexual urges." Often wickedly funny – the children's talents for impersonation and verbal caricature are the equal of their creator's and their production is the most scintillating single scene in Wilson's canon – The Game reveals how qualities of the older generation have become grafted onto the children's personalities. At the same time, the communal need to find a channel for their frustrations and compensatory fantasies is a stimulus to self-expression and helps account for the siblings' unusually high proportion of creative talent. (Even Sukey, the Inge Middleton of *No Laughing Matter*, achieves some regional fame in later life with her West Country radio broadcasts of nauseatingly soppy stories about the days when her children were growing up.)

As the children leave home to enter adult life, the reader is again and again made to see how their successes and failures, their strengths and weaknesses are all shoots from the parental stem. Quentin's Marxism is peculiar because his childhood was not "warm with necessary generosity" like those of his working class confederates. His peculiar gift as a journalist and commentator is exposing the hells of good intentions, the role that his position as eldest child had forced upon him in adolescence, just as it had fed his fantasy of being "the dispassionate, objective outsider ... who, by eliciting the facts, reveals the moral pattern, sets all to right, uncovers the riddle." But the underside of this objectivity is isolation and emotional withering. In the closing pages of the novel a piece of music conjures up for Quentin the face of his long-dead mother and leads him to wish that he had been able to love, and to long for the "warm darkness" where at last he may be able to. Gladys breaks the law to get money for her mendacious lover, who subsequently lets her down, a pattern of exploitation established long before with her father's requests for loans and even for physical favours.

Margaret's coolness towards sex reflects her childhood assumption that it must be awful if it makes one behave like her mother; and her first serious affair ends because her upbringing has left her without the confidence necessary for a deep, sustained relationship. Her creative powers, particularly her gift for lethal irony, have their root in the need to distance herself from the moral squalor of her childhood; and her family are the subject of the acetic stories by which she makes her name as a writer. In The Game, Margaret had taken the part of her great-aunt Rickard, whose favourite she was and who encouraged her to be clever and self-reliant. In later years, Margaret comes to recognize her determining influence, reflecting that "the failure in human sympathy" that has thinned her creative powers can be traced to the aunt's costiveness and protective cattiness.

Rupert, the handsomest child, is his mother's favourite – his self-love the mirror of her narcissism. He helps his fledgling acting career through an affair with an imperious, bitchy leading lady, who is old enough to be his mother. Indeed, when he first realizes what is expected of him, Rupert expostulates: "But I couldn't possibly. She must be over fifty. It'd be a kind of incest." Later in life Rupert rightly reflects that he might never have been an actor if it hadn't been for "his love-hate battle" with his mother. And his successful interpretations of Malvolio in *Twelfth Night* and Andrey Prozorhov in Chekhov's *Three Sisters* – the pinnacles of his professional career – are rooted in his insight into the character of his father, whom Rupert had played in The Game.

Sukey on the other hand has something of the soppy sternness of Granny Matthews, whose part she had taken in The Game. One is initially sympathetic to Sukey, for her yearning for a husband and "children asking to be shaped" and for animals (like the kittens destroyed by her parents) is in wholesome contrast to the semi-Bohemianism of Number 52. But over a period of time, Sukey, the responsible parent and wife, is corrupted by domesticity and self-satisfaction. Her human sympathy shrinks to the limits of her immediate family and proves unequal to the demands made upon it by a Jewish refugee family. When last glimpsed in the "1956" section, Sukey has become pathetic: she is shown making one of her frequent visits to church to tell God cloying anecdotes from the past about PS, her favourite son who was killed while on National Service in Palestine.

Finally there is Marcus, who in The Game had taken the part of his mother and whose homosexuality is shown to be rooted in his mother's rejection of him. "As far as love from 'er goes," observes Regan, "Master Marcus was better born dead." As an adolescent Marcus insists that he will never marry: "I don't see how any of us could. After seeing *them*." Years later, his rich lover complains of Marcus's treatment of a mutual female friend: "Vulgar malice and spite! You sounded just like your awful mother." And later still, while at his most vicious and unreasonable during a quarrel with his cockney lover (incarnation of the "slum chum" he had fantasized about during childhood), Marcus suddenly realizes he "was screaming like a vulgar self-centred bitch. Like my mother, in fact."

There is a good deal more to the Matthews children than the linkages between their childhood and adult life. For example, in Margaret and her feelings about writing, and in Rupert's learning how to play demanding roles, Wilson explores complex questions about the relationship of the creative artist's life to his work. And Marcus's sentimental account of how as a young man he started "selling his bum" – an account from which the wit and irony that sustain the rest of the novel are unaccountably absent – detracts only a little from one's interest in his complex personality and struggle to evolve from a pansy boy and aesthete into an individual with a capacity for human sympathy. But the relation to the parental stem is the key to each of the siblings, and it is the successful incorporation of this theme with a panorama of a swath of twentieth-century English society that is the fundamental reason No Laughing Matter is such an impressive novel.

But there is a third informing principle at work in No Laughing Matter – Wilson's insistence on coming clean, on flaunting the artificiality and fictiveness of the text. We must now examine the results of this insistence, and assess its effect on the novel's social, moral, and psychological reality, which Wilson has so ambitiously laboured to create. The devices used to destabilize the reader have been well studied by several commentators.[41] There are the references to various art forms and their conventions, which repeatedly invite the reader to become aware that the object he holds in his hands is itself a piece of *bricolage*: the silent film in the opening section; the family theatricals; William Matthews's belletristic memoirs; discussions about painting; Sukey's broadcasts; the high camp stylization of Marcus's green ball; the plays and films in which Rupert acts. Most importantly, there is Margaret Matthews, the novelist within the novel. One of her early short stories – it is based on her twin sister's wedding – is reproduced *in toto*; and there are accounts of her grappling with the formal difficulties of her craft. A more blatant device for coming clean is the intermittent use of parody and pastiche: the cinematic techniques in the opening section; the rendering of some scenes in dramatic script: the scene in which the Matthews parents drown their children's kittens, which is presented as a take-off on the murder scene in the second act of *Macbeth* (with the drunken Regan becoming the porter at the gate). Most conspicuous are the five between-the-acts playlets which punctuate the text, each a parody of a kind of play popular at the time when the scene is set: "Before the Week-End" is imitation Maugham;[42] "Parents at Play: A Lesson in Lamarckian Survival" is Shavian; "The Russian Vine: An English Play" has its roots in Chekhov; "French Windows: An Interrupted Play" is à la mode Terence Rattigan; and "Pop and Motor: A Catastrophe" parodies Beckett's *Endgame*.

It is one thing to identify these devices and recognize that they constitute "a very explicit formal attribute" of *No Laughing Matter*.[43] It is more difficult to gauge accurately how the devices relate to the social and moral content of the novel, and how they affect the reader's response to the story. For example, in their salutary attempts to discredit the "folklore" about the non-experimental preoccupations of the contemporary English novel, both Malcolm Bradbury and Robert Burden overemphasize the novel's *anti-roman* features. For its self-conscious and destabilizing devices are clearly subordinate to its traditional mimetic and communicative functions. The novel is not primarily about itself; even Burden must concede that its "disruptive elements never completely subvert the realist text: history and social reality, character and intrigue, are fully sustained aspects of *No Laughing Matter*."[44] Such overemphasis might have been avoided if it had been realized that a better context in which to locate Wilson's novel is not that of contemporary French fictional experiments or American comic-apocalyptic ones but that of Fielding's *Tom Jones* and Thackeray's *Vanity Fair*, both of which employ a self-conscious narrator who through parodic and other devices conveys "a sense of the fictional world as an authorial construct set up against a background of literary tradition and convention," while at the same time offering "an intent, verisimilar representation of moral situations in their social contexts."[45]

The major reason for Wilson's employment of disruptive devices in *No Laughing Matter* should be apparent to anyone who has followed his development as a novelist. These devices provide a means for the expression and diffusion of the obsessive emotions which (to recall Wilson's own comments on the "magical power" of the great nineteenth-century novelists) creates the " 'apport' or atmosphere which is the indefinable personality of the novel." The primary obsessive emotion in Wilson's fiction is his sense of pervasive evil; what is most innovative about *No Laughing Matter* – the title itself calls attention to this (as did *Laughing Mirrors*, a working title ultimately discarded) – is that Wilson attempts "a more ribald, farcical treatment of evil in the hope that, by removing a certain solemnity or portentousness from the subject, I may have acclimatized horror more successfully to the novel form."[46] It is clear from comments in the *Iowa Review* interview that Wilson feels he has been successful in his attempt. It will not be apparent to all readers, however, that the drowning of the Matthews children's kittens in the language of *Macbeth* is any more successful a representation of evil than Simon Carter's shooting his beloved badgers or Celia Craddock's threat to slaughter her son's favourite Muscovy ducks if he leaves her for Bernard Sands. In any event, such considerations should not deflect attention from the central critical question concerning *No Laughing Matter*: the effect of the novel's self-conscious, disruptive *apport* on its social and moral content.

In addressing this question, I would begin by remarking that it is in some ways unfortunate that Wilson has used the term "alienating devices" to describe his novel's destabilizing procedures. For the effect of their intermittent employment is hardly that of the Brechtian *Verfremdung*. Wilson, who has described himself as a reformer, not a revolutionary,[47] has no desire to stir his audience to political action, nor does he want to extirpate sympathy and empathy in the name of critical awareness. The devices employed in *No Laughing Matter* do keep the reader from inferior, sentimental involvement in the life stories of the Matthews children, but they hardly estrange him altogether. They rather assist in the creation of a deeper, more reflective kind of involvement; for the presentational form of the novel mirrors and highlights certain important thematic features of the content. For one thing, the narrator of *No Laughing Matter* is as acutely self-conscious and stagy as are the Matthews children and their parents, who also have a similar taste for parody and impersonation. Indeed, one could plausibly argue, as Wilson himself does in the *Iowa Review* interview, that in the kitten drowning scene it is the Matthews parents themselves and not the parodic narrator who employ the language of Macbeth and Lady Macbeth.

More importantly, the vehicle is a medium for the expression of the novel's vision of human existence. For the self-conscious theatricality of *No Laughing Matter* conveys a sense of a disordered world of false-seeming, a Vanity Fair in which puppet-like characters act out their routines as in a marionette grand guignol. A sense of the futility of human existence, of the artificiality and inauthenticity of human relationships, of the nothingness beneath the surface, is not only declaimed – as it is by Quentin at the end of the 1919 section; it is enacted by the novel's self-conscious narration and employment of what might be called the inauthentic and artificial modes of parody and pastiche. It is in this world that the Matthews children must endeavour to cultivate some degree of authenticity and humanity. Through its self-conscious sense of its own artificiality, then, the reader is led to a sympathetic awareness that however stunted they may be by their parental environment, however bandied about by the *Zeitgeist*, the Matthews children do aspire to wholesomeness, and that whatever form they can impose on the chaos around them is, in Robert Frost's phrase, "velvet ... and to be considered for how much more it is than nothing."[48]

No Laughing Matter is, then, not so different from Wilson's earlier novels as it may initially appear, for what accounts for its strengths is the interpenetration of social, moral, and obsessive concerns within the presentational matrix of diversity plus depth. For this recipe to work, however, especially when the obsessive emotion is disseminated through alienating devices, the ingredients have to be carefully proportioned. In his next novel Wilson was less successful in achieving this delicate balance.

In the closing scenes of *No Laughing Matter*, which are set in Morocco and display several specimens of mid-1960s British youth, one can see Wilson beginning to feel his way into *As If by Magic*. For what is most noticeably new in the novel are the Third World settings (Tokyo, Borneo, Tangiers, Ceylon, and several Indian states, principally Goa) and the full-scale depiction of alienated youth and the hippie life-style, with its outré sexual mores, cultish modes of expression, outlandish costumes, communes, and spiritual quests. The major use to which the Eastern settings are put is expressive – the dissemination of a sense of overwhelming, unattributable evil. As the scenes shift from the West to the East, social and moral concerns become recessive; psychological and "transcendent" concerns become dominant. This fall and rise is nicely adumbrated in the scene in Colombo in which the earnest pleading of a young administrator – "But these are *social* questions ... " – is drowned out by the violent shrieking and clattering in the trees above him of the grotesque flying foxes: "flapping black leathery wings, red furry bodies, beady eyes, greedy mouths." In her novel, Meg Eliot was brought to the brink of an inner abyss by staring down at the desert from the airplane taking her to the country where political violence would soon claim her husband's life. But whereas Meg, after this brief exposure to Eastern evil, was returned to the known worlds of London and the South Coast, in *As If by Magic* Wilson insists on a more sustained exposure to what cannot be contained by categories of right and wrong. The pederasts of Tokyo and Borneo, the chain of causation that leads to the pitiful Sudra boy being stoned to death, the multiple rape of Elinor Tarbutt, and the religious riots in Goa are all examples of pervasive, gratuitous evil. The more he travels in the East the more Hamo Langmuir comes to hear behind quotidian sights and sounds "a high, distant overtone of perpetual desperate woe" and to wonder if this could be "the natural noise of the world" rather than "a sound simply present in his own too little disciplined head." This sound is distinctly reminiscent of the echo Mrs Moore hears in the Marabar caves in Forster's *A Passage to India*, the reverberations of which shatter the fragile liberal-humanist beliefs in order, progress, enlightened rationalism, friendship, and mutual understanding.

Two story lines alternate throughout *As If by Magic*. As in *The Middle Age of Mrs Eliot*, Wilson uses as his novel's central organizing principle the counterpoint of an introspective homosexual male of liberal humanist convictions and a more extroverted female whose crisis of personality is resolved by involvement in the world. In the story of Hamo Langmuir, the dominant theme is the discovery of evil. A plant geneticist, developer of a new strain of rice called Magic that has triple the yield of what it supersedes, Langmuir embarks on a tour of the East to witness at first hand the nutritive wonders of his Magic. What he finds – that the economic consequences of his discovery have led to the rich getting richer and the poor more hopelessly downtrodden – is profoundly disturbing to his liberal-humanist beliefs and is paralleled by an equally jolting internal discovery about the true nature of his sentimentalized and idealized homosexual lusts. During his visits to a homosexual nightclub in Tokyo and a pederastic orgy in Borneo (the two most repellent episodes in Wilson's entire canon) Langmuir comes to see himself in the mirror of the grotesque, aging adults who disguise their lust for young flesh in sickening fantasies of benevolence.

The reader of Wilson's fiction is on familiar ground here. As with Bernard Sands, but much more palpably, the belated recognition in a homosexual context of evil within the self is incapacitating and sets in motion the drift towards death. As is Gerald Middleton, Langmuir is brought to a crisis point located at the confluence of public and private responsibility. But while Middleton came to discover he could do nothing to remedy the harm caused by his private derelictions, he could at least deal successfully, if belatedly, with his professional obligations. Langmuir on the other hand is ineffectual in both realms. The basic reason for the difference is that while Middleton's crisis was primarily moral, Langmuir's is primarily psychological. He comes to realize that the sources of the overtones of perpetual desperate woe are both internal and external, but his pathetic attempts to mitigate both public and private evil accomplish nothing. His life ends in Goa when he is slaughtered by a mob to which he is vainly attempting to explain the limitations of his Magic; and in what follows there is nothing of the post mortem uplift of the close of *Hemlock and After*. Langmuir's posthumous proposals to change his institute's research priorities so as to take account of Third World social and economic realities come to nothing; and Alexandra Grant, his god-daughter and heir, finds in going through his mail that his cheques for generous sums, intended for the benefit of the boys he had coveted, have all been returned uncashed.

The other story line concerns the young Alexandra Grant and her friends. Earlier novels had evidenced Wilson's interest in "representatives of the Younger Generation," but it is unprecedented that he should devote roughly half a novel to contemporary youth. This is of course admirable in intention, and one applauds the boldness of such a remarkable extension of range in a novelist then in his late fifties. And it is true that one of the novel's finest sections describes "the flux and muddle ... as well as [the] deeply self-centred peace" of a commune on a North African beach and that the account of Elinor Tarbutt's quest for dissolution of self is finely done. But the attempt to hurdle such a wide generational and cultural gap is not without its dangers, as Wilson himself warned in 1954 when he spoke of older novelists falling into documentary when they attempted to inform their creations with the world of the young.

After leaving the new university at which she, together with Rodrigo and Ned (the other members of her *ménage à trois*), has read English literature, Alexandra completes the process of rejecting her moneyed background and her awful parents by going abroad to search for the magic of peace and fulfilment through sexual, then maternal and meditative means. At the end of the novel she has returned to England having learned – as expected – what Wilson spells out in his novel's closing sentence: that "no magic spells could solve her problems." The process through which Alexandra goes is a version of the late adolescent identity crisis which it seemed *de rigueur* for university students to undergo in the late 1960s, and there is nothing in Wilson's flamboyant rendering of this process to suggest that Alexandra's problems were any more serious than those of many of her real-life contemporaries. (By 1980, in speaking of "what the Western lost were seeking" in India, Wilson would remark that "I write 'were' for surely they are yesterday's persons.")[49] This becomes clear if we compare her crisis to Meg Eliot's mid-life crisis of personality and to the difficult process of adjustment to old age that Sylvia Calvert makes in *Late Call*. There is authorial sanction for so doing, for Wilson has said that Alexandra's portrait was meant to be the final panel of a triptych of major female characters, each at a different stage of the life cycle.[50] In each case the pattern is the same: dislocation, change of venue, protracted uncertainty and confusion, eventual restoration of balance, and return to the world. Meg Eliot's and Sylvia Calvert's crises are serious, deeply felt, and presented with a sympathetic insight that makes their portraits two of the best things in Wilson. But because he has so little inside sense of Alexandra's conundrums, Wilson's treatment of her necessarily lacks the sense of felt life that he regards as a distinguishing characteristic of great fiction.

Wilson's difficulty with Alexandra is most apparent towards the close of her story, where he seems not to know what to do with her. After she is shaken out of "the sort of false calm you've found, that kind of animal peace, the detachment of the cow concentrating on its udder," which Elinor rightly diagnoses as a malaise of self and which is analogous to Meg's temptation to remain in the nursery world, Wilson contrives various slapdash happenings to bring her story to a close. One of these episodes, the exceptionally forced scene in which Alexandra meets Langmuir just before his death and announces that she wants her homosexual godfather to marry her, underlines the fact that the alternating stories of Langmuir and Alexandra do not reinforce each other in the way they are intended to and that the sum of the novel's parts is greater than its whole. The telling contrast is with the climactic scene of *The Middle Age of Mrs Eliot*, in which Meg and David spend what is to be their last evening together, a scene which gains enormously from everything that has gone before it in the novel.

But the least well integrated feature of *As If by Magic* is its vehicle of presentation – the full-scale, flaunted use of alienating devices, parodic effects, burlesque, and farce – which is markedly different both from the alternation of inside and outside views (the mixture of diversity and depth) that Wilson had used in *The Middle Age of Mrs Eliot* and *Late Call* and from the more sparing, calculated, and thematically integrated 'alienating' devices used in *No Laughing Matter*. Take, for example, the novel's use of parody and its larger strategy of deliberate allusion to or echoes of other literary works. It is one thing when Alexandra, Rodrigo, Ned and Elinor make explicit literary allusions, as they are forever doing; these earnest young seekers after authenticity and enlightenment are fresh from reading Eng. Lit. at university; their holy writ is Lawrence, Tolkien, Forster, Dostoevsky, et al; and Wilson is concerned to dramatize "the terrible second-hand literariness of their lives" and to point up the limitations of "a sort of second hand magic of literature."[51] As Alexandra herself exclaims: "Oh damn Eng. Lit., that brought to one's mind always metaphors, symbols, quotations, and characters from books." But it is quite another thing for Wilson himself to load his novel with overt literary allusions, only some of which – like Langmuir's resemblance to Prince Myshkin – are called attention to by the young people. Examples are the portentously symbolic fog that envelops London in the novel's opening pages and recalls the opening of Dickens's *Bleak House*; the interminable drawing room scene soon after which recalls similar seemingly endless scenes in Dostoevsky; the parodies of American folk literature in the Tokyo brothel scene and of Sade's *Hundred and Twenty Days of Sodom* in the Borneo picnic of the "uncles"; the Feydeau farce scene in Ceylon; and the contrast between the upper class Langmuir and his demotic assistant Erroll, which has echoes of Don Quixote and Sancho Panza, as well as of Tolkien's Frodo and Sam.

Wilson has not contrived these allusions in order to add a vicarious symbolic heightening to the events in his narrative nor to have them serve as reminders of the second-hand literariness of his younger characters' lives. They are rather employed in the interests of farce, for in *As If by Magic* Wilson seems determined not to have the form and content exist in a mutually vivifying tension, but to take out of his novel with one hand what he has put into it with the other. The stages in Hamo's discovery of evil are repeatedly reduced to a series of "humiliating farces," including several pratfalls. Scenes involving Alexandra are made similarly grotesque and farcical, like the elaborate description of her, Rodrigo, and Ned sprawled asleep in her parents' baroque bedroom, with Ned's bearded face lolling over the bedside "like a pet animal asleep where it should not be," or the account of the bald, obese swami escaping in female disguise from a mob like Mr Toad from prison (another of Alexandra's literary associations).

In a subsequent commentary, Wilson explained that he clothed the story of Alexandra's self-discovery and Langmuir's discovery of evil in the garments of farce and parody in order to get for them "some kind of sense of sympathy ... a little sympathy for someone who might otherwise be rather repulsive to a number of people who might be reading the book."[52] In doing so, however, Wilson would seem to have neglected the fundamental importance of the quality and the intensity of the sympathy. Martin Price says that in *As If by Magic* "one is not so much struck by the game of self-conscious artifice as by the moral insight."[53] My own reaction is the opposite. Angus Wilson has used farce and other alienating devices to prevent his audience from indulging in certain kinds of inferior involvement. But he has not provided the wherewithal for a more appropriate and intense involvement as he did so successfully in *No Laughing Matter*. The involvement of the reader is the prerequisite for capturing his feelings (and thereby communicating the moral insight), which as late as the *Iowa Review* interview Wilson described as the novelist's goal, and which, as we have seen, he often emphasized in his earlier critical writing and strove with notable success to achieve in his earlier novels. But in *As If by Magic* the central characters and the reader are manipulated so gratuitously and bizarrely that they make considerations of sympathetic identification merely notional, and weaken the novel's energetic and insightful examination of the important subjects of Third World inequalities, the fragility of liberal humanist beliefs, and the search for the key to an integrated life.

V

It was not until 1980, seven years after *As If by Magic*, that Wilson's next novel was published. *Setting the World on Fire* begins with a brief foreword giving the historical "facts" about Tothill House, "the only great house in London with large formal gardens and a park remaining in private hands, [which] is situated just behind Westminster Abbey." This account closes with a little flourish of self-consciousness: "It only remains to say that the house and its history are of course the inventions of the author." A reader coming to this novel from Wilson's previous two fictions might well assume this to be the first of a fusillade of devices intended to flaunt the fictiveness of the text and to destabilize the reader. But the foreword contains virtually the only occurrence of such devices; and by itself Wilson's admission is no more disruptive of the representational surface of *Setting the World on Fire* than are the routine disclaimers of resemblances to real persons and places found in the prefatory notes to many realistic novels.

One reason for Wilson's return to a more traditional vehicle of presentation is that, unlike *No Laughing Matter* and *As If by Magic*, his eighth novel is relatively uninformed by obsessive energy or a sense of pervasive evil. The exception to this generalization is Marina Luzzi, an Italian jet-set millionairess, who is one of the more memorable supporting players in Wilson's canon. With her "breathless cascade of smart talk" and wicked mimicry, Marina tirelessly strives to keep at bay the worm of boredom by seeking out what is amusing: "Michelangelo, Raffaele, that's boaring. No. People *talk* about Verrio these days. That's what matters. And all Sir Francis and 'is little page boys called by numbers. They say 'e was very cruel to them. That's amusing." Her taste for the baroque reflects her dislike of order and regularity: "Chaos is the only exciting thing left. I adore chaos. Throwing all the rules out of the window at the old bores." There is "a lack of propriety, even a note of hysteria, to the absurdity and fun" that Marina communicates, and she increasingly becomes a minatory figure: "The Paris riots were boaring. Everyone looks for 1848 there. But not in *London*! I wish I could 'ave seen those London riots. But not the bombs. They are ugly and boaring like all technology." Even this qualifier is waived at the novel's close when Marina associates herself with terrorists intent on "setting the world on fire" with incendiaries.

But the title of Wilson's novel does not refer principally to Marina. At its centre are Piers and Tom Mosson, brothers whose nicknames for each other – Van and Pratt – call attention to the commanding presence in the novel, as both locus and symbol, of Tothill House itself. Renowned for its architectural union of opposites, the house had been designed by Sir Roger Pratt in the late seventeenth century. To its "marvellous sense of proportion" and classical restraint had been added the baroque extravagance of John Vanbrugh's Great Hall – one hundred feet high, one hundred long and fifty wide, with twisting black marble pillars, a lantern, and an enormous mural by Verrio depicting the fall from the chariot of the sun of Phaethon, the too-aspiring youth who before his fatal spill had come close to setting the world on fire.

Piers and Tom are the grandsons of Lady Mosson, who presides over Tothill House. Piers, the elder sibling, stands to inherit the house and the vast family fortune if his uncle Hubert dies childless. This seems likely after Hubert's engagement to Marina Luzzi is broken and it is revealed that the uncle's ruling passion is, so to speak, setting his bum on fire through having women beat him. Of the two siblings, Piers (Van) is dominant; Tom (Pratt) recessive. The latter "has all his feet on the ground. That's how he is." Even in adolescence Tom is terrified by the experience of walking alone over Westminster Bridge. The one exception to his cleaving to the ground – to the organized, planned, and measured, "the necessarily flat life of daily duty" – is his boundless admiration for his high-flying "wonderful brother" Piers, who has the charm and charisma that Tom lacks, and who yearns for the heights his brother eschews. The novel opens in 1948 with Piers, on his first visit to Tothill House at the age of eight, standing in the Great Hall awed by the grandeur of Phaethon's flight, which becomes in time the "symbol of all he aspired to, [in which] every sense was united, even sex." It becomes Piers's ambition to set the world on fire as a theatrical producer-director. His first production is a school performance of *Richard II*, which insists on the greatness of that king's fall ("Down, down I come like glist'r-ing Phaethon ... "). The novel's second and third quarters are devoted to events surrounding the plans of the precocious Piers (then in his eighteenth year) to stage Lully's opera *Phaethon* in Vanbrugh's Great Hall, an ambition only fulfilled a decade later in 1969, by which time Piers has inherited Tothill House.

Most of the characters in *Setting the World on Fire* are nicely hit off, and Wilson has a fine time describing Tothill House, its library, saloon, stables, gardens, and especially its Great Hall. And in addition to the centrepiece of the novel, Piers's triumphant production of Lully's opera, there are several social gatherings, at the depiction of which Wilson has always been very good: the headmaster's reception after *Richard II*; a family lunch at Tothill House; the first-night supper there after the début of *Phaethon*. But on the whole, for a novel by Angus Wilson, *Setting the World on Fire* is unusually spare of detail and incident. Just as there is little obsessive energy, so too there is a marked diminution of social breadth and moral depth, the two other principal sources of strength in Wilson's previous novels.

The social spectrum of *Setting the World on Fire*, for example, is restricted. Most of the novel's characters belong to the world of the enormously rich. Two other characters are genteel but in reduced circumstances – Piers's mother and her brother Eustace, the one plucky, the other a sponge. Both are types that Wilson has often done before. There are two characters from nearer the bottom of the social scale: Magda Sczekerny, Hungarian refugee and sub-librarian at Tothill House; and Ralph Tucker, estate factotum, aspiring playwright of the angry-young-man sort, and latterly a terrorist. But neither characterization goes much beyond the repeated comparison of the features of each to those of Dutch dolls. Moral depth is similarly cur-tailed, for no character is given any ethical, spiritual, or psychological quan-daries, and no character, not even Piers or Tom, is shown to grow or change. Though we see both siblings over an extended period of time, neither develops in personality or character; nor do we come to know them more deeply.

The reason for this is that *Setting the World on Fire* is different in both *apport* and kind from any of Wilson's previous fictions. If not nostalgic, the novel's mood seems reminiscent; its principal subject might be described as the intensities of adolescence and one might even suggest that for obsessive energy Wilson has substituted the less volatile fuel of remembrance. Westminster School, which the brothers attend, was Wilson's public school; the Christian Science beliefs of Lady Mosson recall those of Wilson's mother; and Piers's passion for the theatre recalls that of his creator, who had once considered making acting his career. Whatever its genesis, this mood is well suited to the kind of novel Wilson has written. *Setting the World on Fire* has a strong fabular or parabolic quality and Tom and Piers necessarily lack depth of characterization and moral complexity because they are subservient to the static symbolic patterning of Pratt/Vanburgh, classical/Romantic, order/freedom, soaring/earthbound. This contrast is the major organizing principle of the novel and an unprecedented departure from Wilson's previous methods of construction, which had resulted in sturdy edifices made with the brick, mortar, and wood of social notation, moral complexity, and expressive energy.

At the end of the novel's extremely foreshortened conclusion, Tom is bizarrely killed while protecting his brother – the side-effect of a terrorist plot in which Marina Luzzi is involved. In the novel's closing sentences, Piers reflects that the show must go on and that he must continue "to ascend the towers of imagination." It is clear that the reader of *Setting the World on Fire* is meant to be sympathetic to the heroic interpretation of the Phaethon myth and to Piers as a type of the ever-aspiring creative artist. Should the reader take one further step and regard Piers as an epitome of his creator? Like Angus Wilson, Piers is an impresario, a mimic, a contriver of splendid effects, and feels he "has a right every now and then to shake the audience out of a clichéd sense of piety." Piers, however, was only in his late twenties when he produced Lully's *Phaethon* in the Great Hall of Tothill House; Wilson was in his late sixties when *Setting the World on Fire* was published. And as we have seen, there is a great deal more than splendid effects and expert audience manipulation to be found in *Hemlock and After*, *The Middle Age of Mrs Eliot*, *Late Call*, and *No Laughing Matter* – novels which form part of one of the most impressive canons of any contemporary novelist.

Chapter Two

Brian Moore's Grammars of the Emotions

I

If one includes the novella *Catholics* and excludes *The Revolution Script*, a semi-documentary potboiler about the 1970 terrorist kidnappings in Quebec, Brian Moore has published twelve novels since *Judith Hearne* came out in 1955. The major pattern formed by these novels becomes visible when they are grouped according to their settings, which correspond to the stages of Moore's own life. Four of them have been set wholly in Ireland (the first three in his native Belfast): *Judith Hearne, The Feast of Lupercal* (1957), *The Emperor of Ice-Cream* (1965), and *Catholics* (1972). The Second World War gave Moore the opportunity to leave Ireland when he was in his early twenties, and for much of the 1940s he lived in different places on the continent before emigrating to Canada in 1948. This period of his life is represented in his fiction by *The Doctor's Wife* (1976), which is set in France and concerns the adulterous passion of its title character, who leaves husband and son behind in Ulster, *The Temptation of Eileen Hughes* (1981), which takes place in London, and *The Luck of Ginger Coffey* (1960), the story of a n'er-do-well Irish immigrant trying to make it in Montreal. After a decade in Canada, principally in Montreal, Moore moved to the United States where he has since lived, first in New York, then in southern California. These locales are the setting of the four ambitious works which comprise the apex of his achievement as a novelist: *An Answer from Limbo* (1962), *I Am Mary Dunne* (1968), *Fergus* (1971), and *The Great Victorian Collection* (1975). In their different ways all four novels involve a confrontation of the Old World of Roman Catholic Ireland and the secular New World of America. In Moore's own words, they are "balanced on that seesaw of emotion and memory which has been the fulcrum of my novels – the confrontation between now and then, between there and here, which was and is the fruit of my decision to choose exile."[1] *The Mangan Inheritance* (1979) seems in some respects the completion of this pattern. The confrontation of then and now, past and present is continued, but whereas in the earlier novels the movement had been outward from Ireland to North America, that of *The Mangan Inheritance* reverses the direction and begins a return trip.

While not so well known or widely acclaimed as Angus Wilson, John Fowles, or V.S. Naipaul, Moore does have a distinguished reputation and has received a degree of critical recognition. He has even been described as "a novelist's novelist."[2] It is not hard to find reasons why: the clarity of · his prose; the excellence of his ear – for example, his mastery of the inflections and idioms of American speech, which usually present insuperable difficulties for trans-Atlantic novelists (even for such resourceful stylists as Anthony Burgess and Angus Wilson); and his "great talent" for characterization, for "that exact description of common feelings which both individualizes the character and generalizes the experience."[3] Christopher Ricks has spoken of the "simple excellence" of Moore's novels, of their "concentrating, simply, directly and bravely on the primary sufferings and passions that everybody feels … In none of his novels is anything concealed except the art by which they transmute 'an ordinary sorrow of man's life' into something we care about. He does not, in fact, need the services of a literary critic."[4] In short, Brian Moore is a professional, the favourite living novelist of that consummate professional Graham Greene, who has praised "a quality of realism" in Moore's novels "which gives the reader a kind of absolute confidence – there will be no intrusion of the author, no character will ever put a foot wrong."[5]

Despite these encomia, however, Brian Moore's name is seldom mentioned in overviews of contemporary fiction, and while he is unquestionably an accomplished journeyman, some would hesitate to call him a major contemporary novelist, a designation all would apply to Wilson, Fowles, and Naipaul. Nigel Dennis, for example, added a codicil to the declaration of Graham Greene: "The author and his characters have only limited ambitions, so neither the unobtrusiveness of the former nor the Indian tread of the latter is a matter of great magnitude."[6] Certainly the subject matter of Moore's fiction – varieties of failure, crises points in the lives of unexceptional people, the hang-ups of a lapsed, self-exiled Irish Catholic writer – is restricted. And one could also say that his presentation of these concerns is similarly circumscribed. Even when his premise is fantastic, as in three of the later novels, the treatment follows the well-worn grooves of traditional realistic fiction and is as predictable as the novels' standard commercial lengths (*Catholics* aside). There is no big novel in Moore's canon, no predominant work showing all of his powers at full stretch; nothing, that is, comparable to *No Laughing Matter* or *The French Lieutenant's Woman* or *A House for Mr Biswas*.

One might further complain that no big themes of prime contemporary concern are wrestled with in Moore's fiction. One of his *revenants* says of the novels of the title character of *Fergus*: "The problem here is that this man is not living in history. His work, such as it is, ignores the great issues of the age." One might similarly remark that while most major novelists struggle to break new ground, to affirm, to make a positive statement, Moore remains content to lick familiar wounds and to play over and over again his personal record of failure, loneliness, exile, meaninglessness. His fellow Ulsterman James Simmons has even argued that Moore is not primarily concerned with human life but with art – that he is committed to "the Flaubertian error": an art for art's sake aesthetic which (as another of the *revenants* in *Fergus* suggests) is his substitute for religious belief. Because of this self-withering, Simmons argues, Moore is content to exercise his artistic talents in the depiction of characters to whom fulfilment, felicity, vision, and transcendence are denied.[7]

My own view of Brian Moore is that he is an exceptionally interesting, affecting, and accomplished novelist, as I hope to show in what follows. For when Christopher Ricks said that Moore did not need the services of a literary critic there were only five novels in the canon; there are now twelve and there is a need for critical mediation between novelist and reader if the essential distinction and cumulative richness of Moore's work is to be appreciated.

One of the reasons his body of work is seldom pointed out in surveys of contemporary fiction is that Moore's peregrinations have denied him a readily identifiable regional or cultural base. Another is that it is not easy to type Moore's fiction as belonging to any of the dominant trends in the novel during the last twenty-five years. For example, while the winds of the *crise de roman* have blown around him, Moore has had the confidence to chart his own course. "The Novel House is empty," as he has hyperbolically put it: "Its tenants have wandered out witlessly into Barthian byways, through Borgesian mazes, to squat, disconsolate, at Beckett's crossroads, waiting for some faceless God."[8] In a "sort of camp period with novels," during which "black humor, Beckett's influence, [and] the *anti-roman*" are all "considered to be important," Moore has had the strength to be his own man and set his own standards.[9] He has remained committed to self-exploration, to the dramatization of his own vision of human existence through the presentational medium of character, and to the novel's traditional communicative purposes: "I try to explore my own experience in ways that will also prove meaningful and satisfying to other people."[10]

Any consideration of Moore's ambitions as a novelist or his views on the state of the contemporary novel must begin with the recognition of the tremendous influence upon him of James Joyce. His first two novels, *Judith Hearne* and *The Feast of Lupercal*, are much indebted to the example of Joyce's *Dubliners*: their central characters, both "outcast from life's feast" like Maria in "Clay" or Mr Duffy in "A Painful Case," are observed against a *Dubliners*-like urban background of social and religious stagnation, and the style of presentation of both novels is close to that of Joyce's "scrupulous meanness." These resemblances suggest what Moore's subsequent novels and certain comments he has made on his own work confirm: that the influence of Joyce, and the desire to avoid his over-influence, have been determining factors in his artistic development. Moore has said that Joyce, the "literary hero" of his youth, was a "tremendous influence" and that *A Portrait of the Artist as a Young Man* "seems to me, as it does to almost every Irish writer, even today, almost the story of one's early life. It's our generation's *Catcher in the Rye*; our *Huck Finn* – all those things. The retreats, the hellfire, the feeling of hopelessness with girls, etc." Moore goes on to explain how *Portrait* was the negative determinant of his first moment of creative choice: "When I came to think about writing a novel, one thing I didn't want to do was an autobiographical novel because I thought "Who can compete with *Portrait?*"[11] He determined to write about a woman rather than a man because of the fear of being autobiographical and, as he elsewhere explains, the "abstract idea" of this woman's story was similarly determined because of the territory his precursor had previously appropriated: "Joyce and other people [had] written about loss of faith in intellectuals: no one [had] written about loss of faith in a very ordinary person."[12]

Moore's initial conservatism as a novelist – for a long time he eschewed anything even remotely smacking of the experimental, expressionistic, fantastic, or pyrotechnical – seems similarly influenced by the awesome shadow of Joyce. For there seems something *parti pris* about his limiting assessment of Joyce's greatness: "Joyce thought of himself as a great innovator, but I think the true value of his novels rests in ... the 'celebration of the commonplace.' And the finest things in *Ulysses* and in the *Portrait* rest on a naturalistic basis, on character and on his ability to write about ordinary people and ordinary – even banal – situations. I think that is [his] strength; take that away and the books disappear ... The best part of *Ulysses* is the beginning."[13]

It is interesting to note that similar distinctions are found in Moore's comments on other writers. He admires the parts of Fowles's *The Magus* that are set "in a real world": the early scenes in London and the interlude on mainland Greece. But the rest of the novel he regards as close to preposterous.[14] Similarly, Moore thinks that Saul Bellow's grittily realistic *Seize the Day*, the story of a single day in the life of Tommy Wilhelm, a middle-aged failure forced to confront the reality of his existence and driven to the recognition of his true needs, is "a magnificent book – it's one of the best books written in the last fifteen or twenty years." But Moore does not like the parabolic *Henderson the Rain King*, and "I don't really like *Herzog.*"[15] As for the French writers of the *nouveau roman*: "they are interested in furniture. I am anti *anti-Roman*." Like V.S. Naipaul, Moore has "an interest in clarity and [has] the sort of mind that doesn't want my reader to be deceived or awed by technique ... if you find the perfect way to tell [a good story] nobody will even notice that there's a technique."[16] As for Nabokov, Moore finds him: "very overrated, especially by himself; he believes he is continuing the Joycean tradition, but he has none of Joyce's sense of real life, that down-to-earth sense: what Joyce called in a wonderful phrase about his work 'the celebration of the commonplace'."[17] Contemporary writers, Moore feels, "are losing sight of that real world in which our parents and relatives still live ... [that] real, ordinary, dull world ... That's one of the crises of the novel that nobody discusses nowadays."[18]

It is against the background of his views on the contemporary fictional scene that criticism of Moore's novels should be assessed. As to the complaint that his subject matter is limited and parochial: it is true that an Irish Catholic background is helpful in becoming habituated to the nuances of his fiction, and in what follows I have not tried to pretend otherwise. But all novelists render human experience in concrete terms, and good novelists are able to show how that experience is representative. Only a few have Moore's particular background; but everyone has a personal, and almost everyone a familial past, just as everyone has a childhood. And while there may be many emotional languages, they have one underlying grammar which, as the narrator of *Fergus* says, is formed by our parents. Similarly all adults have special moments in their lives – crisis points or situations of stress – in which they are forced to confront the reality of their lives. As Moore rightly says, it is in precisely these situations that the drama of his novels is found, in "the moment in a person's life, the crucial few weeks or months, when one suddenly confronts the reality or unreality of one's illusions."[19] And if Moore's central characters are all in various ways exiled or alienated – is that not widely representative, indeed is it not what Moore himself has called "the classic pattern" found in contemporary writing?[20]

Concerning the charge that Moore's novels lack big themes of overriding contemporary importance: if this is taken as an observation, not an accusation, one cannot but agree. During the Second World War Moore witnessed "the great happenings of my generation": he saw the Germans fleeing Naples; the dead brought off hospital ships at Anzio; collaborators shot dead in the streets of Marseilles; the death camp at Auschwitz; and the advance of the Russian armies across Poland. But when at the age of thirty he quit his job as a reporter for a Montreal newspaper and sat down in a cabin in the Laurentians to find out at last if he was meant to be a novelist, it was not about these cataclysmic events that he found himself writing, but of his native Belfast and an unattractive middle-aged spinster, a secret drinker trapped in genteel poverty, who is forced to confront the terminal emptiness of her life. "In that first novel," Moore has said, "I discovered a subject which was, over the years, to become central to most of my writing. It is loneliness. It is, in particular, that desperation which invades the person who discovers his life has no meaning."[21]

Since then Moore has continued to write about more or less ordinary people in commonplace situations and their attempts to cope with themselves and their burdens. One such burden is the past, which, says Moore, "is landed on our doorstep, for all of us. We're trapped by the past, it's rubbish we can't get rid of."[22] Another is the opposite side of the coin: "this new sense of rootlessness which so many people experience today ... [this] loss of identity ... [this] feeling we are no longer able to relate to our own past, that we no longer know the person we were ten years ago."[23] A third burden is failure, for one of the quintessential givens of Moore's fiction is that "failure is a more interesting condition than success. Success changes people; it makes them something they were not and dehumanizes them in a way, whereas failure leaves you with a more intense distillation of that self you are."[24] Failure, like loneliness and the discovery that life has no meaning, may be desolating but at least it "clarifies" and leaves one "less deceived" about oneself and about the nature of the world.

The last two phrases in quotation marks are from poems of Philip Larkin, Moore's junior by a year, whose work has a number of close similarities with Moore's. Both are accomplished craftsmen and technically conservative. Both have a narrow range of subject matter and theme and both are committed to the depiction of the sufferings and burdens of ordinary people living in a post-Christian world in which all beliefs are known to be illusory. For Moore's characters, as for Larkin's, the "long perspectives / Open at each instant of our lives" serve only to "link us to our losses"; and life

Whether or not we use it ... goes,
And leaves what something hidden from us chose,
And age, and then the only end of age.[25]

In both writers portraits of the artist are unflinchingly de-idealized; in both, pity and compassion usually remain implicit, though sentimentality is sometimes risked in the interests of conveying a sense of the ordinary truths that make life bearable. This comparison of the two writers could be developed further, but enough has perhaps been said to explain why more than once in what follows poems of Philip Larkin will be used as points of reference in bringing into focus distinctive features of the fiction of his contemporary peer.

II

In his first two novels Moore tried "to depict the moment of crisis in the lives of ordinary people, the moment when all the things they were and have become rise up to confront them – the two or three crisis weeks in a life when the climactic decision is made or not made."[26] Both *Judith Hearne* and *The Feast of Lupercal* are studies of losers, whose fates are determined by the claustrophobic gentility of Belfast and the suffocating weight of Irish Catholicism. *Judith Hearne* has been called "perhaps the finest novel to come out of Northern Ireland" and is unquestionably a more powerful work than *The Feast of Lupercal*.[27]

It is also more rough-hewn. One reason (Graham Greene to the contrary) is Moore's inability to refrain from authorial intrusions, which are an index of his residual bitterness concerning the religion of his fathers and the city of his birth. For example, an empty Catholic church is described as "cleared of its stock of rituals, invocations, prayers, a deserted spiritual warehouse waiting new consignments." And as Judith Hearne and James Madden walk down Wellington Place, Moore interjects this comment on "the designated centre of the city, the staring white ugliness of City Hall":

There, under the great dome of the building, ringed around by forgotten memorials, bordered by the garrison neatness of a Garden of Remembrance, everything that was Belfast came into focus. The newsvendors calling out the great events of the world in flat, uninterested Ulster voices; the drab facades of the buildings grouped around the Square, proclaiming the virtues of trade, hard dealing and Presbyterian righteousness. The order, the neatness, the floodlit cenotaph, a white respectable phallus planted in sinking Irish bog. The Protestant dearth of gaiety, the Protestant surfeit of order, the dour Ulster burghers walking proudly among these monuments to their mediocrity.

Another reason for the novel's comparative crudity of presentation is Moore's concern to give outside as well as inside views of his central character. This leads to the awkward device of a series of one-paragraph soliloquies assigned to Judith's fellow guests at Mrs Henry Rice's seedy boarding-house and to interruptions of pace near the end of the novel caused by brief shifts to the points of view of a bank cashier and a wine-and-spirit merchant. The purpose of these outside points of view is the same as that of the authorial intrusions and of a number of successfully integrated features of the novel (for example, the characterizations of Mrs Rice and Father Francis Xavier Quigley): to give the reader a sense of the grey, venal world in which the unloved and desperately lonely Judith Hearne, an unattractive, snobbish, and impecunious spinster in her mid-forties, must live our her life.

Before the novel's present time, Judith Hearne had spent years caring for her Aunt D'Arcy, a selfish, domineering woman whose life, like that of Eveline's mother in Joyce's *Dubliners* story, ends in a "final craziness," but continues to lay "like a spell on the very quick" of Judith's being.[28] *Faute de mieux*, Judith remembers "her dear aunt" fondly and in the opening paragraphs of Moore's novel her photograph and a coloured oleograph of the Sacred Heart are the first belongings she unpacks as she settles into the latest in a series of one-room lodgings. Judith has had a lifelong devotion to the Sacred Heart, "her guide and comforter. And her terrible judge," and early in the novel her religious observances are shown to be the one bright spot in her drab life. Not only can she "put loneliness aside on a Sunday morning" and become one with the congregation at mass; her belief allows her a sustaining hope: "She had always prayed for guidance, for help, for her good intentions. Her prayers would be answered. God is good."

Judith allows herself to feel that God has brought into her life James Madden, her landlady's brother. Also lonely, with time to kill, Madden has returned to Ireland after three decades of menial employment in New York, though he leads Judith to believe his trans-Atlantic station was more exalted. This misapprehension helps strengthen Judith's illusion that God is finally providing for her. At the same time her breeding and an expensive watch of her aunt's lead Madden to the incorrect conclusion that Judith has money. Thinking her a likely business partner, he feeds his illusion that he can "get going again, make a new start" in Ireland. When the truth of Madden's background and his intentions is forced upon Judith, the reader discovers a final affinity between the two characters: a problem with drink. As her illusion concerning Madden begins to crumble, the alcoholic Judith locks herself in her room, puts on her nightdress, turns the picture of the Sacred Heart to the wall, takes a bottle of cheap whiskey from her trunk, and pours. "The yellow liquid rolled slowly in the glass, opulent, oily, the key to contentment. She swallowed it, feeling it warm the pit of her stomach, slowly spreading through her body, steadying her hands, filling her with its secret power. Warmed, relaxed, her own and only mistress, she reached for and poured a tumbler full of drink."

In this way the major crisis of Judith Hearne's life is precipitated: her loss of faith. In a dark, empty church she beseeches her God: "O Sacred Heart, please, I need Your strength, Your help. Why should life be so hard for me, why am I alone, why did I yield to the temptation of drink, why, why has it all happened like this? O Sacred Heart, lighten my cross." She raises her tear-filled eyes to the altar, but the "tabernacle was silent. Behind the door, God watched. He gave no sign." Then, unexpectedly, the per-functory, undevout manner of an old sacristan brings into Judith's mind "the terrible doubt" that perhaps there is no God in the tabernacle, only round wafers of unleavened bread: "Supposing, just supposing, her heart cried, supposing nobody has listened to me in all these years of prayers. Nobody at all up above me, watching over me ... Was there nothing to pray to? ... What if there was no God? ... if it is only bread? If no one hears? No one? ... and if I am alone?"

Her faith shaken, Judith goes on a binge, which becomes a gamut of humiliation. She defies God, "if You're there," to show her a sign; she takes her meagre savings from the bank and checks into Belfast's best hotel; she smuggles gin into Earnscliffe Home for the friend who had taught her the assuagements of drink but is now – it is a prevision of Judith's own fate – "a forgotten old woman, mumbling in a corner in a house run by nuns"; she insists to the wife of the only family who is kind to her that she has never liked her. Finally, exhausted and despairing, Judith attacks the tab-ernacle door in hatred after having reached the nadir of the black truth of her existence: "There are no reasons for this terrible thing [her suffering]."

In the novel's final scene, Judith Hearne, now convalescent at Earnscliffe Home, utters the one minimal, hopeless prayer that is left her: "I do not believe. O Lord, help my unbelief." But her final action in the novel is identical with her first: putting out in a strange room the pictures of her aunt and even of the Sacred Heart, for as she reflects "No matter what you are, it [the picture] is still part of me." Though one would sorely like to do so, it is not possible to find at the end of *Judith Hearne* anything positive or uplifting. Although Judith has come to know the illusionless truth about herself it does not make her free (as the reappearance of her pictures reminds us) and will do nothing to change her terminally lonely and unfulfilled life. Though her suffering is, in Wordsworth's phrase, "permanent, obscure and dark," it has nothing of "the nature of infinity," for Judith is not a visionary poet, but an ordinary person incapable of the long perspectives necessary for such transcendent intimations.

One can reflect that her faithless faith, though it gives her only a clear-sighted view of the desolation of her reality, is superior to the alternative faiths (or illusions) of other characters in the novel. James Madden's religion, for instance, consists of "making your Easter duty once a year, going to Mass on Sunday morning. Religion was insurance. It meant you got security afterwards. It meant you could always turn over a new leaf. Just as long as you got an act of perfect contrition said before your last end, you'd be all set"; and his illusions of success do not keep him from loneliness, from drinking away his afternoons in the company of sponges, or from forcing sexual intercourse upon a sixteen-year-old servant girl. Bernie Rice's undergraduate atheism is as fatuously and self-servingly maintained as his claims to be an artist. And the institutional beliefs represented by Father Quigley are thoroughly repulsive. But such comparisons offer only cold comfort to the sympathetic reader, and it would be a disservice to Moore's novel and to the intensity of his concern for his central character to point a constructive moral to adorn Judith's story.

In Philip Larkin's "Deceptions," the poet asks what comfort he could possibly offer the girl he has read about in Mayhew's *London Labour and the London Poor*, who was drugged, raped, and left desolate in a London bedroom a century ago. For she would hardly care to know that she was "less deceived" than her ravisher who (like James Madden going to the bedroom of his teenage prey) stumbles up "the breathless stair / To burst into fulfilment's desolate attic." One can properly say of Judith Hearne only what Larkin says about the subject of his poem:

> What can be said,
> Except that suffering is exact, but where
> Desire takes charge, readings will grow erratic?[29]

It is in the unillusioned clarity of this perception that much of the power of Brian Moore's first novel lies.

The Feast of Lupercal, published two years after *Judith Hearne*, resembles its predecessor in setting, subject, theme, and presentation. Once again Moore studies the effect of the repressively genteel, authoritarian culture of Roman Catholic Belfast on a lonely, emotionally underdeveloped character unskilled in human relations and locked into a sterile privacy. The novel recounts a few crucial weeks in the life of Diarmuid Devine, a bachelor in his late thirties, whose infatuation with Una Clarke, the twenty-year-old Protestant niece of a fellow instructor at Saint Michan's College, solidifies into love, but begins to evaporate as soon as the heat of cultural authority, mainly represented by the administration of the school, begins to be felt. Both product and victim of his culture, Devine, like Judith Hearne, is made to run a gamut of humiliation, the only reward of which is the bitter cup of illusionless self-knowledge.

The Feast of Lupercal is more polished, dispassionate, and understated than its predecessor – qualities that Moore later ascribed to "a sort of natural pulling back in the second novel" and to a deliberate attempt to write in an "anti-melodramatic" vein.[30] The novel does contain passages like the following about Belfast: "It was all a clique, this city made up of cliques, drama cliques, religious cliques, school cliques, and God knows what else"; but these are the reflections of the central character and not the result of authorial intrusion. And the characterization of Father Keogh, the president of the school, is so evenhanded that, as Moore later complained, many readers have mistakenly taken for "a kind old man" this "very spirit of authoritarianism and Catholicism at its worst. He is Realpolitik all the way."[31] This is a mistake that not even the most inattentive reader of Judith Hearne could make concerning Father Quigley, who in the confessional was "the efficient foreman, setting the belt of sins in motion" while thinking about his next meal and reflecting that rissoles gave him heartburn.

But what The Feast of Lupercal gains through evenhandedness and the eschewal of melodrama it loses in intensity and depth of reader involvement. Indeed, Moore came to feel that his novel was "terribly underplayed … and a little too quiet."[32] There are real gains, like the splendid description of the group of elderly guests at a party, in which the still, sad music of ordinary humanity grown old is piercingly heard:

Here were the old ones. Tim Herron's mother and his wife's father, an aged uncle, a solitary aunt. Five or six unmarried females, silly, elderly, out of things. All of them dressed in their Sunday best, wondering what to do with themselves. For they had so looked forward to this party, and now, as usual, they were not enjoying it. They sat in a stiff oval on the sofas and chairs, trying to think of small, useless remarks. Unwanted, even by each other, they were the kind of relatives who must be invited to every function because, being the least noticed, they were quickest to take offense. Someone had given them glasses of sherry and there were a few small biscuits on a plate. All waited for supper, like children for a treat …

And when that had been said, there was nothing more to say. They sat waiting for him to say something – and after a few moments of silence, the old ladies turned to each other; the micelike whispering began, talk in tiny contrast to the laughter and liveliness from the floor below. Out of it, in this room, the old ones and the maiden ladies waited for Mr Devine to bring some of the party to them. And when he could not, they wished that he would go, they could discuss him then, they could use him as a starting point to begin again that familiar conversational pilgrimage from the unsatisfying present to the familiar past. And soon, supper would come. A nice supper. They could discuss the meal. They waited, therefore, watching him, willing him away.

Still, the emotion evoked by this description is pathos and no deeper chords are struck elsewhere in the novel, for one can feel for the story of Diarmuid Devine's journey towards the truth about himself only a quality of pity that is not far removed from embarrassment. One reason for this is that the novel goes on too long; its emotional charge would have been greater if it were more concentrated and pared down to novella length. This is especially true of Devine's developing relationship with Una, which is treated in too much detail. The object of Devine's growing affections is not a sharply focused or interesting characterization. This is not necessarily a weakness, for Una is similarly undeveloped in personality and character – indeed, if she were less a fledgling it would be difficult to imagine her giving Devine the time of day. Virtually all one needs to know about Una is nicely conveyed by one sentence early in the novel: "She was young and there was something wild and unfinished about her, as though she were in her first year of nylon stockings and lipstick and not yet used to them." After this, the more one sees of Una the less interesting she becomes and the less involved one becomes with Devine's passion.

The major reason *The Feast of Lupercal* is a less engaging, less powerful work than *Judith Hearne* lies in the difference between the plights of the two central characters. Judith is tormented by the loss of the religious faith that has been her sole refuge and support; Devine on the other hand is threatened merely with the loss of respectability, and his crisis never goes qualitatively beyond "a heavy apprehension, reminiscent of childhood when something has been broken and someone will tell." In interviews Moore has twice insisted that, unlike Judith Hearne, Devine "had choice – he could have gone away with that girl"; "his fate was, finally, his own fault."[33] The reader of Moore's novel would be well advised not to take these afterthoughts too seriously, for Diarmuid Devine is about as capable of changing the circumstances of his life as Eliot's Prufrock, whom he resembles in a number of particulars, including being "Deferential, glad to be of use, / Politic, cautious, and meticulous" and in giving social convention priority over desire.

The initial description of Devine's appearance is distinctly Prufrockian:

He was a tall man, yet did not seem so: not youthful, yet somehow young; a man whose appearance suggested some painful uncertainty. He wore the jacket and waistcoat of a business suit, but his trousers were sag-kneed flannels. His black brogues clashed with loud Argyle socks. The military bravura of his large mustache was denied by weak eyes, circled by ill-fitting spectacles. Similarly, his hair, worn long and untidy behind the ears, thinning to a sandy shoal on his freckled brow, offset the Victorian respectability of his waistcoat, gold watch chain and signet ring.

He does try to cultivate a more up-to-date appearance when he determines for the first time in his life to bid for a female's attention. And in the novel's climactic scene, he has even come to find himself alone in his basement flat with a not unwilling Una. But his attempts at seduction are pathetically inadequate and Una, who is also a virgin, does not know how to take the lead. On the bed where he has masturbated thousands of times, Devine is unable to consummate his love for Una, "his sinful imagination" having "atrophied reality."

His private humiliation over, Devine's public humiliation begins the next day with adolescent scribblings on the walls of a school lavatory and with his spineless inability to admit to her uncle that Una has spent the night in his flat. His love for her pales before the overwhelming question: "*Oh Merciful God, how did I get mixed up in a thing like this?*" The public humiliation reaches its climax when Devine, a teacher who has long used the cane as a pedagogic aid, is himself caned by Una's uncle – a punishment that under-lines the emotionally stunting nature of the authoritarian culture of Saint Michan's, epitome of the Irish Catholic culture that has made Devine what he is.

On the last page of *The Feast of Lupercal* Devine says good-bye to Una, who is leaving for a new life in London. He reflects that "She was right, he couldn't change. For the rest of his life he'd go on telling people what they wanted to hear." One is free to reflect that a positive result of Devine's penitence is self-knowledge, but such constructive implications are sharply qualified by the striking image with which the novel ends – an example (like the description of the old people at the party) of the quietly understated artistry of *The Feast of Lupercal* at its best. As he watches Una walk away, the blinkered horse standing beside him becomes the perfect emblem of Devine himself and of the irreparable nature of his existence:

Beside him, in the avenue, a horse and cart waited idle, as their owner offered wood blocks by the bag at a front door across the way. The horse's head moved like a mine detector along the gutter, reins slack over the strong back. Mr Devine, watch-ing as Una turned the corner, absently put out his hand and fondled the horse's neck. The powerful muscles fluttered at his unexpected touch and the horse swung its head up, looking wildly down the avenue in the narrow focus of its blinkers. Horse and man looked down the avenue, and there was no one there. The horse, harnessed, dumb, lowered its head once more. The man went back into the house.

In *The Emperor of Ice-Cream*, Moore's fifth published novel, the third with an Irish setting, another point of comparison between him and Joyce is apparent. Richard Ellmann has remarked that Joyce was more interested in parental love than in sexual love. In Brian Moore's novels parental relationships are at least as important as sexual relationships, usually more so. *The Emperor of Ice-Cream* is the *Bildungsroman* that Moore chose not to attempt a decade earlier at the beginning of his career. The novel's subject is the late adolescence of Gavin Burke in Belfast during an eighteen-month period from November 1939 to April 1941. The historical background – the Phony War, the Battle of Britain, and the bombing of Belfast by the Germans – frames the stages of Gavin's drift towards manhood and provides a shape for Moore's episodic, low-key novel. So does the *Harmonium* poem of Wallace Stevens which runs through Gavin's mind more than once, the importance of which Moore calls attention to in the novel's flamboyant title. The refrain of "The Emperor of Ice-Cream" urges an end to phoniness ("Let be be finale of seem"), and while its first stanza speaks of whipping "in kitchen cups concupiscent curds" (a splendid image for the tempests of adolescent sexuality), its last stanza contains a sobering image of death – a woman's horny feet protrude to show "how cold she is, and dumb."

While *The Emperor of Ice-Cream* has the same setting as *Judith Hearne* and *The Feast of Lupercal*, it differs from Moore's first two novels in several ways. It is more comic in terms of both its sometimes funny incidents and its positive conclusion; more loosely organized because of the extended time period; and more panoramic. There are a number of scenes and characters that relate only tangentially to Gavin's growth: for example, his fellow workers at the Air Raid Precautions post: "an illiterate ex-weight lifter ... an old soldier who dyes his hair black, a drunken officer type, a hod carrier, a dwarf, some old charladies, and a blonde semi-whore"; or the people Gavin encounters on his forays outside his family's middle class Catholic world: "Jews, left-wing ministers, pansies, poets, boozers, puppeteers: this was a grown-up world, undreamed of in the St Michan's school philosphy."

One reason for the comparative lightness and optimism of *The Emperor of Ice-Cream* is that Gavin Burke is not a loser. Though for most of the novel he thinks of himself as "a failure in life" and midway through is so judged by his father, Gavin has the youthful capacity to outgrow and to avoid being trapped by his environment. Another reason is that there are no ambiguities or qualifications surrounding his actions. He is not an embryonic artist, and he does not have to injure others or cross moral minefields to reach the threshold of adult life. And his emergent point of view is shown to be unequivocally superior to that of the novel's two principal representatives of his community's values: his father and his on-again, off-again girl friend. Gavin's view of his father as "one of the most prejudiced, emotional, and unreasonable of men" is corroborated by the description of how Mr Burke reads his morning newspaper: "shuffling through a page of stories until he found one which would confirm him in his prejudice. A Jewish name discovered in an account of a financial transaction, a Franco victory over the godless Reds, a hint of British perfidy in international affairs, an Irish triumph on the sports field, an evidence of Protestant bigotry, a discovery of Ulster governmental corruption: these were his reading goals." Sally Shannon's values are equally clear-cut: she makes crisp distinctions between the venial sin of necking and the mortal sin of going beyond, urges Gavin to get a grip on himself in a way that reminds him of "confession in the days when he had believed in confession," and tells him to think of his future security in a way that reminds him of his mother. In short, there is much to confirm Gavin's description of Sally as "a little Catholic bourgeois prig whose main interest in life seems to be the rules of courting etiquette."

The most important element in Gavin's successful escape from the prison of Catholic Belfast is fortuitous: the German decision to bomb his native city. At one point in his story Gavin had reflected that nothing would ever change in Ireland and that Yeats was wrong in 1916 to think that he and his countrymen could be "changed, changed utterly." But when the bombs begin to fall and the fires start at the beginning of the novel's powerful closing section, Gavin feels "an extraordinary elation" and a sense of release in which there is joy but no fear. For him all is utterly changed by his liberating encounter with death during the long day he voluntarily spends in a hospital morgue placing randomly piled corpses in coffins:

in the stink of human excrement, in the acrid smell of disinfectant, these dead were heaped, body on body, flung arm, twisted feet, open mouth, staring eyes, old men on top of young women, a child lying on a policeman's back, a soldier's hand resting on a woman's thigh, a carter, still wearing his coal sacks, on top of a pile of arms and legs, his own arm outstretched, finger pointing, as though he warned of some unseen horror.

Until this extraordinary experience, Gavin's reflections and debates with himself had been orchestrated by the antiphonal voices of his White Angel and his Black Angel, the two guardians whose presence had indicated that despite his loss of faith Gavin's consciousness was still defined by the religious culture of his family. But he now begins to hear "a new grown-up voice" that tells him Sally Shannon will never change and that he has outgrown her.

The termination of this relationship is, however, a relatively minor matter. In the novel's final scene, during which his new voice again counsels wisely, the subject is the parental relationship which in Brian Moore's novels can never be terminated. Gavin returns to his family's bomb-damaged, now condemned house and enters its sitting room, "unchanged since his childhood," to discover it has changed at last. His father also enters the room, for he has returned from Dublin, to which he had removed the rest of his family, out of worry for the son who had earlier thought his father no longer cared about him. Moved by the evidence that his world too has changed, changed utterly, Mr Burke begins to cry and says he has been a fool while Gavin maintains a new-found manly silence and reaches for his hand.

At one point in *The Emperor of Ice-Cream* Gavin had reflected with disgust on the part of his world that seemed most unchanging: "the frozen ritual of Irish Catholicism perpetuating itself *in secula, seculorum*": "the diurnal dirge of Masses all over the land, the endless litanies of evening devotions, the annual pilgrimages to holy shrines." These were of course some of the seemingly immutable ceremonies of pre-Vatican II Catholicism. The subject of *Catholics*, Moore's eighth novel, are the profound changes that have taken place in the Roman Catholic Church since Pope John XXIII first opened the windows to let in fresh air. In this spare and resonant tale, which illustrates what a powerful pressure the religion of his parents and of his youth has continued to exert on Moore's imagination, the antagonism of the early novels to Catholicism is replaced by a sense of loss and regret for what is now gone. Indeed, *Catholics* is a triumph of the sympathetic imagination, for the kind of post-Vatican II ecclesiastical novel that one would surely have expected from the author of *Judith Hearne* and *The Feast of Lupercal* would have been a work like the excellent *Three Cheers for the Paraclete* of the Australian Irish Catholic novelist, Thomas Keneally, which sides with a young, intelligent, and humane priest in his struggles against Down Under replicas of Father Quigley, Father Keogh, and Father McSwiney (the sadistic Dean of Discipline in Moore's second novel). But what Moore has masterfully brought off in *Catholics* is something different and more difficult.

Catholics is mildly futuristic, being set in the closing years of the twentieth century. By this time the forces of ecumenism have carried the day: the Church is no longer interested in souls but in "the good of mankind"; the World Ecumen Council in Amsterdam seems more powerful than the Vatican; there is talk of an *apertura* with the Buddhists; the "best thinking saw the disappearance of the church building as a place of worship in favor of a more generalised community concept, a group gathered in a meeting to celebrate God-in-others"; and it is even the case that Holy Orders are taken by those who feel that the Church, "despite its history and its dependence on myth and miracle, exists today as the quintessential structure through which social revolution can be brought to certain areas of the globe."

This situation is sketched in the novel's background; in the foreground is Muck Abbey, an isolated monastery on a small island three miles off the coast of Kerry, the Romanesque church of which embodies "that hush, that bareness which contains all the beauty of belief." Here the young "James Kinsella, Catholic priest" (as he calls himself) has come on behalf of his ecumenist superiors in Rome to terminate a revival among the monks of the abbey and their mainland parishioners of customs that are now frowned upon, indeed virtually prohibited: the venial sins of benediction, private grace, the sign of the cross, and other anachronisms; the mortal sins of the Latin mass and private confessions. Kinsella is skilled in *Realpolitik* and knows how to shade the options. His reaction to the monks, whose simple, childlike way of life is nicely evoked, is rather that of Matthew Arnold to the monks of the Grande Chartreuse: "For the world cries your faith is now / But a dead time's exploded dream." Kinsella's task on Muck is to insure that the new orthodoxy of a "uniform [ecumenical] posture within the Church" is maintained. The abbot of Muck is the humble Tomás O'Malley who is in his late sixties and whose sole concern is for the way of life of his monks and the faith of their parishioners. It is on the polite struggle between him and Kinsella that the novella concentrates.

Catholics, however, is not only about ecclesiastical politics and liturgical reform; it is also about the much more important matter of belief, and what it is like to have to learn to live without it. Its true subject is precisely that of *Judith Hearne*: an ordinary person's loss of faith; what happens when one comes to feel that the tabernacle contains only "round wafers of unleavened bread" (both novels use exactly this phrase) and that there is no one to hear the despairing prayer that Judith utters near her story's end: "I do not believe. O, Lord, help my unbelief." Only after the middle of *Catholics* does it become clear that its central character is not Kinsella but Tomás. We discover that the spiritual leader of the monks – whose most cherished belief is that the mass is a miracle and a mystery and not, as the ecumenists would have it, merely a "symbolic act" or "pious ritual" – is himself a man who no longer believes. Years before, the tawdry excesses of Lourdes ("that sad and dreadful place") and its "miraculous" bathing pool had revolted Tomás, and first caused him to doubt. Since then he has intermittently had to enter "the hell of those deprived of God ... the hell of no feeling, that null, that void." Tomás can avoid this hell only by not praying: "sometimes he tries to say the words; 'Our Father Who Art in Heaven,' but there is no Father in heaven, His name is not hallowed by these words, His kingdom will not come to [him] who sits and stares at the tabernacle; who, when he tries to pray, enters null; who, when in it, must remain, from day to day, weeks becoming months, and, sometimes, as after Lourdes, a year."

In the novel's closing scene, Tomás attempts to rally his dispirited monks, for of course they have lost to the forces of ecumenism. He first tells them that no matter how they are now expected to consider the mass "No one can order belief ... It is a gift from God." But this is to no avail and Tomás finally realizes that in order to save the others he must lose himself by leading them in prayer. "Prayer is the only miracle," he tells them. "If our words become prayer, God will come." But as he leads them in saying the Our Father, he feels himself once again entering the void. And this time "He would never come back." Tomás fate is tragic, and it is small consolation for the reader to reflect that the tortured, despairing abbot is a man of much greater dignity than the smooth *apparatchik* Kinsella.

III

A final instance of the tremendous influence of Joyce is Brian Moore's self-exile from Ireland: "I was – and am – a great admirer of Joyce and I think it was reading Joyce that inspired in me all those idiotic Stephen Dedalus ideas of going forth and doing something. And also tempted me into exile – I had a great pattern to follow."[34] The early years of Moore's expatriation are reflected in the settings of *The Doctor's Wife* and *The Luck of Ginger Coffey*. Together with *The Temptation of Eileen Hughes*, these novels are Moore's least satisfactory fictional performances. It is not so much that there is anything manifestly deficient about them: it is rather that by Moore's own standards there is not enough that is right with them.

The Luck of Ginger Coffey concerns the belated coming to terms with himself of a n'er-do-well Dubliner (Moore has described him as a "classic Irish type" to which Stephen Dedalus's father also belonged)[35] who when the novel opens has been living in Montreal for six months with his wife and fourteen-year-old daughter. Ever the eternal optimist ("the old saying is true. The darkest hour is just before the dawn ... While there's hope, there's life"), Ginger Coffey anticipates at every moment the commencement of his "rags to riches rise the New World was famous for ... At home it was Chinese boxes, one inside the other, and whatever you started off as, you would probably end up as." As expected, however, events in the novel are so contrived (in its closing section rather too contrived) that by the end of the story of several crucial weeks in his life, Ginger has gained a certain measure of self-knowledge and come to accept the truth about himself: "He knew something now, something he had not known before. A man's life was nobody's fault but his own. Not God's, not Vera's, not even Canada's. His own fault. *Mea culpa* ... weren't most men losers? ... He had tried. He had not won. He would die in humble circs ... There would be no victory for Ginger Coffey ... he had learned the truth. Life was the victory, wasn't it? Going on was the victory."

The main trouble with *The Luck of Ginger Coffey* is what Moore has himself called its "flat realism," a condition he tried to remedy (as he retrospectively explained) by mixing "three styles ... realistic style, comedy, and tragedy," and by doing "something that actually could happen realistically ... in a farcical way."[36] But Moore did not try hard enough, for all the parts of his novel seem written at the same energy level and are uniformly tinged with the same greyish hue. Some of the minor characters do provide spots of brightness: for example Fox, the alcoholic cripple with a wicked tongue; and MacGregor, the managing editor of the newspaper for which he and Ginger read proof: "Bony old arms hanging naked from shirt sleeves, blue vein pumping in his pale forehead, fanatic eye starved for trouble." But the three most important non-title characters in the novel – Ginger's daughter Paulie, his wife Vera, and Grosvenor, who is in love with her – are all flatly presented and never really come to life. Concerning the last, Moore does try to enliven things, but when one reads of the thirty-year-old Grosvenor that "adolescence, like an incurable disease, had never quite left him" one's delight at the crispness of the phrase is tempered by the realization that it is out of key with the dominant tone of the novel and that at his best Brian Moore has no need to write so snappily.

Even with Ginger himself the reader has difficulty in keeping his attention engaged throughout. With the exception of four brief switches to an outsider's point of view (which are all unexpected and unnecessary, and therefore annoying) Ginger's story is narrated from his point of view, much of it through a kind of internal monologue. Ginger does have a distinctive voice and there is a certain zip and pungency to his perceptions and reflections. But even this voice loses its fizz after a while, for the style is the man and Ginger's character and personality do not have sufficient depth and complexity, nor his reflections sufficient acuity (Moore has described him as "a relatively stupid man"), to sustain the reader's interest throughout.[37]

In *The Luck of Ginger Coffey*, then, Moore failed to avoid a danger for any novelist devoted to a celebration of the commonplace: the danger that the novel as well as its subject will come to seem commonplace and flat. This is avoided in *Judith Hearne* and *The Feast of Lupercal* because in the stories of a few crucial weeks or months in the lives of their central characters the subject was not simply the end of a protracted adolescence but the determining influence of environment on character. One was shown the weight of a whole culture pressing down on Judith Hearne and Diarmuid Devine and one felt continually the intensity of Moore's bitterness about life in Northern Ireland and the irremedial nature of the central characters' situations, which left no possibility for an upbeat ending and the attendant risk of sentimentality.

In *The Luck of Ginger Coffey*, on the other hand, Canadian culture and society are never more than a backdrop to Ginger's story and his situation is never felt to be extreme, let alone terminal. And at the novel's conclusion sentimentality is not avoided. Moore has said in retrospect that "the whole thing at the end" of *Ginger Coffey* "didn't quite come off for me."[38] Because it raises central critical questions concerning his practices as a novelist it is worth pondering a little the reasons for Moore's difficulty. At the end of his story Ginger experiences two moments (extremely rare in Moore's fiction) of liberating insight, even of self-transcendence. The first occurs on the steps of a courthouse after Ginger is released from the overnight grip of the law and the threat of further incarceration: suddenly "his heart filled with an unpredictable joy. He was free ... For one liberating moment he became a child again; lost himself as a child can, letting himself go into the morning, a drop of water joining an ocean, mystically becoming one." In the second, with the wife whom he thought he had lost restored to him, Ginger has an insight into the nature of love:

love isn't just going to bed. Love isn't an act, it's a whole life. It's staying with her now because she needs you; it's knowing you and she will still care about each other when sex and daydreams, fights and futures – when all that's on the shelf and done with. Love – why, I'll tell you what love is: it's you at seventy-five and her at seventy-one, each of you listening for the other's step in the next room, each afraid that a sudden silence, a sudden cry, could mean a lifetime's talk is over.

A major difficulty with both these moments is that they are totally unprepared for by what has gone before. Unlike the equally stupid Tommy

Wilhelm in Bellow's *Seize the Day*, a work Moore extravagantly admires, Ginger is never shown to have a need so deep that only an overwhelming emotion can fill it. Moore is surely guilty of special pleading and a confusion of life and art when he defends Ginger's moment of joy by arguing that everyone experiences such instants and that they are always unexpected.[39] Similarly the reader's response to the declaration about the true nature of love can only be notional because earlier in the novel Ginger had never been shown seeking any kind of love – wasn't a decent job all he was after? Since Moore's definition of ordinary, long-term love is unrooted in what has preceded, it is defenceless before the charge of being different neither in quality nor kind from the fatuous apothegm in Erich Segal's *Love Story*: "Love is never having to say you're sorry."

One might speculate on the deeper reasons for the flatness of these affirmative moments and reflect that happiness is a condition of which Moore, like Philip Larkin, seems to have little experience and that, except for sexual love, emotional relationships between men and women have never seriously engaged Moore's imaginative attention. Over and over again in his novels it is on the chords of parental relationships that his deepest emotional notes are struck. One might also reflect that Larkin is more successful in conveying a moving sense of such ordinary truths not only because he works in a poetic medium but also because he and his work are rooted: as a resonating context for his simple truths Larkin has available the traditional pieties and customs of English provincial life – Whitsun weddings, a chapel funeral, seashore bathing, show Saturday, church-going. But whatever the reason for their flatness, the most interesting point (one entirely to his credit) is that Moore feels that these common truths, these ordinary ecstasies, are so important that it is worth the risk of sentimentality to present them: "One must run right up to the edge of sentimentality to get at [the] ordinary truth, because the thing that makes sentimentality move so many people is that it's within a hair's breadth of that beautiful ordinary truth. So many modern writers are scared of that. Tears are not acceptable in our society."[40]

Sentimentality is not the problem in *The Doctor's Wife*; melodrama is. The novel's subject is that of a number of famous nineteenth- and twentieth-century novels, as well as of a legion of other novels: adulterous passion and its consequences. In form the novel is a conventional middlebrow romantic drama of the type of *Brief Encounter* or Graham Greene's *The End of the Affair*. There are two settings: France (Paris and a sunny Riviera interlude) is in the foreground; in the background, only as far away as the nearest telephone or airport, is rainy, violent Belfast. The year is 1974, but Belfast is essentially the same city it was in Moore's first two novels. The continuity is underlined by a reference to Bernie Rice and his mother, two characters from *Judith Hearne*.[41] Sheila Redden, the title character of *The Doctor's Wife*, is an attractive woman of thirty-six who has come from Belfast to Paris to begin a holiday on which her overworked husband is not immediately able to join her. Almost overnight she finds herself totally involved sexually and emotionally with Tom, a blandly wholesome American in his late twenties, with no past at his back, who is all that Sheila's dull husband and the stagnant, repressive culture he epitomizes are not.

Once this triangle has been established, familiar changes are rung upon it: the woman's realization of the dullness of her existence, "all that laundry list of events that had been her life since she married"; her initial resistance followed by her sudden capitulation; her dissimulation, counterpointed by the spouse's growing suspicions; the husband, initially distraught, then vindictive, with the weight of family, society, and the law on his side; the authenticities of passion. ("It was as though wrong were right. Her former life, her marriage, all that had gone before, now seemed to be her sin. These few days with Tom were her state of grace"); guilt over the child left behind; the husband's confrontation with his wife; and finally, the crisis, the moment of decision and, in the case of *The Doctor's Wife*, of renunciation. For the novel ends with Sheila living alone and anonymously in the limbo of London and working in a laundry.

In the novel's most powerful scene, Dr Redden confronts Sheila in a Paris hotel room. When she refuses to return to him he becomes irrational, violent, obscene, and sexually aroused to the point of beating and raping her. Before this happens, he tells her: "It's books, of course, that you got all your notions from. Not from real life. All these novels and trash that's up there in your room at home." The most serious shortcoming of *The Doctor's Wife* is that one might similarly accuse Brian Moore. Of course there is nothing necessarily debilitating about a writer employing a well-worn popular form, even a dated one, and no reason why such a form cannot be adapted to serious artistic purpose. In *The End of the Affair*, for example, Greene appropriated the same vehicle as Moore in order to dramatize the workings of divine grace. And in Moore's novel one does find the same serious concerns that inform much of his fiction: belief and what it is like to live without it; the pressure of the past on the present; parental and familial ties versus sexual ties (Sheila's older brother Owen, a father figure whose embrace reminds her that "family ... allegiances antedated all others," is an important character in the novel).

The trouble with *The Doctor's Wife* is that these themes are not freshly incarnated in character, setting, and situation. On the contrary, they seem to have been programmatically dropped into the narrative in order to provide thematic weight. The gratuitous insertion of a conversation about belief and non-belief between Sheila and a priest in Notre Dame (with his drinker's nose and faithless faith he seems drawn more from the pages of Graham Greene than from life) is one example. Another is that for all her eager couplings with Tom, not to mention their mutual soapings in the shower and a naked piggyback gambol, one never comes to feel that Sheila Redden has sexual and emotional needs of the depth and intensity of those ascribed to her. The major reason for this is the outside point of view from which Moore has chosen to narrate most of Sheila's story. While the narrator is close enough to his subject to note the menstrual blood flowing down her legs during a bath, he is rarely able to report what is going on inside her mind. The obvious contrast is with the strikingly successful first person characterization of the thrice-married title character of Moore's 1968 novel, *I Am Mary Dunne*, whose fears of madness, contemplations of suicide, and celebrations (in Catholic images) of the ecstasies of the sexual present all suggest that there are elements of recycling in Moore's characterization of Sheila Redden. The novel's weakness is also instanced in the perfunctory characterization of Tom, who is not even given a distinctive voice, something that Moore does extremely well. All one remembers of Tom is that he was tall, nice, thought people should be allowed to do what they wanted to, and often had erections. Finally, except in the rape scene and part of a scene between Sheila and her brother, Belfast and Paris, puritan and erotic, parental and sexual, never satisfactorily confront each other.

Like the story of Sheila Redden, *The Temptation of Eileen Hughes* is a tri-cornered romantic melodrama set in a European capital and full of the tourist-eye detail of hotels, restaurants, and airports. Unlike its predecessor, the destabilizing passion that precipitates the novel's action is platonic, not sexual. The three principals are Bernard McAuley, "the richest Catholic in Lismore," a town thirty miles from Belfast; his good-looking wife Mona, whose major holiday activity is sexual promiscuity; and their junior by more than a decade, the twenty-year-old Eileen Hughes, a shop-girl in the McAuleys' store who has been invited to join her employers on a trip to London, all expenses paid. The novel opens with Bernard berating an assistant hotel manager because Eileen's accommodation has been overlooked. His annoyance seems the impatience of a well-to-do man of the world accustomed to first class service. But it soon becomes clear that Bernard's concern for Eileen is obsessive; the "innocent" and "unspoiled" young woman has become his ruling passion, the only thing that makes his life worth living. On their first day in London Bernard tells Eileen of his love, outlines his plan to buy a big country house and have her come to live with him and Mona, and describes the nature and intensity of his passion:

sex isn't love. I know that. It's the opposite of love. Love, real love, is quite different from desire. It's like the love a mystic feels for God. It's worship. It's just wanting to be in your presence, that's enough, it's more than enough, it's everything there is. That's what it's been like for me since the first day I saw you in there, working in the shop. I've worshipped you. In silence. In devotion ... It's funny, the parallels between religion and love ... I only thought I was in love with Mona. That wasn't love. I know that now. Desire isn't love. Desire is something you can control ... But love isn't like that. When you fall in love with someone, really fall in love, it's a sort of miracle, it's almost religious. The person you love is perfect. As God is perfect.

What Eileen wants from life, however, is not worship but simply the chance to do nursing and to get to know "some nice boy." When she realizes the true nature of her situation in London, she determines to return to Lismore despite the pleas of Bernard and Mona. But Eileen is unable to get a flight to Ireland before the night on which the two climactic events of the novel occur: her first sexual experience, into which she is drawn by wine, marijuana, and the niceness of their purveyor, a counter-cultural American who is the novel's most sharply delineated character; and Bernard's suicide attempt, for which the stronger drugs of whiskey and sodium amytal are used. In the novel's short closing section, Eileen, returned to Lismore, resolves to leave the McAuleys' store and work as a doctor's receptionist; on the last page the reader is tersely informed that Bernard's second suicide attempt three months later was successful.

The major weakness of *The Temptation of Eileen Hughes* is the presentation of character. The hard edge of Mona's self-interest is nicely conveyed, but her sexual rapacity seems gratuitous and little attempt is made to supply a credible motivation. Eileen is a convincing representation of an unexceptional young woman of pinched background and modest expectations. The problem with her, as with Una Clarke in *The Feast of Lupercal*, is that while the characterization is adequate, the character is uninteresting. But the missing centre of *The Temptation of Eileen Hughes* is not the personality of its title character but the inner life of Bernard McAuley. Moore has not cared to provide the reader with an extended inside view of Bernard. Through rumination and dialogue, Mona is made to supply some information about her husband's private life: that in his early twenties he had left university to enter a Benedictine monastery and suffered a nervous breakdown half a

year later; and that several months into his marriage he had discovered that
he "just couldn't stand being dependent on another person's body," and
that sex was only an urge that might just as well be relieved through
masturbation. But this is all that one learns about the Bernard McAuley
within. While elsewhere in his fiction Moore masterfully explores the atrophy
of desire and the loss of faith, the sparse information supplied by Mona is
not sufficient to make Bernard's description of his extraordinary love even
as resonant and involving as Ginger Coffey's flawed description of the nature
of ordinary human love.

In several of Moore's New World novels the themes of artistic integrity
versus commercial pressures and the dangers of success for the writer are
blended with his quintessential themes – failure, loneliness, exile, the past
– in complex and enriching ways. *The Doctor's Wife*, from which he made
upwards of half a million dollars, and *The Temptation of Eileen Hughes*
suggest that Moore did not pull these themes out of his hat and that the
forces of the commercial enemy are not entirely outside his gates.[42] He once
made the penetrating observation that the trouble with the ambitious fictions
of Anthony Burgess was he didn't "put the sweat into it."[43] In the stories
of Sheila Redden and Eileen Hughes, Brian Moore seems to have suffered
the same creative acedia.

IV

The four novels set in the United States – *An Answer from Limbo, I Am
Mary Dunne, Fergus,* and *The Great Victorian Collection* – have important
features in common. First, the American settings have given Moore the
opportunity for a genuine extension of his novelistic skills, for each novel
contains more than one sharply observed New World characterization. More
important, the central characters of each novel are not commonplace
persons like Judith Hearne, Diarmuid Devine, and Ginger Coffey. On the
contrary, Brendan Tierney, Mary Dunne, Fergus Fadden, and Anthony
Maloney are talented, in one way or another creative, and successful in
worldly terms (though this does not preclude their being failures in more
fundamental ways). Two of them are self-exiled from their native Ireland,
while the other two find themselves in settings far different from those of
their Canadian upbringing. As in V.S. Naipaul's novels, the more *déraciné*
the characters, the more importantly sexual relationships figure in their
lives. At the same time, there is for Moore's protagonists an intensified
preoccupation with parental relationships, to which sexual relationships are
ultimately shown to be subordinate.

As their central characters are more complex than those of Moore's Irish novels, so the novels themselves are more sophisticated in structure and style. In them Moore moves beyond the naturalistic realism of his earlier work. His basic paradigm – dramatization of the crisis point in a person's life – remains intact, but whereas *Judith Hearne, The Feast of Lupercal,* and *The Emperor of Ice-Cream* dramatized the conflict of the individual with his society and culture, in the New World novels the central characters are in conflict with themselves. Since the interest is more psychological than social, these novels tend to be intensive rather than extensive: two of them reduce the time frame to a single day, and a third juxtaposes three inside points of view in order to show with diagrammatic clarity the past–present opposi-tions. For the same reason the realistic surface of one novel is expression-istically distorted (owing to the first-person narrator's distraught emotional state); in two others a fantastic premise is introduced.

The principal reason for this shift in emphasis is patent: in the New World novels Moore's primary concern is not so much with the ordinary sorrow of others as with his own particular afflictions. The central characters of each novel are at some level portraits of the artist – as an exile, as a man whose only belief is in his own creative powers, as a person forced to confront the meaninglessness of his existence. All the novels are concerned with self-exploration and self-expression, and attest to the fact that for the exiled writer "there will exist, within his consciousness, two worlds, mov-ing in counterweight, one against the other. And in his fiction, as in his life, the past will rise up, challenging and confronting the present."[44] This juxtaposition of present and past, New World and Old World, Catholic and secular, parental and sexual, is the major structural principle in the four novels. As John Wilson Foster points out: "The crises weathered by Moore's later characters may be *aggravated* by life in a dehumanising cosmopolitan society but they are *caused* by the radical difference between that society and the provincial ... communities from which the characters hail. It is this difference, the sense of limbo, that throws up all the fantasies and ghosts and upsetting memories."[45] Or as Moore had put it in a comment on Malcolm Lowry's work which is equally true of his own: "And so, almost despite himself, his subject becomes, as always, the fall of man, his remorse, his incessant struggle 'towards the light, under the weight of the past, which is his destiny'."[46]

I Am Mary Dunne is the least pessimistic in conclusion. It describes a single day in the life of its title character and narrator, an attractive, worldly woman of thirty-two who lives with her third husband in a swanky Man-hattan apartment. Mary has come to New York from her native Canada and Moore has described her novel as "my first book without any Irish characters in it."[47] For all practical purposes, however, this distinction is without a difference. Mary is a third-generation Nova Scotia Irish Catholic, has attended Catholic schools, is steeped in the habits of mind and expression of the faith in which she no longer believes and, like Moore himself and a number of his protagonists, has a mother of deep, simple faith – her response to the possibility that she may have cancer is to "say my prayers and put myself in God's hands. That's all any of us can do." But Mary's background does give Moore an opportunity to introduce two provincial English Canadians on which to exercise his considerable powers of characterization: Janice Sloane, a sophisticate *manqué* lacking in authenticity and emotional intelligence; and the almost unbelievably boorish Ernie Truelove, "a large lumpish man, very Canadian square, in his navy blazer, white shirt, maroon tie, flannels, and sensible black brogues."

Unlike any other of his novels, *I Am Mary Dunne* is narrated entirely in the first person. Mary is wholly characterized through her way of speaking, her perceptions, sensations, and thoughts; everything depends upon her being accepted by the reader as a fully convincing, sharply focused individual. This is no mean technical feat, and Moore has successfully brought it off. It is true that there are traces of soap opera in Mary's story, that her tone is too consistently high-pitched and breathless, and that once or twice she sounds rather too much like Molly Bloom. (In fact, at its conclusion the reader discovers that, like Molly's long interior monologue at the end of *Ulysses*, the whole of Mary's narrative is a transcription of her thoughts and memories as she lies in bed with her husband at the end of a long, eventful day.) But on the whole *I Am Mary Dunne* is finely realized. One might almost call it a *tour de force* of characterization – and of plotting: for while the present-time action of the novel is a single day, the narrative is managed in such a way that memories triggered by present events make the day an epitome of Mary's entire post-adolescent life. Indeed, on the second page, Moore alerts the reader to his artistry and dexterity by having Mary point out how unsatisfactory a chronological exposition of her life would be:

I mean if I were to try to tell anyone the story of my life so far, wouldn't it come out as fragmentary and faded as those old snapshot albums, scrapbooks, and bundles of letters everyone keeps in some bottom drawer or other? What would I remember about my life, wouldn't it be just some false, edited little movie, my version of what my parents were like, the places I lived in, the names of some of the people I've known, and would any of it give you any idea of what I feel about, say, sex, or children, about something trivial like cleaning the oven broiler or something terrible like this thing about Hat [her second husband]?

The self-conscious awareness of artifice calls attention to the closeness of the novelist to his subject. Though Moore chose a female character as the subject for his first novel in order to maximize the distance between himself and his creation, in *I Am Mary Dunne* he is just as deliberately exploring his own dilemmas and his own creative processes through the impersonation of Mary:

I am Mary Dunne because I have taken my own life and transmogrified it into hers. I have taken my years of wandering from country to country, my changes of nationality, my forgettings, rememberings, my feelings of being lost and a stranger and have, I hope, made them hers. For two years I have wakened in the mornings, gone into a room, sat at a typewriter and, like any actor going on stage, like a medium trying to induce a trance, I have tried to think myself into the skin and into the mind of a young, troubled, pretty woman. And, like a medium speaking in the voice of another person, I have written the book in the first person singular, in her voice, the voice of Mary Dunne.[48]

In her critical study of Moore, Jeanne Flood makes an important point when she says that "the reader is at every point made aware that the closely woven realistic density of the novel is a triumph of the creative imagination. Moore's title echoes Flaubert's '*Madame Bovary, c'est moi,*' and in so doing establishes the fact that the character Mary Dunne is the creation of the novelist Brian Moore, and that in the character ... he will reveal himself. The epigraph of the book reinforces the point: 'O body swayed to music, O brightening glance, / How can we know the dancer from the dance?' "[49]

As her day begins, Mary is already in the grip of a pre-menstrual tension, her "dooms" or "down tilt," which is at times so intense as to seem an anxiety neurosis. This tension is making her painfully aware of the gaps between the various persons she has been at different times in her life (Mary Dunne, Mary Phelan, Mary Bell, Maria, Mary Lavery), undermining her sense of identity ("who is that me I create in mirrors ..."; "I am a changeling who has changed too often") and causing her to question whether there is any meaning in her life. As the novel unfolds, Mary is made to undergo a day of reckoning in which various incidents, including visits from Janice and Ernie (friends from her days in Montreal), force her to recall key events from her past, particularly her second marriage, which (like her first) had foundered on the rock of her husband's sexual inadequacy, for whose death

– a probable suicide – both friends suggest Mary is largely responsible. While they do have a point, it is clear that Janice and Ernie's feelings towards Mary are laced with resentment, and it would be wrong to follow their lead, as some commentators have, and read Mary's story as a moral reckoning. Her intensely self-involved first-person narrative and the compact past-present fusion do not give the reader the perspective or the time for moral evaluation. What they do provide is an intensity of reader involvement and an excellent vehicle for the exploration of the theme of identity.

For most of the novel, Mary's battered sense of identity is shown to have two dominant, contrasting constituents: memory (that is, *notre maître, le passé*, to recall the Quebec political slogan mentioned by Janice), and sexuality (that is, fulfilment in the present). Concerning the former, *I Am Mary Dunne* opens with Mary remembering the day in school back in Nova Scotia when she had annoyed Mother Marie Thérèse by changing Descartes' famous axiom to "I remember, therefore I am" – for even at the age of fifteen she was certain that identity is determined by the past: "we are what we remember." Concerning the latter, Mary rapturously describes her third husband, who "never thinks of the past," as "My resurrection and my life ... Terence maketh me to lie down in green pastures ... he restoreth my soul ... He's my new religion. He's life after death." The reason Terence can be so described is that his body "fits mine as no other body ever did." During their intercourse, "that Mass of the senses ... that fuck that encompasseth me," Mary seems wholly fulfilled, everything is made new, and "there is no past."

Mary's instability and her questioning of her identity are shown to be principally caused by the tension between her celebration of a Lawrencian sexual present and her Faulknerian sense of the primacy of the past. *I Am Mary Dunne* does not, however, conclude with a resolution of the tension between memory and sexuality or, as some commentators have claimed, with the vanquishing of the former by the latter. The novel rather concludes with the supersession of this conflict by Mary's recognition of a more fundamental constituent of her being, the parental bond which for her, as for most of Brian Moore's protagonists, is the bedrock of their identity. Early in the novel Mary's sexual fantasies, confusions, and needs were shown to be radically connected with her learning at fifteen, the same age at which she had rewritten Descartes' axiom, that her father had "died screwing, that some woman was in bed with him" when he expired in a New York hotel room. And near the end of the novel, during a long distance phone call with her mother, Mary asks:

"Mama?" I said. "Mama? I want to ask you something. Do you think I've changed much in these last years?"

Again she laughed. "You haven't changed at all, you're still talking over the time limit."

"No, seriously."

"Look," said my mother, "good night, now. You haven't changed for me. You're my daughter, you'll always be the same to me. Good night, darling."

And she hung up.

It is this exchange that Mary recalls when on the novel's final page she desperately wills herself to affirm her identity by repeating not any of the names she had taken from her three husbands, the first two the principal figures in her gloomy post-adolescent memories, the third her phallic saviour, but the name her father and her mother had given her:

I am the daughter of Daniel Malone Dunne and Eileen Martha Ring, I am Mary Patricia Dunne, I was christened that and there is nothing wrong with my heart or with my mind: in a few hours I will begin to bleed, and until then I will hold on, I will remember what Mama told me, I am her daughter, I have not changed, I remember who I am and I say it over and over and over, I am Mary Dunne, I am Mary Dunne, I am Mary Dunne.

Such unchanging parental bonds, unaffected by time, distance, or circumstance, and the indelible sense of identity they confer, are both a blessing and burden to the protagonists of the two novels I shall next discuss. Brendan Tierney in *An Answer from Limbo* and Fergus Fadden in the novel named after him are both writers, émigrés from Ireland trying to make it in America. Both are preoccupied with questions of artistic integrity and acutely aware of the relation of the serious artist to the commercial forces upon which his livelihood depends. Both recognize what the writing and careers of Hemingway, Fitzgerald, and Mailer all bear witness to: that in America the greatest danger for the writer is success, not neglect.

In both novels, the theme of artistic integrity is mixed with more fundamental concerns. In *An Answer from Limbo*, Brendan is only one of three central characters: the other two, his mother and his wife, are diametrically opposed representatives of parental love and sexual love, the Old World and the New, "Irish Catholicism against the rootless wasteland of North America," to quote Moore's description of his novel's organizing theme.[50] We enjoy inside views of each of the three characters, who are given more or less equal time. Each is shown to have a dominant belief or illusion which shapes his or her conduct towards others and which is put to the test during the novel. Brendan's mother believes in God, "in hell and purgatory, penance and indulgences, baptism and extreme unction. She believe[s] that God placed her on this world for a purpose." Brendan has lost his mother's faith and in its place made a religion of his writing: the novel on which he is working is "the belief that replaces belief." Jane has an assortment of stock liberal beliefs, but for much of the novel her consciousness is dominated by secret belief in a "dark ravisher" who will fulfil her sexual needs as her husband has never been able to do.

Brendan has brought his widowed mother from Ireland to New York to look after his two obnoxious children so that Jane can work to support the family while he finishes his first novel. The mother has all of the rigid beliefs, pieties, and prejudices of her background, and had she appeared in any of Moore's Belfast novels would not have been treated sympathetically. But against the background of New York, Mrs Tierney appears in a most attractive light. She is shown to possess a simple dignity and a concern for others that contrast with the consuming self-centredness and neurotic needs of Brendan and Jane. She does impose her own values when she clandestinely baptizes her grandchildren (while her son and his friends are talking in the next room about "phallic females" and "penis envy"), but compared with the programmatically liberal Jane the mother seems almost too pure an embodiment of tolerance and humanity.

At one point Jane's mind is described as "dithering among the catch phrases of her time: affluent society, beat generation, existential decision, nuclear holocaust." Jane lives in and for the engagé present. Having no past, she has no counterforce to limit and shape her sexual drives. Her secret dream of a dark ravisher is incarnated in the repellent Vito Italiano, a stud of consummate vulgarity. Usually dismissed, perhaps because of the unfortunate overtones of his name, as a macho caricature, Vito is, alas, an accurately rendered New World type. The only mitigating feature of his characterization – it is as if Moore is placing his signature in the corner of his portrait – is that even Vito has a mom, who makes one appearance in the novel. Old, heavy, and varicosed, she snores in a nearby room while her son services Jane in an episode that is the nadir of her degradation.

Brendan Tierney, proud and haughty, with more than a little of Stephen Dedalus in him, is consumed with artistic ambition and jealousy and prepared to sacrifice both his marriage and his mother for his art. His point of view is the only one rendered in the first person, and his prose style is a central aspect of his characterization. Brendan does not write like Brian

Moore's third person narrators; his style is mannered, self-conscious, and derivative, sounding sometimes like a less fey Salinger, once like Norman Mailer, and at other times recalling the over-articulateness and sterile self-absorption of Joseph in Bellow's *Dangling Man*.[51] This inauthenticity of voice is important, for through it, despite the tendency to identify with a first person narrator, the reader is kept at a critical distance from Brendan. It also indirectly suggests something about the nature of the novel Brendan is writing – that it will be mannered and coldly intelligent – a point missed by critics who complain that since one does not know the quality of Brendan's novel, one has no way of knowing whether the sacrifices he forces on others, and on himself, are justified.[52]

At the end of the novel, Brendan tries to avoid dwelling on his responsibility for the grotesque circumstances of his mother's death: a broken hip, a stroke, two days in agonizing pain on the floor of a borrowed apartment while above her the television blared out its New World banalities. In a moment of unusual self-insight, Brendan is led to ask himself if his belief – the religion of literature – is "sounder" than his mother's belief in God. The answer is indirectly given in the novel's final scene. During his mother's burial, Brendan realizes he is observing the ceremony with such care only because he intends one day to write about it. His illusion and his success (for his publishers have great hopes for his novel) have dehumanized Brendan and made him a shrivelled human being. He can no longer feel; he can only record: "I have altered beyond all self-recognition: I have lost and sacrificed myself." His void is worse than that of Tomás in *Catholics*, for it is of Brendan's own making.

Fergus is regarded by many as one of its author's least satisfactory novels. As Moore ruefully observed: "When I wrote *Fergus* I worried extremely because I was bringing back fictional *revenants* or ghosts or hallucinatory figures or whatever, and I was sensible enough to realize that this would not be acceptable to many people who've read my other books, a prediction which turned out to be crashingly accurate."[53] While my own view is that the novel is among Moore's finest works, what is indisputable is that *Fergus* is an extremely interesting work for anyone interested in the informing patterns of Moore's fiction and in his attempts to give artistic expression to his obsessive concerns.

In structure and technique, the novel may be described as a cross between Fellini's *8½* and the Nighttown (or Circe) section of Joyce's *Ulysses*, both almost certainly direct influences. But the seed of what was to become *Fergus* was sown in *An Answer from Limbo*. In one of that novel's scenes a photograph album falls to the floor while Brendan is helping his mother pack. He picks it up and opens to a series of snapshots of a long-ago Tierney family outing on the beach at Portstewart. The photographs seem to be accusing him, and after a minute he shuts the book. In another scene Brendan reflects that "if I were granted the wish to bring back to this world for one hour any human being I have known or read of, I would put in the call tonight for my father. We would not be friends. I might be shocked at his bigotry, his vanity, his platitudes. But there, standing in the kitchen, holding his signet ring, I suddenly, desperately, wished that he were with me."

In *Fergus*, this wish is granted to the title character. The novel recounts one extraordinary day in the life of Fergus Fadden, a writer in his late thirties with two good novels to his credit, who has somewhat against his better judgment come from New York to southern California to write a screenplay which will earn him the money to pay for a messy divorce. Fergus is living in a rented beach house in Malibu with Dani, a girl barely out of the teeny-bopper stage, whose mother Dusty joins them for an overnight visit. Mother and daughter, both splendid characterizations, are rightly regarded by Fergus as a dual "personification of the American way." Yet in their strained relationship even these *déraciné* and shallow females bear witness to the *sine qua non* of Moore's fiction: that "parents form the grammar of our emotions."

Dusty is not the only visitor to the beach house: the more important visitors who appear intermittently throughout the day – only Fergus can see or hear them – are a number of matter-of-factly presented apparitions from Fergus's Catholic Belfast past, his father (who seems identical to Gavin Burke's and Brendan Tierney's) chief among them. As with Mary Dunne during her long day of reckoning, the presences from Fergus's past force him to recall some unpleasant facts about himself and disrupt his attempts to cope with the present: "Until now, he had thought that, like everyone else, he exorcised his past by living it. But he was not like everyone else. His past had risen up this morning, vivid, uncontrollable, shouldering into the present. How can I live a life with Dani, he wondered, if my mother keeps coming into the room?" When he tries to tell Dani about his apparitions, her reply helps Fergus realize that while his past and present are juxtaposed, they are immiscible: " 'Ah-so,' said Dani in her Chinese impersonation, one which secretly depressed Fergus and made him wonder if he overestimated her intelligence. 'So now we make-um food appear. All light?' "

The *revenants* initially seem to Fergus "like one of those miracles [his father] used to believe in, like Lourdes"; but as the day advances a more naturalistic explanation presents itself. Fergus comes to see that people from his past appear to him because for one reason or another he thinks of them. (One shortcoming of the novel is that these visitations do not always seem triggered by telling correspondences between past and present.) The people who appear to Fergus are as palpably "real" to him as Dani, Dusty, and Boweri, the film producer who stops by to give him a glimpse of the iron fist inside his velvet glove, or, to complicate matters, as Winston Churchill, whom Fergus dreams he encounters in a public lavatory. Indeed, in some ways the apparitions are more real; since most of them are people he has known in childhood, they are "seen, smelled, and sensed with the special strong perceptions of a very young child." Compared with his mother and Aunt Kate, who fill his living room "with a presence stronger than that of the living women," Dani and Dusty seem "improbable characters in a wide-screen color film of American life." Even his mother's best friend, Mrs Findlater, the subject of Fergus's first sexual fantasies, is "a woman whose excitative quality could not be matched by any other female in the whole world." Indeed, the moment he realizes he can smell and touch, as well as see and hear, his apparitions, Mrs Findlater, her skirt raised provocatively, materializes on the chaise longue before Fergus and submits to his molestations.

Fergus holds extended conversations with his apparitions in the intervals of attempting to relate to his girl and her mother and to resolve a crisis of his artistic conscience concerning his screenplay, the ending of which is unsatisfactory to the director and producer who hired him: "I keep telling you we need some hope. Some little lift, so's the audience can walk out, they don't want to commit suicide." The relationship between Fergus's past and his hypersensitive literary conscience, two of the novel's three main threads, is made explicit by his sister Maeve during her visitation: for Fergus, as for Brendan Tierney and Stephen Dedalus, literature is a substitute for religious belief, particularly faith in a life after death: "You start worrying about your reputation outliving you. Your work becomes your chance to beat the grave. That's a very attractive thought, particularly for ex-Catholics. That's why you care so much about your literary status ... Your trouble is, you can't be sure of anything. You have no laws, no rules, no spiritual life at all. You have to make up your own rules of conduct. You have to become your own wee ruler, and found your own wee religion. You are your own god." That the novel's third major thread, Fergus's relationship with Dani, is similarly rooted in and shaped by his past is made clear in several ways; particularly striking is the contrast between the two times Fergus kneels, once during an apparition to join his family in saying the rosary, once to bury his face in Dani's "soft bush."

The reader initially feels, as does Fergus, that like most ghosts in literature the *revenants* will spark some revelation or transmit some important secret. But as the novel unfolds it becomes more and more clear that since the apparitions are simply the incarnations of Fergus's memories they can offer no cure for that quintessential malaise of Brian Moore's central characters: "that desperation which invades a person who discovers his life has no meaning." They can tell Fergus nothing he does not already know about himself, however dimly.

This finally becomes clear to Fergus during the novel's long climactic scene, which mixes a Fadden family picnic (transposed from the sands of Portstewart to Zuma Beach), an angry mob, and a woman from Fergus's past whom for a long time he cannot quite place. She turns out to be Elaine Rosen, for whom Fergus had done a good deed when he knew her on Long Island some years before. It does seem a violation of the novel's ground rules that Fergus should be able to remember someone whom he cannot remember; but this inconsistency should not keep one from seeing the point Moore is making. Not only has the memory of Elaine Rosen faded because it dates from a post-childhood and post-adolescence period of his life; for the same reason Fergus's good deed is not efficacious and can bring no remission of his crisis.

That Fergus's condition is as irremissive as Judith Hearne's becomes clear in the novel's closing pages. Dr Fadden's last remark to his son is "Don't you see? If you have not found a meaning, then your life is meaningless." Although the dawn comes up in the novel's closing sentences, *Fergus* ends on as hopeless a note as *The Feast of Lupercal, Catholics,* and *An Answer from Limbo.* As they have done in the novel's opening pages, waves continue to slam on the shore "monotonous as a heartbeat," as monotonously as Fergus's memories, whether or not in apparitional form, will continue to slam on his consciousness – their regularity only broken by catastrophe, as Fergus's pulse had been by the minor heart attack he suffers near the end of his story. For Fergus, as for the characters in Naipaul's later novels, the only truth to be extracted from experience is that the life you have led is the life you will lead.

Fergus, then, is a diagnostic, not a remedial work. There is no "little lift" at the end and nothing emotionally cathartic, like the apparition of Bloom's dead son Rudy at the end of the Nighttown section of *Ulysses.* That Moore was himself ill at ease with the desolating implications of *Fergus,* his most transparently autobiographical novel, is suggested by the fact that as soon as *Catholics* was behind him he returned in his next novel (also similar in several matters of detail) to the same California setting, the same juxtaposition of past and present (with a more fantastic premise), and the same complex of themes.

At first glance, however, even at first reading, *The Great Victorian Collection*, Moore's most peculiar invention, appears to have little in common with his other novels. For one thing, it is his only work in which the central character is not of Roman Catholic upbringing; nor are any of the other characters Catholic. The novel opens with Anthony Maloney, a young historian at McGill University in Montreal, going to sleep in a motel room in Carmel, California. Maloney, whose field is the Victorians, dreams that the empty parking lot outside his window contains an enormous, department-store size collection of "Victorian artifacts, *objets d'art*, furniture, household appliances, paintings, jewelry, scientific instruments, toys, tapestries, sculpture, handicrafts, woolen and linen samples, industrial machinery, ceramics, silverware, books, furs, men's and women's clothing, musical instruments, a huge telescope mounted on a pedestal, a railway locomotive, marine equipment, small arms, looms, bric-a-brac, and curiosa." Like Adam, Maloney wakes from his dream and finds it truth. What he has wrought – one character calls it "the first wholly secular miracle in the history of mankind" – brings him instant notoriety: reporters, scientific investigators, art experts who argue over the originality and authenticity of the items in the Collection (which Moore has a grand time describing), businessmen interested in "creative decisions" regarding the Collection's commercial potential, a weird-looking man with a sign saying "God alone can create: do not believe this lie": all beat a path to the Collection's door. Maloney becomes intimate with two of these strangers: a local reporter called Vaterman, a colourless, crass young man interested only in manipulating Maloney for his own advantage; and his good-looking, coltish-legged girl friend Mary Ann, who says she believes in the Collection and to whom Maloney becomes attracted, especially after she becomes associated in his mind with the Collection.

It is not long before Maloney makes some disturbing discoveries about his creation. One is that artifacts of the "other Victorians" are represented in the Collection: a chamber full of flagellation equipment, including punishment costumes for women; a library of illustrated Sadean literature; and the receiving room of a brothel, its walls adorned with obscene paintings. Another is that as soon as it is tampered with the Collection begins slowly to lose its initial, mint-condition lustre. A third discovery concerns his inability to realize a fresh fantasy: Maloney can dream only of the Collection and his increasingly custodial relation to it. The dream becomes a nightmare when it shrinks to a monochromatic image of a television set, "the screen of one of those surveillance monitors one sees in supermarkets," in which one stationary black-and-white view of an aisle of the Collection succeeds another. Maloney attempts to escape from the Collection by travelling first to Los Angeles and its all-night dance clubs, then to Montreal, his birthplace. Not only is he unable to rid himself of his nightmare; his relationship with Mary Ann reaches a sour climax in Montreal and he returns to Carmel a defeated man resigned to subservience to his creation: "He was the prisoner of what he had wrought."

In the final chapter of *The Great Victorian Collection*, the documentary, clinically dispassionate style of presentation records the fate of Maloney and his dream. The Collection becomes the nucleus of a lesser Disneyland, though most visitors prefer to the Collection itself the more conveniently located and tourist-oriented Great Victorian Village (the Lourdes, so to speak, of this secular miracle) with its motel units, shopping plazas, and vulgar emporia. Though only Maloney seems to notice or care, his Collection continues to deteriorate: "The fountain, for instance, Osler's great crystal fountain: those perfect blocks of polished glass are now mostly dull, light in weight, dead as plastic." Maloney turns to drink to get through his days and make bearable his nights. *In extremis*, he tries without success to burn the Collection and even with a hammer is "unable to shatter a single fragile piece of the Staffordshire." A bourbon bottle and jar of pills – New World, post-Victorian artifacts – are beside him when he dies in the same motel room in which he had first dreamed up the Collection that has destroyed him.

So described, *The Great Victorian Collection* must sound like a cross between Oscar Wilde's *Picture of Dorian Gray* and contemporary inner-space fictions like Doris Lessing's *Briefing for a Descent into Hell*. While it would not be unrewarding to pursue these analogies, the most important points of reference in fixing the location and determining the magnitude of *The Great Victorian Collection* are the other stars in Moore's fictional galaxy, which have a great deal more in common with the story of Anthony Maloney than they may initially seem to.

On one level, *The Great Victorian Collection* is a grim fable about artistic integrity and its pitfalls, "a shrewd allegory about the situation of the artist in contemporary society."[54] Works of art do not spring up *ex nihilo*, and Maloney is right to think that if his Collection "was not wholly original in concept, it was, nonetheless, his own." The Collection soon becomes the subject of disputation by academics: one denies its originality; another straddles the fence ("neither original nor fake"); all seem as interested in their reputations and in scoring points off each other as in understanding what is before them. The authorities at McGill (that is, Canadian critics) first scoff at the creative achievement of a native son, but jump on Maloney's bandwagon as soon as his achievement is ratified by British and American experts. As time passes, the Cold Pastoral of the Collection comes to seem more and more lifeless to its creator, to have "the stillness of a burial ground" and to be "a web of artifice as different from the reality it sought to commemorate as is a poem about spring from spring itself." Finally, Maloney's creation is seized and squeezed by the hands of commercial profit and vulgarization virtually from the moment it comes into being; and what survives in the public's mind as Maloney's artistic legacy is not his creation but a meretricious simulacrum of it.[55]

This fable is so ingeniously contrived that it seems ungenerous to say that it is not as focused as it might have been and that, since it begins with the realization of Maloney's dream, it has nothing to show us about the *sine qua non* of any artwork: the creative processes and the sweat that have gone into its creation. There are, moreover, two other important parabolic dimensions to *The Great Victorian Collection* that are at least as suggestive as, though less overt than, the allegory of the artist.

The Collection is like Brendan Tierney's religion of art in that it tends gradually to absorb into itself all of the creator's life. But the sexual underside of the Collection suggests that it may be taken to represent not only an artist's ruling passion but anyone's fantasy which, if not controlled, can grow to destructive proportions and come to distort and suffocate reality. That we may think of Maloney's fantasy as potentially any man's, not only an artist's, is suggested by the uncreative Vaterman being placed in the grip of a fantasy that resembles Maloney's in that they keep both men from acting upon their desires for Mary Ann. (Vaterman imagines that her father means to kill him if he finds them in bed together and that he is constantly following them with this end in mind.) Maloney's fantasy (the Collection) begins to absorb Mary Ann into itself when he spies her changing out of Victorian costume in one of the Collection's bedrooms. This erotic image grows in his mind and blends with a later image of her as a Victorian servant girl at the mercy of her young master and as "the older of the pubescent sisters in Baxter's Victorian portrait." Maloney eventually comes to understand what has happened: "His manner of falling in love with Mary Ann was another symptom of his curious fate. There could no longer be any real life for him – no life at all apart from the Collection." The one time they do try to make love, at the very moment when Mary Ann is attempting to stimulate him sexually, her reality breaks through his fantasy, spoiling their coupling and presaging the end of their relationship: "And so, as he was and always would be, a dreamer, this reality undid him."

On the third level of parabolic meaning the Collection represents the pressure and the persistence of the past. Although Maloney is not a Catholic and although his Collection is made up of English artifacts, it is very hard to avoid going behind Maloney to his creator and interpreting *The Great Victorian Collection* as another attempt on Moore's part to come to terms with his Irish Catholic past. Maloney says at one point that "A man can only dream what he knows. And my field is the Victorians." Similarly a writer can only write about what he knows and Moore's creative field, like Fergus's apparitions, largely consists of his Irish Catholic past. Moore has more than once cited Mauriac's statement that " 'the door closes at twenty', meaning that after that age nothing important happens to us: the important events occur in childhood and adolescence."[56] Such an interpretation of the Collection makes sense of the otherwise incongruous Catholic similes scattered through the text ("as though she were in a pew," "as though beginning the Lord's Prayer," "like a penitent in the confessional," "he had been granted instant canonization as a patron saint of youth"), and allows us to understand the reason for the extraordinary similarities between the bedroom scene described above and the climactic moment in *The Feast of Lupercal*, the wrenching scene in which the pathetic Diarmuid Devine is unable to consummate his love for Una because of his Irish Catholic inhibitions and sense of sin. Like Devine's, Maloney's "sinful imagination [has] atrophied reality."

From this point of view the collection of Victorian artifacts suggests the ornate paraphernalia of pre-ecumenical Catholicism – the vestments, monstrances, tabernacles, confessionals, and rosaries; the pictures and statues, like Judith Hearne's oleograph of the Scared Heart, the reproduction of Guido Reni's insipid *Ecce Homo*, which hangs on Diarmuid Devine's wall in pious memory of his father, the statue of the Divine Infant of Prague which adorns Gavin Burke's bedroom and is described in the opening sentences of *The Emperor of Ice-Cream*, and the crucifix Mrs Tierney puts up on the wall of the bedroom her daughter-in-law has so inappropriately decorated for her. The sexual underside of the Collection becomes an emblem of the impure thoughts, concupisable longings, and masturbatory fantasies that were the cause of the anxieties and the hell-fire sermons to which Joyce in the *Portrait* gave such definitive artistic expression that it forced the young Brian Moore to search for less autobiographical subject matter. This is the past that impinges remorselessly upon Maloney's present, that binds with briars his joys and desires. For although *The Great Victorian Collection* is set in the sunny warmth of a California coastal town, like all of Moore's novels it has its imaginative roots in the cold, rainy northern city of his birth.

V

The confrontation of past and present is continued in *The Mangan Inheritance*, but from a perspective different from that of Moore's New World novels. Its early scenes are set in New York and Montreal. Alone in the former at New Year's because his American wife Beatrice, a rich and successful actress, has recently walked out on him, Jamie Mangan returns to the city of his birth to visit his father and his second wife, Margrethe, who is less than half the father's age. Jamie's phone call to his mother, who is living in Santa Monica, allows Moore to touch all the bases of his New World exile, but before long Jamie leaves for Ireland, the setting of two-thirds of the novel. It would seem important to Moore to have his reader recognize this change of direction, this new elaboration of the dominant figure in the carpet of his fiction, for he has included in *The Mangan Inheritance* an otherwise pointless scene in which Jamie, now in rainy southwest Ireland and enthralled with a girl young enough to be his daughter, has an apparition of Beatrice, epitome of the bounty of the New World in her dark mink coat and cognac-coloured boots. This is patently an allusion to *Fergus*, in which the title character, living in affluent circumstances in sunny southern California with a girl young enough to be his daughter, experiences a series of visitations from his Irish past.

    The Mangan Inheritance conforms to the paradigm of most of Moore's fiction in that it presents "the moment in a person's life, the crucial few weeks or months, when one suddenly confronts the reality or unreality of one's illusions." Like his New World novels, it also concerns "this new sense of rootlessness which so many people experience today," the sense of a "loss of identity ... that feeling that we are no longer able to relate to our own past, that we no longer know the person we were ten years ago." His wife's leaving is painful to Jamie mainly because it has forced him to realize the emptiness of his life: "it's as if there's nobody there any more. Sometimes I feel as if I'm going mad. Except that there's no me to *go* mad ... It's as though I'd ceased to exist." Jamie reflects that "Primitives fear the photograph, the shutter click, their image stolen, then given back to them as a lifeless souvenir, entombed in a piece of paper. Beatrice had snapped the shutter, stealing away the man he once had been, presenting him with himself as her useless husband."

But if one photograph has magically robbed Jamie of his identity, he soon comes to find himself held by the power of another – a daguerreotype of an ancestral double which seems to promise the recovery of identity. Looking through Mangan family documents in his father's possession, Jamie comes upon "A small, shimmering, mirror-bright picture on silver-coated copperplate ... What made Mangan stare as though transfixed by a vision was that the face in the photograph was his own." The face may even be that of the Irish poet James Clarence Mangan (d1848), Europe's first *poète maudit*. Himself a *poète manqué*, Jamie feels an "unearthly excitement," a "strange elation" whenever he looks at the photograph, which almost instantaneously becomes for him an icon of miraculous power. He calls it "his cure, his antidote ... [his] resurrection," and feels that its glittering eyes are "urging him to start again, to pursue his true vocation." Jamie resolves to visit Ireland and discover whether the photograph – initialled J.M. and dated 1847 – is that of the poet Mangan. Meanwhile Beatrice and her lover have died drunk in a New Year's Eve car accident, and after her grotesquely secular funeral service – massed flowers on a leafy green stage, a duo playing Mozart, a fatuous eulogy, the reading of a sentimental poem that meant nothing to her, the absence of her body – Jamie puts behind him this striking instance of New World deracination and leaves for Ireland to discover who he is through searching his ancestral past.

Once he reaches the village of Drishane in the wilds of West Cork – its life "the obverse of his life in New York" – *The Mangan Inheritance* begins to becomes a rather different kind of novel. To recall Moore's comment on the shift of scene from London to an exotic Greek island in John Fowles's *The Magus*, "it almost seems as though a new writer [has] taken over the narrative."[57] As in Fowles's novel, the new writer has the same tone of voice and the same eye as his predecessor, but he does not feel bound by the realistic conventions that obtained in the novel's opening section and introduces some of the conventions and appurtenances of romance. Thus is seems to Mangan as if he "had gone back in time" and entered a world as "different and distant" from the world he knew "as is a fairy tale from the evening news," as if he had entered "a dream which like all true dreams moved at its own mysterious pace, without logic, toward a purpose he did not understand." And another character describes what is happening to Jamie as being "like a ghost story."

Jamie meets several Mangan kin who live in the vicinity of Drishane, including the eighteen-year-old Kathleen, whose childish good looks belie the fact, soon discovered and savoured by a sexually intoxicated Jamie, that she is a veteran slut, a skilled and willing performer of all the acts of venery. But Kathleen is also prey to nightmares which suggest, as do other incidents, that there is some dark secret in the Mangan family past. When Jamie explains that he, like so many North Americans before him, has returned to the old country because "I want to know who are the people who made me what I am today" he does not heed the warning that "if you keep looking over your shoulder, sir, you'll find things you don't want to find." This thought had already crossed Jamie's mind when he reflected that the Drishane Mangans seemed "people left over from another time, their speech debased, their lives mean and pointless as that of cur dogs snuffling around a trash heap." But Jamie remains committed to his illusion: that the discovery of the truth about his double in the photograph (and of its other avatars, for he learns that there have been in intervening generations other Mangans of whom he is the spitting image) is synonymous with self-discovery, the acquisition of identity, and the beginning of a new life.

In the novel's long climactic scene Jamie learns the full story of his ancestral inheritance from Michael Mangan, an older double of himself, also a poet, who lives with his books in a ruined Norman tower with a winding stair in an isolated setting overlooking the sea – an appropriately Yeatsian setting for Jamie's discovery of the desolation of reality, which is the sole reward of his ravening, raging, and uprooting among the Mangan past. Jamie's *Doppelgänger*, the "image of himself as an old man," is able to confirm that the face on the daguerreotype is indeed that of Europe's first *poète maudit*, and at first it seems to Jamie that "something more than chance" has guided him to Michael Mangan, "this poet who bore his face, his true spiritual father." But Jamie's double goes on to explain that facial identity among the Mangans is accompanied by temperamental similarities. He next tells Jamie (with no emotional inflection, no hint of shame or regret) the horrifying story of what has made him *maudit*: incestuous relations with his only daughter over a period of years beginning when she was twelve; the ravishing when she was the same age of his niece Kathleen, the minor whom Jamie has also penetrated; his daughter's ending his sexual outrages with a sharp kitchen knife. In the same tone Michael Mangan then asks Jamie to help him get his poems published in America, and invites him to admire an old poem dedicated to his infant daughter, in which he writes wishes for her protection. Jamie is appalled by this "foul fawning child molester," this spiritual father revealed to be "a brute." He rushes from the tower, leaving behind his no longer cherished daguerreotype, which breaks at his feet when his double hurls it after him. Thus ends Jamie Mangan's quest for identity through the search for his roots, and thus ends the novel – except for a six-page epilogue set back in Montreal.

The Mangan Inheritance is intensely readable, has a strong thematic thrust, and is technically interesting in its attempts to accommodate romance elements within a realistic frame. One nevertheless senses a certain thinness and flatness in the novel and one leaves it with the feeling that not all its parts are vitally related to the whole. Much of this feeling is owing to the fact that the novel goes on too long. The bleak landscapes of western Ireland, for example, are wonderfully described – but described a little too often. This is only one indication of the fact that there is too much social and topographical notation for a novel that has as its theme the search for identity and the discovery of evil. In *I Am Mary Dunne* copious social notation and the theme of identity went well together because they were fused in the first person narrative of the dynamic central character. But like most of Moore's male protagonists, Jamie is passive and undynamic, and the novel's romance motifs and its supra-realistic premise are of themselves not sufficient to provide strength and cohesiveness.

Like *The Great Victorian Collection*, the plot of *The Mangan Inheritance* rests on a fantastic premise involving the persistence of the past and its determining effect on the present. In the later novel the premise is that through over four generations identical facial features, together with poetic ambitions, a dissolute life, the tendency to have an upper front tooth knocked out, and a bad end can all be genetically transmitted. One accepts the fantastic premise of *The Great Victorian Collection* because it is introduced early in the novel and it is thereby clear to the reader that the Collection is part of the fictional contract he agrees to if he continues to read. Once he has done so, everything that follows is thoroughly plausible.

The Mangan Inheritance proceeds in the opposite manner. It begins realistically and introduces its fantastic premise only gradually and long after the reader has signed a contract for a realistic novel. In addition, throughout *The Mangan Inheritance* the fantastic premise is tinged with melodramatic and Gothic effects, some of which rather smack of the factitious. One imagines that Moore felt these effects to be necessary because, unlike the multifaceted symbol of the Victorian Collection, the daguerreotype and its genetic implications were not by themselves a strong enough premise (or symbol) to sustain an entire novel. This of course helps explain Moore's choosing to include extensive social and topographical notation throughout.

This brings me to the novel's puzzling last chapter. Jamie hastens from Ireland to the bedside of his father in a Montreal hospital. The father has suffered a serious stroke but manages to whisper to his son that he knows he is dying, that Margrethe is pregnant, and that wife and infant will need Jamie's financial support. The novel ends with Jamie and Margrethe, a plastic cup of coffee in her hand, watching the father "labor to breathe, watching him die." On first reading it is hard to know what to make of this brief scene. If one assumes that Jamie's leaving Ireland does not mean that the reader has to leave behind interpretative habits appropriate to romance, it would be easy to see the newborn Mangan child, presumably male, and the comely young wife's future dependence on Jamie as suggestive of any of several things. But this kind of critical exercise would be merely notional, and is not the kind of operation the good reader of Brian Moore should perform.

A better way to think about the ending is to remember that in the world of Brian Moore "suffering is exact, but where / Desire takes charge, readings will grow erratic," and to note that like no fewer than four of his novels, *The Mangan Inheritance* ends with a scene or a memory involving the central character and his or her mother or father, in all of which the primacy of the parental bond is underlined. It is this bond, not sexual relationships or hundred-year-old daguerreotypes, that is for better or worse the bedrock of the identity of Moore's characters. This is Jamie's real inheritance as a Mangan. As the narrator of *Fergus* says, it is parents who form "the grammar of our emotions." This realization may not lighten the desolating implications of what is left when one is forced to confront "the reality or unreality" of one's illusions; for in Brian Moore's world one can no more escape into the past than one can escape from it. But at least the parental bond is no illusion. There are hospital bedsides or their surrogates in everyone's life, and though they lack the romance of ruined Norman towers or the bed on which Kathleen fulfils Jamie's sexual fantasies, it is in such quotidian places that a person's essential inheritance is realized.

Chapter Three

John Fowles's Variations

I

John Fowles said of *The Ebony Tower*, his 1974 collection of four long stories and a novella, that its working title was *Variations*, "by which I meant to suggest variations both on certain themes in previous books of mine and in methods of narrative presentation." He went on to say that he was led to change the collection's title when its "first professional readers, who do know my books, could see no justification for *Variations* whatever."[1] If this is actually so, one can only marvel at the insensitivity of editors. *The Ebony Tower* is full of thematic parallels to the three novels of Fowles which preceded it (and to *Daniel Martin*, which followed it in 1977), and its contents are not only interesting variations on several fictional genres; their more important formal variations are on the "methods of narrative presentation" used in the novels. As Fowles has himself said: "the major influence on any mature writer is always his own past work."[2] Acquaintance with these longer fictions adds a dimension of considerable critical interest to the shorter fictions of *The Ebony Tower*, and vice versa; for Fowles's thematic and presentational variations are deliberate and calculated; they are never simply repetitions. Apprehending the specific differences within the general similarities not only enhances understanding of each of Fowles's fictions, long or short; it also sharpens awareness of his stylistic and narrative gifts, of the complexity and resonance of his informing fictional concerns, and of the cumulative richness of his canon.

The first of Fowles's longer fictions was *The Magus* (1965; revised 1977), which was written before but published two years after *The Collector*, his fictional début.[3] While an impressive, sometimes dazzling, and always readable performance, the extended account of the seemingly endless mysteries that engulf Nicholas Urfe on an exotic Greek island contained some characteristic first novel features: a strongly autobiographical and self-conscious flavor; narrative, stylistic, and thematic excesses; and a less than exacting sense of form. Fowles himself came to call it "a novel of adolescence, written by a retarded adolescent" and admitted that "I tried to say too much ... like all first novelists, I wanted to say all sorts of things about life, and it got too complicated."[4] In *The Collector*, on the other hand, Fowles was in full control. This work, his only underrated novel, possesses the very qualities *The Magus* sorely lacks: comparative brevity, formal tightness, no extraneous detail or incident, and a powerful cumulative thrust. Another important feature of *The Collector* was what Angus Wilson called its "remarkable mimetic powers";[5] the alternating first person accounts of Clegg and Miranda in this claustrophobic story of imprisonment, non-communication, and death are impressive stylistic achievements. *The Collector* and *The Magus* were both large-scale commercial successes, but it was not until the publication in 1969 of *The French Lieutenant's Woman*, which is set in Victorian England and utilizes many characteristically Victorian fictional techniques, that the majority of critics rejoiced to concur with the common reader's estimation of Fowles. It was eight years after *The French Lieutenant's Woman*, undoubtedly his major achievement, that Fowles's most recent novel was published. In *Daniel Martin*, which he has described as "about what one twentieth-century man feels about his century and generation in one particular country,"[6] Fowles returned to the autobiographical flavor of *The Magus* and to a re-examination from the perspective of middle age of the same novel's concern with his Oxford generation. But compared with *The Magus*, there is little that is dazzling in *Daniel Martin* and, however thematically interesting its pattern of loss and symbolic repair, the novel even crosses the frontiers of boredom during certain stretches of the title character's journey away from artistic underexpression and frustration in the present, towards renewal and a deeper authenticity through creative activity and repossession of the past.

The appreciable differences of subject matter, setting, style, and genre among these four ambitious novels can have misleading implications concerning Fowles's development as a writer. For, to borrow a distinction of Northrop Frye's, John Fowles is one of those artists who unfolds rather than grows. Since he began to publish in the early 1960s his informing fictional themes and underlying strategies of narrative presentation have to a remarkable degree remained constant. This is perhaps not especially surprising in an artist who did not begin to publish until in his late thirties; but the more important reason has to do with Fowles's views on the nature and function of art. These have been set forth in his occasional prose – essays, prefaces, reviews, interviews – and in the non-fictional works he has published, especially *The Aristos* (1964; revised 1968), Fowles's intellectual self-portrait, a collection of numbered *pensées* inspired by the fragments of Heraclitus. Didactic in intention, though deliberately uncongenial in presentation and sometimes rebarbative in style (Fowles was later to describe it as begun "in my twenties" and "very arrogant"),[7] *The Aristos* contains reflections on the human condition, on contemporary reality, and on art that encapsulate what his novels seek to dramatize. Finally, there are the views on art that are directly or indirectly expressed in the fiction itself, for in their different ways all of Fowles's novels and stories are centrally concerned with the imagination and its productions.

Fowles's aesthetic may be described as conservative and traditional. He does not share "the general pessimism about the so-called decline of the novel," for the novel is "inalienably in possession of a still vast domain," and "countless ... forms of human experience" can only "be described in and by it."[8] He believes that the novel's traditional purposes – "to entertain, to satirize, to describe new sensibilities, to record life, to improve life, and so on [are still] viable and important" and that the duty of all art "is in some way (if only in terms of pure entertainment) to improve society at large."[9] He even asserts that "didactic teaching" is a genuine function of the novel, for "All the great novelists of the past have been more or less didactic ... The danger is when that tone dominates."[10] For himself as a novelist, he considers it essential to have a "view of the purpose of literature absolutely clear. I don't see that you can write seriously without having a philosophy of both life and literature to back you ... The novel is simply, for me, a way of expressing my view of life."[11] It follows that Fowles does not believe in "hermetic" art, but in "writing that wants to get read."[12] In *The Aristos* he distinguishes between artists "who pursue their own feelings and their own self-satisfaction" and artists "who exploit the desire of the audience to be wooed, amused and entertained."[13] At least until *Daniel Martin*, there could be no doubt to which group Fowles himself belonged. His choosing to work with such popular forms as the detective story, the thriller, and the historical novel is one piece of evidence. Another is the primary emphasis that Fowles has always placed on telling a story – on performing the primal narrational act of making the reader want to learn what happens next. A third is his commitment to "the great tradition of the English novel – realism": "For *me* the obligation is to present my characters realistically. They must be credible human beings even if the circumstances they are in are 'incredible,' as they are in *The Collector*. But even the story, no matter how bizarre, no matter what symbolisms are involved, has to be possible ... Believability must dominate even the most outlandish situation."[14]

Fowles denies that the function of art is self-expression, a doctrine he regards as tyrannizing the modern artist and leading to depreciation of the craft of the art, even to " 'insincere' and 'commercial' craftsmanship." The concomitant modern emphasis on forging a distinctive style is similarly deplored. Style, says Fowles, should not "signal one's individuality [but] satisfy the requirements of the subject-matter." Just the opposite is said to be true of much modern art: "There is the desperate search for the unique style, and only too often this search is conducted at the expense of content ... This accounts for the enormous proliferation in style and techniques in our century; and for that only too characteristic coupling of exoticism of presentation with banality of theme."[15] In short Fowles is against artists who are "high on craft and low on humanity"; against creative writing courses which spread the notion "that it is sufficient to learn the technique to achieve the value"; against the "sort of rococo cleverness which may be interesting to literary cliques and other stratospheric elements in the literary world, but which basically says nothing about the human condition, which teaches nothing, which does not touch people's hearts"; against those post-war American novelists who "write so much better than we (the British) do. They have much more skill at describing, at cutting, at dialogue, at all the machinery; and then at the end one takes the sunglasses off and some-thing's gone wrong. One hasn't a tan"; and against the practitioners of the *nouveau roman* who reduce "the purpose of the novel to the discovery of new forms" and who, in their "jettisoning all the old methods of conveying character and narrative" and claiming to know of their characters only what can be tape-recorded and photographed have responded to the impasse of the novel by sitting down and describing the wall at the end.[16]

Fowles's fiction puts into practice his aesthetic dicta. He has something he believes important to communicate to the reader (the theme or content) and is concerned to communicate it in as effective a way as possible (the style and method of narrative presentation). In *The Aristos* he is concerned to point out that many of his ideas go back as far as Heraclitus, called elsewhere by Fowles a "proto-existentialist"; in his essay on Kafka he sim-ilarly insists that most of the themes of that great modernist go back at least as far and that what fundamentally matters in Kafka is "*the articulation, not the articulated*"; and in *The Ebony Tower* he has Henry Breasley, a major twentieth-century painter, say: "Don't care a fart in hell where my ideas come from. Never have. Let it happen. That's all."[17] These are salutary reminders, for it is not in his ideas and themes themselves, but in their artistic embodiment in his chosen medium of prose fiction that Fowles's originality and distinction as a creative writer lie.

The principal thematic concerns of Fowles's fiction may be called exis-tential: "I'm interested in the side of existentialism which deals with free-dom: the business of whether we do have freedom, whether we do have free will, to what extent you can change your life, choose yourself, and all the rest of it. Most of my major characters have been involved in this Sartrian concept of authenticity and inauthenticity."[18] Elsewhere he has similarly insisted: "How you achieve freedom. That obsesses me. All my books are about that. The question is, is there really free will? Can we choose freely? Can we act freely? Can we *choose*? How do we do it?"[19] For

Fowles, any consideration of these questions presupposes an awareness and an acceptance of the primacy of mystery in human existence: "Unknowing, or hazard, is as vital to man as water."[20] As Conchis explains to Urfe in *The Magus*: "mystery has energy. It pours energy into whoever seeks an answer to it ... I am talking about the general psychological health of the species, man. He needs the existence of mysteries. Not their solution." Transience, randomness, contingency, flux, the aleatory: all of these notions help to describe man's state, as does Arnold's splendid line about "The unplumb'd, salt, estranging sea" which is quoted in the last sentence of *The French Lieutenant's Woman*. Fowles insists that there are no intervening gods, no absolute truth or reality, and that any *Weltanschauung* – social, cultural, intellectual, religious, aesthetic – that says there are and consequently gives man a feeling of security and certainty is inimical to authentic human existence. "Being an atheist," he has said, "is not a matter of moral choice, but of human obligation."[21] This is the cruel but necessary truth that Charles Smithson, the protagonist of *The French Lieutenant's Woman*, comes to recognize in the church at Exeter: "You stay in prison, what your time calls duty, honor, self-respect, and you are comfortably safe. Or you are free and crucified." For Fowles, "we must evolve to exist."[22] For him, as for Wallace Stevens, loss of faith is growth and is desirable even though freedom may lead to crucifixion and the black hole of unknowing prove bottomless.

Despite differences of style and setting, the vehicle of narrative presentation through which the theme of the necessity of mystery is carried is the same in each of Fowles's novels. (It must be borne in mind, however, that *The Collector* is a negative exemplum of Fowles's quintessential narrative paradigm: Clegg proves incapable of change or growth because of his blinkered class notions and because his only sexual stimulus is pornography. And in *Daniel Martin,* as we shall see, there are complex variations in the pattern owing to the fact that the title character is middle-aged.) In each novel a central male character undergoes a rite of passage from the known to the unknown. Fowles's description of the "basic idea" of *The Magus* is equally true of his subsequent novels and of the title novella of *The Ebony Tower*: "a secret world, whose penetration involved ordeal and whose final reward was self-knowledge."[23] The catalyst of this movement from the quotidian to the mysterious is "the great alchemy of sex,"[24] of which an aura of strangeness and contingency, intensified by real or imagined deception, is a part. "There is something erotic in all collusion," as Urfe notes in *The Magus*. The agent of sexual attraction is one of those cool, intelligent and comely young English females without which – it almost seems – no work by Fowles would be complete. In fact, "Poor Koko," one of the stories in *The Ebony Tower*, is his only work of fiction to date in which such a character does not appear.

This attraction runs a course indicated by Fowles in a generalization about his novels: "My female characters tend to dominate the male. I see man as a kind of artifice, and woman as a kind of reality. The one is cold idea, the other is warm fact. Daedalus faces Venus, and Venus must win."[25] The sexual attraction leads to an "ordeal" for the male, a situation of stress in which growth becomes possible. In *The Aristos* anxiety is called "an antidote to intellectual complacency (petrifaction)" and is said to be of value in helping man realize his need "to learn to choose and control his own life."[26] The crucible in which this destabilizing attraction takes place is in one way or another a "secret world" removed from ordinary reality: the Undercliff near Lyme Regis where Sarah begins to make Charles Smithson "aware of a deprivation"; Bourani, Conchis's estate on Phraxos where "Second meanings hung in the air; ambiguities; unexpectednesses" and where Urfe meets "Julie"; the isolated house in which Clegg incarcerates Miranda; the remote Breton *manoir* of *The Ebony Tower*, an island in "an arboreal sea," where David Williams meets "the Mouse." Behind these young women and closely associated with them are older, preceptorial male figures, all of them creative artists. Behind Miranda is the painter G.P.; behind Julie is Conchis, "an omniscient artist who lives inside the world of the novel" as one critic describes him;[27] behind Sarah is her novel's narrator, as warm to her as he is cold to Charles, and, latterly, Dante Gabriel Rossetti, in whose house she finds refuge from the petrifying conventions of her day; and behind the Mouse is Breasley.

A second major thematic interest of Fowles's fiction concerns the relation of the individual to his cultural and historical situation and to his society: for these determining forces are what most threaten freedom and corrupt authenticity. "The ordinary man and woman," Fowles has said, "live in an asphyxiating smog of opinions foisted on them by society. They lose all independence of judgment and all freedom of action."[28] This smog is the opposite of the cloud of mystery and hazard, in which atmosphere alone freedom and independence can breathe. Since Fowles is English, his concern for the individual in society is mainly focused by that without which (it sometimes seems) no English novel can be conceived: a preoccupation with class. Fowles is concerned to show the necessity for an individual to understand the ways in which he has been shaped by his class background and to transcend the limitations imposed on his selfhood by class consciousness. In *The Magus* and *The French Lieutenant's Woman* the vehicle of narrative presentation of this theme is the same paradigm described above. Woman, the stimulus of mystery, is also the agent of social transformation. At the end of his story Urfe has become "speciesless"; shriven of the snobbish class attitudes that earlier led him to treat Alison so callously and to be so willingly taken in by Julie's chic impersonations, he is able to form friendships with Kemp and Jojo, two *déclassé* females who function as surrogates of Alison. As Charles Smithson is pulled towards the enigmatic Sarah he is uprooted from the self-satisfied security of his age and his inherited position in society and led towards a liberating classlessness like that to which he is subsequently attracted during his travels in America.

In *The Collector* G.P. speaks of an individual's need to cauterize the part of himself which binds him to the class in which he was brought up. Miranda's diary entries, which take up the middle of the novel, are inspiriting because in them we see her growing away from the shallow liberal humanism of the privileged young towards a deeper, richer conception of human existence; her end is all the more horrible because she dies just as she is learning to be more authentically alive. Clegg, on the other hand, is as incapable of throwing off his lower middle class notions of respectability as he is of being brought to a sense of mystery through the alchemy of sex. Genteel to the end, he calls Miranda "the deceased" as he carries her corpse out to the garden for disposal. All he has learned from his months with her is to choose as his next victim a girl from lower down the social ladder. In *The Collector* the social theme is brought into focus through the creation of a situation that makes possible a direct confrontation of class extremes, the Few and the Many as Fowles calls them in his interesting description of the novel's "deeper message":

history – not least in the twentieth century – shows that society has persistently seen life in terms of a struggle between the Few and the Many, between "Them" and "Us." My purpose in *The Collector* was to attempt to analyse, through a parable, some of the results of this confrontation ... unless we face up to this unnecessarily brutal conflict (based largely on an unnecessary envy on the one hand and an unnecessary contempt on the other) between the biological Few and the biological Many ... unless the Many can be educated out of their false assumption of inferiority and the Few out of their equally false assumption that biological superiority is a state of existence instead of what it really is, *a state of responsibility* – then we shall never arrive at a more just and happier world.[29]

The Few who have rid themselves of the shackles of class and the smog of received social opinion are members of an elect. Conchis uses this term early in *The Magus* and explains to Urfe that "Hazard makes you elect. You cannot elect yourself." The most significant quality the representatives of the elect have in common is imagination; to cite Iris Murdoch: "contingency is destructive of fantasy and opens the way for imagination."[30] The importance of imagination in human existence is a third major theme in Fowles's fiction. All of the novels and stories are much concerned with art and aesthetics. Miranda, an art student, is constantly thinking about art and its relation to life. Paintings, music, and Conchis's metatheatre figure importantly in *The Magus* and it is one of the symptoms of Urfe's disease of self that he has used his aesthetic sense not to intensify life but to freeze it: "all my life I had tried to turn life into fiction, to hold reality away." There are numerous references to paintings and painters in the title novella of *The Ebony Tower* and the work's thematic hinge is the contrast – as persons and as painters – between a young artist and an old one. In *The French Lieutenant's Woman* Charles's movement from security to hazard, his painful discovery that there are no intervening gods or absolutes, is counterpointed by the creative difficulties of the self-conscious mid-twentieth-century narrator who cannot assume the omniscient point of view of the Victorian novelist but must create in an atmosphere of contingency and unknowing. And *Daniel Martin* may be described as a reflexive novel about the central character and sometime narrator's attempt to move towards freedom and authenticity through beginning to write a novel about what the novel that contains him is about. The interrelationship of what he calls "the aesthetic theme" and "the existential theme" is the subject of the best of the three chapters of William J. Palmer's *The Fiction of John Fowles* (1974), and there is little one would want to quarrel with in his judgment that "Fowles's greatest strength as a novelist lies in his continuous and artful linking of these two themes."[31]

But in Fowles's novels imagination and its workings are not only a supporting theme which strengthens and helps to elaborate the movement from the prison of the known into the dark freedom of the unknown. Imagination, active or potential, is a *sine qua non* of change and growth because it is through this faculty that a sense of mystery and hazard is not only communicated in works of art, but initially apprehended in human experience. In Fowles's existentialist interpretation of the Garden of Eden myth, Adam is "hatred of change ... stasis, or conservatism" and Eve "the assumption of human responsibility, of the need for progress." The serpent is imagination – "the power to compare, self-consciousness."[32] Fowles has said: "One cannot describe reality; only give metaphors that indicate it. All human modes of description ... are metaphorical. Even the most precise scientific description of an object or movement is a tissue of metaphors."[33]

That is to say, one's perception of reality, one's phenomenological world, is the work of the imagination. The failure to replace culturally and socially conditioned metaphors of reality by one's own, or to move beyond stale metaphors, is an imaginative failure. What lies beyond one's metaphors is the unknown, and it is at the point where the imagination and the unknown meet that an awareness of mystery and hazard begins. As the king tells his son in the tiny parable interpolated into that elephantine parable, *The Magus*: "There is no truth beyond magic."

For John Fowles, the essential value of the productions of the imagination is that "human freedom lives in human art"; the best works of art "are essentially demolishers of tyranny and dogma; are melters of petrifaction, breakers of the iron situation."[34] Since mankind's most human and most evolved tool is language, "it is the art that communicates through language that must be the most important." For Fowles "poetry is obviously the highest and most concentrated form of that art,"[35] but since it is equally obvious that prose fiction is the natural medium of his imagination, Fowles understandably has most to say about the magic of the novel and about the freedom it allows the writer. For Fowles faith in the novel and its future, which he has more than once reaffirmed, is based on the fact that "For all its faults, it is a statement by one person."[36] Indeed, "The novel is an astounding freedom to choose. It will last just as long as artists want to be free to choose. I think that will be a very long time. As long as man."[37]

Fowles also thinks that the novel allows freedom to the reader as well as to the writer, especially in comparison with the non-literary art of the film, a medium about which he has some disturbingly negative things to say – especially in *Daniel Martin*. The well-known unresolved endings of two of his own novels are obvious examples of places where readers are made to work. And the reader's active collaboration with the text in the production of meaning is an important theme in *The Magus* and the implied subject of two of the stories in *The Ebony Tower*. More fundamental than deliberate authorial strategies, however, is the fact that there is something in the very nature of the literary medium that activates the reader's imagination: "The marvelous thing about a novel is that every reader will imagine even the very simplest sentence slightly differently."[38] Take, for example, the "essential difference in the quality of image" evoked by the novel as compared with the film: "The cinematic visual image is virtually the same for all who see it; it stamps out personal imagination, the response from individual *visual* memory. A sentence or paragraph in a novel will evoke a different image in each reader. This necessary co-operation between writer and reader, the one to suggest, the other to make concrete, is a privilege of *verbal* form; and the cinema can never usurp it."[39]

One final aspect (a qualifying one) of Fowles's belief in the imagination and its productions remains to be remarked on. As we have seen, his metaphors for the interface of the known and the unknown tend to assume a female shape. (Indeed, in "Le Voyeur vu," one of the better poems in his 1973 collection of verse, a woman seen undressing in a window across a midnight garden becomes to the "dark Zeiss eyes" of the poet nothing less than "imagination / new-bodied in a nakedness / made real across the reason's void.") In *The French Lieutenant's Woman*, the narrator says at one point of Sarah, the mysterious title character, that she possesses two distinguishing qualities: passion and imagination. But if we ask what evidence the novel offers of the second quality, the answer must be Sarah's power of creating illusions, specifically the deception she practises on Charles which culminates in his ravishing her. The power to create deceptions and illusions makes Sarah (as it does Conchis) something of a John Fowles-type novelist, for Fowles has described the novelist as "a dealer in plausible hypotheses, a confidence trickster," defined the novel as "a hypothesis more or less ingeniously and persuasively presented – that is, first cousin to a lie," and at the end of *The French Lieutenant's Woman* he brings himself on stage in the guise of a rather vulgar impresario.[40] These designations and this costuming are quite different in their implications from most of the confident and unequivocal claims quoted above that Fowles has made for the primacy and importance of the imagination's productions in human existence. It is, of course, not surprising to find in a twentieth-century author such contrasting conceptions of the role of the creative artist: one thinks for example of Wallace Stevens's "Notes toward a Supreme Fiction" on the one hand and his "The Man on the Dump" on the other. But one feels that in Fowles's case the contrast more particularly suggests an awareness both of what Bergonzi calls "the essentially problematic nature of fictional form in our time" and of his very ambitiousness as a writer of fictions designed to contain "a sort of quantum of mystery"[41] that will seize his readers' imaginations in ways that will be a stimulus to the recognition of the possibility of freedom and consequently of growth. For at a time when many of his contemporary English novelists are "too insular, too privately embroiled," playing it "so bloody safe most of the time" and content "just to be read in England" Fowles has clearly aspired to be a major novelist of international stature.[42]

II

Critical consideration of John Fowles's fiction might well begin with the five relatively short and straightforward variations of *The Ebony Tower*, which may be regarded as a primer to the more sustained, complex, and engaging variations of the novels. The setting of "The Cloud," the volume's closing story, is a warm, brilliant day in central France in late May. The story recounts in detail the country picnic of eight English people: the hosts Paul and Bel, an expatriate, best-selling novelist and his wife; their two young daughters; Bel's younger sister Catherine, recently widowed and deeply disturbed; Peter, a BBC producer on a working visit; his trendy girl friend Sally; and Peter's young son. Except for Catherine, the adult characters are depicted, and exposed, in a way that distinctly recalls the fiction of Fowles's older contemporary Angus Wilson, on whose methods of narrative presentation in his short stories "The Cloud" may be regarded as a variation. The social and professional background of the characters, their fatuities, banalities, and self-deceptions, and the skilful use of children as reflectors of adult behaviour all recall Wilson's short fiction, as does the way in which the narrator of "The Cloud" slips in and out of the minds of several of the characters. Here, for example, is the description of the self-satisfied drift of Bel's consciousness while her husband reads aloud from "The Scholar Gypsy" (it sounds like nothing so much as a piece of Wilson's satiric portraiture): "Bel believes in nature, in peace, drift, illogically in both the inevitable and a beneficent order of things; not in anything so masculine and specific as a god, but much more in some dim equivalent of herself watching gently and idiosyncratically behind all the science and the philosophy and the cleverness. Simple, poised, flowing like the river; the pool, not the leap ..."

Its first two paragraphs set the scene of "The Cloud" and establish the reader's attitude to the characters. A discordance of colours signals the abrasive contrast between the soaring blue-and-green country day and the synthetic brightness of the humans in the same way that the song of the hidden oriole – "so leafy, so liquid, so richly of its place and season" – clashes with the din of Anglo-Saxon voices. Only Catherine is shown to be exempt from the unflattering contrast of natural and human: sunning herself she is "like a lizard; sun-ridden, storing, self-absorbed; much more like the day than its people"; and, responsive to the song of the oriole, she later makes lovely use of its characteristic sound in the tale of the lost princess she tells her niece. As the story develops, it gradually becomes clear that Catherine is the focal point of "The Cloud" and that its concerns have more in common with Fowles's existential premises than with the endless subtleties of Angus Wilson's liberal humanism. Catherine's keen intelligence, her concern with authenticity (revealed in her discussion of Barthes's *Mythologies*), her imaginative powers (demonstrated in her fairy-tale), and most of all her awareness of mystery and hazard (the leap, not the pool), set her apart from the other characters. Her metaphors for reality are as different from those of her sister, whose substitution of cosy muddle for mystery is instanced in the above quotation, as she herself is from the loathsome Peter, the "smart little rhesus [whose] cage is time," the "worthless, shallow little *prick*; who saw nothing in trees but wood to build his shabby hutches of ephemeral nonsense from. To whom the real, the living, the unexplained is the outlaw; only safe when in the can."

Catherine's mixture of passion, imagination, and exacerbated sensibilities has led to a pathological depression that has brought her to the brink of self-destruction. As such she is strikingly reminiscent of Sarah in *The French Lieutenant's Woman*, and there can be no doubt that Fowles deliberately intended her to be a contemporary version of Sarah. Catherine is associated with the song of the oriole and its natural setting just as Sarah is with the wren which Charles hears singing in the Undercliff. Catherine, like Sarah, is discovered alone in an evocative natural setting brooding on her absent lover, and her tears, like Sarah's, are forced from her eyes "by a profound conditional, rather than emotional, misery." At the end of *The French Lieutenant's Woman* Sarah seems (one cannot be sure) to have attained a certain degree of independence and psychic balance, which allows her to live in the presence of, but not be destroyed by, the existential void within her, what Fowles in *The Aristos* calls the Nemo. Catherine, on the other hand, must enter "The black hole, the black hole" from which she is unable to return. Sexual violation by an uncomprehending male had been for Sarah a therapeutic necessity; for Catherine the defilement of Peter's sodomizing her can only be the step that takes her over the brink of the black hole. She cannot be found when the picnickers prepare to leave; her un-narrated but probable suicide – certainty is again denied the reader – is intimated at the story's end by the sudden appearance of a lowering storm cloud come to obliterate the beautiful day. The cloud, emblem of unknowing, takes the place of Catherine at the end of her story. In its closing line, the oriole (the princess of Catherine's fairy-tale vainly calling for her lover) sounds again, "but there is no one, now, to hear her."

A disappearance and presumed suicide also figure in "The Enigma," the penultimate story in *The Ebony Tower*. The title refers to the puzzling, indeed inexplicable, disappearance of John Marcus Fielding, a rich, Conservative Member of Parliament. The police make extensive inquiries, but no evidence can be found to substantiate any of the explanations that suggest themselves: kidnapping, temporary amnesia, private scandal, mental breakdown, sexual-romantic passion. In fact no leads of any kind are discovered and the investigation is eventually placed in the hands of a junior detective, Mike Jennings. His inquiries also get nowhere (Fielding's wife, "a woman welded to her role in life and her social status, eminently poised and eminently unimaginative," is particularly unhelpful) until he interviews an ex-girlfriend of Fielding's son. Isobel Dodgson is an aspiring novelist with "a quicker and more fastidious mind in the field of emotions and personal relationships" than any other character in the story; with the help of a small piece of information known only to her, but mainly because of her imagination and sensitivity, she is able to evolve a plausible explanation of the disappearance.

"The Enigma" is of course a variation on the popular literary genre of the detective story. Fowles has suggested that the reason for "the enormous popularity" of this form and of the thriller is that "they are obviously fulfilling a deep need"; for "situations of mystery have become very rare in the personal lives of the twentieth century."[43] In an afterword he wrote for an edition of *The Hound of the Baskervilles* Fowles had a number of interesting things to say about the form: one point concerned "an innate flaw in the detective-tale genre. However fantastic and far-reaching the first half of the detective 'mystery,' the second half is bound to drop (and only too often flop) towards a neat and plausible everyday solution."[44] In "The Enigma" Fowles has handled this inherent generic difficulty in an extremely clever way that has enabled him not only to ring some fresh changes on a limited and cliché-ridden literary form but also to make some striking variations on his own informing themes and methods of narrative presentation.

Isobel's analysis of the disappearance, which recalls the reflections of the narrator of *The French Lieutenant's Woman* on the life-and-will-of-their-own that fictional characters sometimes seem to acquire, turns "The Enigma" into a self-referential story that merges the existential theme and the aesthetic theme into a parable about imagination, mystery, and freedom. Isobel invites Jennings to assume that they and Fielding are all characters in a detective story being written by someone else (as of course they are). When she says to Jennings that "A story has to have an ending. You can't have a mystery without a solution. If you're the writer you have to think of something," she makes the same aesthetic complaint about detective stories that the author who has given her these words to speak makes in his remarks on *The Hound of the Baskervilles*. Isobel dismisses a *deus ex machina* solution as bad art, and when Jennings suggests that the author of the story they are in should not have begun it because he has neglected to plant any decent leads and implies that "detective stories have to end with everything explained" she replies that if the story "disobeys the unreal literary rules, that might mean it's actually truer to life." Isobel prefers to imagine what John Fowles has imagined in writing "The Enigma": that Fielding, the mystery's central character, has walked out on his creator and left the story "without a decent ending." Fielding is imagined by Isobel to have come to feel "like something written by someone else, a character in fiction," just as in the story it is learned that he has devoted his life to playing various establishment roles: successful lawyer, conscientious company director, country squire, master of foxhounds, dutiful back-bencher. The logic of Isobel's scenario leads to the conclusion that just as her Fielding has walked out of the story she imagines herself and him to be in, thereby leaving it without an ending, so Fielding, the character in Fowles's "The Enigma," has chosen to walk out on the inauthentic social roles that have imprisoned him in the security of the known, and has desperately affirmed his freedom by killing himself. In this way Isobel supplies for Fowles's story "The Enigma" a "plausible" but hardly "everyday" solution. For while Miss Parsons, Fielding's long-time secretary, had earlier suggested to Jennings that her employer had taken his own life she had hastened to add that "He couldn't have done it of his own free will. In his normal mind. It's unthinkable."

At the same time that Jennings is listening to Isobel's "plausible hypothesis" (what Fowles says all novelists deal in), he finds himself being more and more sexually attracted to her. This is hardly surprising, for the lovely young Isobel is one of those delicate vessels in which are borne onward through the pages of John Fowles's fiction the seeds of mystery, imagination, and existential growth: "Something about her possessed something that he lacked: a potential that lay like unsown ground, waiting for just this unlikely corn-goddess; a direction he could follow, if she would only show it." Since the Fielding who is led to destroy himself is a creation of Isobel's imagination, the two characters may be thought of as functions of each other, the two halves of a whole that in "The Cloud" were both embodied in the single figure of Catherine. Fielding plunges into Catherine's "black hole," but at the end of "The Enigma" Isobel, whose imagination can encompass this extreme assertion of freedom, and Jennings, who can apprehend something of the truth of her imagination (her magic), are allowed something virtually unprecedented in Fowles's fiction: a simply and happily consummated sexual relationship; what at the end of "The Enigma" Fowles calls the "tender pragmatisms of flesh [which] have poetries no enigma, human or divine can diminish or demean – indeed it can only cause them, and then walk out."

This concluding lyrical flourish suggests another way in which in "The

Enigma" Fowles has had his fictional cake and eaten it too – satisfying the detective story reader's demand for an ending without dissipating the sense of mystery that as a serious artist, even when working in a commercial medium, it is his concern to generate. For "The Enigma" had hardly begun lyrically: a dryly sociological paragraph of statistical generalizations about suicides had introduced a straightforward account of police procedures. But about a third of the way through the story, the narrative perspective had begun to shift from that of impersonal reportage to the point of view of Jennings, the first (and only) character into whose thoughts the reader is granted access. By the time he is buying Isobel tea on Hampstead Heath, the subject of "The Enigma" has become not a disappearance but a process of growth – for Jennings and for the reader. Through Fowles's corn goddess both come to realize that it is enigmas that are important, not their solution.

"Poor Koko," the third story in *The Ebony Tower*, precedes "The Enigma," which it resembles in its generic affinities with low-brow literary forms, in this case with what the story's unnamed first person narrator calls "certain melodramatic situations derived from the detective story and the thriller" that have been "done to death by the cinema and television." The narrator is an older man of letters: "books – writing them, reading, reviewing, helping to get them into print – have been my life rather more than life itself." For some years he has been at work on a biographical-critical study of Thomas Love Peacock and has been lent a cottage in an isolated North Dorset combe so that he can work uninterruptedly on his manuscript. It is on his first night alone there that the narrator undergoes an "ordeal," the first situation of stress or hazard of his "safe sixty-six years of existence." For the cottage is burglarized by a masked young thief who, the narrator decides, belongs "to that baffling (to my generation) new world of the classless British young." Initially startled by finding the cottage occupied, the thief soon enters into conversation with the narrator, whom he has at his mercy. He is most considerate of the older man, offering him coffee and brandy and suggesting he dress warmly in preparation for being bound and gagged. But his final action is as startling as it is apparently unmotivated: he carefully incinerates every scrap of the Peacock manuscript and every volume of the narrator's heavily annotated edition of that author's works. The narrator is able to dine out for months afterwards on the strength of the story of what he calls "this bestial and totally gratuitous act of vandalism." The closing pages of "Poor Koko" describe the interpretative difficulties of this professional critic in uncovering the meaning of the difficult text, so to speak, of the burglar's action.

The isolated setting, the physical detainment of a weaker person by a

stronger, their unbridgeable differences of class, culture, and speech: all
these features of "Poor Koko" point to the unquestionable conclusion that
the story is meant to be seen as a variation on the theme and the presentational vehicle of *The Collector* which, as we have seen, Fowles describes
as a "parable" of the unnecessarily brutal conflict of the Few and the Many.
"Poor Koko" is, however, a lighter, less involving, and more cerebral
fiction than *The Collector*. No inside view of the representative of the Many
is offered, and the reader's attitudes to both representatives are manipulated
in different and more equivocal ways than they are in the novel.

Like "The Enigma," "Poor Koko" is an extremely clever and self-referential story. The first critical problem it sets the reader is assessment of
the narrator. Since he is a professional writer/critic and since in his retrospective attempt to understand what has happened he comes to attach great
importance to the thief's "linguistic usages," it is appropriate that assessment
begin with consideration of his own prose style. Not to put too fine a point
on it, the narrator's style is stilted, dated, and belletristic in a way that
suggests we are listening to a second-rate, back-number man of letters.
Hopeful thoughts instance "the latterday Pangloss in all of us"; the thief is
a "new-style Raffles"; their discussion an "obscene simulacrum of a quiet
chat between chance-met strangers"; the cottage "my humble temporary
version of the Sabine farm"; the title he gives his story is simultaneously
recondite and corny; and genteel clichés abound: "Thomas Hardy has never
been my cup of tea"; "this rude awakening in the night"; "torn, so to speak,
from the womb"; "a bright young genius from the BBC." The prose style
suggests what other aspects of his characterization tend to confirm: that the
narrator has made himself smugly secure in a cocoon of stale metaphors
and hand-me-down mandarin values, and that he has the appearance of
intelligence and literary distinction without the reality. Nothing in "Poor
Koko" gives one any reason to think that the narrator's Peacock biography
will be any more distinguished a work than "my most successful potboiler,
The Dwarf in Literature, [which was not] quite the model of objective and
erudite analysis it pretended to be."

A similar discrepancy between appearance and reality is found in the
narrator's social attitudes. His beliefs are the standard liberal-humanist ones
of Maurice and Jane, the London friends who own the cottage: he believes
in what is "humane, intelligent and balanced," in "Humanism. Good manners" and says that he stands second to none in his detestation of class
snobbery. But his brand of liberal humanism and his claimed superiority
to class prejudice do not keep him from judging the burglar a "semi-literate"
even before he has seen him or heard him speak or from revealing "un-

necessary contempt" – for instance, in thinking that "any attempt at serious argument with this young buffoon would be like discussing the metaphysics of Duns Scotus with a music-hall comedian: one could only become his butt."

It is not as easy to analyse the thief's use of language because of the relative paucity of data. There is little more than a handful of pungently demotic one-liners: "Why you so shit scared, man?"; "We'll play it by ear. Right?"; "what a fucking fraud the whole business of property is"; "You're just saying words, man." But the narrator is eventually forced to attempt such analysis because of his "continuing inability to make sense of what happened." He seems at his most intellectually engaged and most incisive as he works through to the interpretation that "the fatal clash between us was of one who trusts and reveres language and one who suspects and resents it." But it is hard not to regard this reading as partial and self-serving, for as we have seen the burglar's speech is no more stereotyped or cliché-ridden than the narrator's. But if the latter's interpretation is not accepted as authoritative, what, then, is the meaning of the thief's burning up four years of the narrator's work? The reader is denied the wherewithal to answer this question, but he is able to gauge the effect of the incineration on the narrator, who is precipitated into at least some awareness of contingency and enigma. And that surely is all to the good.

The second story in *The Ebony Tower*, the fourth in my back-to-front movement through the text, is not by John Fowles; it is his prose translation from the Old French of the medieval verse narrative "Eliduc," one of the Breton lays written in the late twelfth century by Marie de France, whose work – together with the rest of the corpus of what he calls "Celtic romance" – Fowles highly regards. "Eliduc" is not without a certain interest and charm, though some will think that Fowles claims rather too much for it in the "Personal Note" prefaced to his translation. In a way that will presently become clear, the function of "Eliduc" in *The Ebony Tower* is as a pendant to the title novella that precedes it (which I shall cite in quotation marks in order to avoid the confusion of part with whole), the strongest, as it is the longest, of the collection's fictions.

"The Ebony Tower" recounts the two-day visit of David Williams, a decent, sensible, tolerant, tactful, fairminded, and articulate young art critic and abstract painter, to the isolated Breton *manoir* of Henry Breasley, an old and "indisputably major" expatriate English artist, a non-abstract painter of scandalous reputation, with a contempt for everything conventionally middle class, including David's sterling qualities, and "an almost total inadequacy with words." His *ménage* includes two young English women, the Mouse and the Freak as Breasley calls them, one classy and one *déclassé*, to the former of whom, herself an apprentice painter, David soon finds himself strongly attracted despite thoughts of his children and wife back in England, and his conventionally enlightened, happy marriage. During his two-day visit David undergoes a rite of passage which culminates in the crushing realization that he has arranged his life in such a way as inextricably to trap himself in a prison of rational, humane values: "He was crippled by common sense, he had no ultimate belief in chance and its exploitation ... he had refused ... a chance of a new existence ... what he was born, [he] still was, and always would be: a decent man and eternal also-ran."

"The Ebony Tower" is designed as a prose variation of some of the central motifs of medieval romance, and Fowles goes to some pains to make sure that the reader becomes aware of this. We are reminded that the forest in which Breasley's house is located is the Broceliande of the *lais* of Chrétien de Troyes, and the novella's epigraph – four lines from that writer's *Yvain* – speaks of the perils of a journey into the strange, wild places of this forest. In addition, Fowles has Breasley mention to David the story of "Eliduc," calling it a "damn good tale ... What's that old Swiss bamboozler's name. Jung, yes? His sort of stuff. Archetypal and all that." Like Eliduc in his story (or Tristram in his), David is torn between marriage and passion: a lawful wife on one side of the channel and a beautiful, irresistible female on the other. A *deus ex machina* involving a weasel with a red flower in its mouth happily resolves Eliduc's dilemma; but there is no supernatural dispensation to end David's ordeal: the weasel he runs over near his story's end has only a flower-shaped stain of blood trickling from its mouth.

These specific romance allusions, however, are much less important in "The Ebony Tower" than the aura of mystery, strangeness, and ordeal imparted by romance motifs. These motifs are "pervasive in the mood if tenuous in the actual symbolism," to recall the relationship said to exist between the paintings of Breasley's last period and "Breton medieval literature," in particular its "preoccupation with love and adventure and the magical," and the "extraordinary yearning" evoked by wandering knights and "lost damsels and dragons and wizards." Thus, David comes to believe he is undergoing "a kind of ordeal" at the *manoir* and feels "a little bewitched, possessed" in the "spell-like and legendary," "faintly mythic and timeless" atmosphere and "mysterious remoteness" of the forest. And he comes to see the Mouse, who describes herself as if "under a spell," as a lady in distress whom he is appointed to rescue.

But like the other fictions in *The Ebony Tower*, its title story is not only, and in the final analysis not most importantly, a presentational variation on a particular literary form. It is also a variation, indeed a potent distillation, of Fowles's informing fictional themes and his dominant narrative paradigms. The author is equally concerned that this not go unnoticed, for he arranges to have the Freak found reading *The Magus* during a *déjeuner sur l'herbe* which, like Manet's painting, mixes nude females and clothed males. The narrative movement of "The Ebony Tower" not only corresponds to that of medieval romance; it answers exactly to the "basic idea" of *The Magus*: "a secret world, whose penetration involved ordeal and whose final reward was self-knowledge." As Fowles has himself explained: "In a way I wanted to de-mystify *The Magus*, which I think was altogether too full of mystery. This is a kind of realistic version of *The Magus*."[45]

"The Ebony Tower" is, however, only comparatively realistic, for Fowles needs every bit of the timeless ambiance of romance he can generate in order to depict convincingly in the space of a few fictional hours and in only a hundred pages the same complex process of sexual attraction, awareness of deprivation, apprehension of mystery, suspicion of deception, and arrival of the crunch that in *The Magus* and *The French Lieutenant's Woman* is developed over a much more extended and psychologically credible time span, and in many more pages. In the same way he needs to associate his fictional characters with the stylized characterizations of romance, for how else can Fowles forestall the reader from realizing that the thematic thrust of "The Ebony Tower" hinges on the dubious premise "that a non-conformist personal life is a precondition for great art."[46] It is a measure of Fowles's virtuosity that in "The Ebony Tower" he has brought things off so well, linking a romance vehicle to an existential tenor in a more artistically successful way than he was able to do in *The Magus*.

David is, of course, the novella's variation on Nicholas Urfe and Charles Smithson, and the Coëtminais *manoir* which generates a sense that "everything remains possible" and seems "haunted and unpredicted" the secret place of natural beauty and mystery, the crucible in which – beginning with his glimpse of two naked girls on the lawn – "the great alchemy of sex" begins to transform David. Just as Sarah is contrasted with the vapid Ernestina, so the Mouse is contrasted with Beth, the sensible, perky, but unmysterious wife who waits for David in the quotidian world outside the pristine ("freshly apprehended") forest.[47] And just as Urfe's "disintoxication" leads him to appreciate the worth of Alison, so David comes to "learn" the Freak, to see her as a vulnerable and kind human being, not "the absurd sex doll" he initially imagines her to be. Breasley, a rogue painter whose pristine characterization owes nothing to earlier fictional renditions of the type, is the older preceptorial figure – one of the elect – who stands behind the Mouse.

The contrast between David and Breasley is Fowles's most sustained and explicit attempt to link the existential theme and the aesthetic theme. Like G.P. in *The Collector*, Breasley has a consuming hatred of abstract art. He believes that "full abstraction" (which, remembering *The Aristos*, may be described as pure style devoid of content) represents "a flight from human and social responsibility," that its practitioners are castrators and eunuchs, and that "Art is a form of speech. Speech must be based on human needs, not abstract theories of grammar." The title of the novella is Breasley's image for abstract art. By the end of "The Ebony Tower" the anguished David has come to feel the truth of Breasley's denunciation and to realize that both his art and his life are similarly impoverished. He sees that "the surface liberties of contemporary art" spring "from a profound frustration, a buried but not yet quite extinguished awareness of nonfreedom" and that in the same way his "sense of loss, of being cleft, struck down, endlessly deprived ... and deceived" because of his failure with the Mouse – for he has hung back when he should have gone forward and substituted for the hazardous step into the unknown the "fatal indecision" of "if onlys" – was "metaphysical: something far beyond the girl; an anguish, a being bereft of a freedom whose true nature he had only just seen." At the same time David realizes that his loss also includes severance of any meaningful connection with the past, for while Breasley has "an umbilical cord to the past," to the mystery and livingness of nature and of past works of art, David has only what is epitomized by his wife, who brings to their meeting at the Paris airport "the relentless face of the present tense." It is there that David surrenders himself permanently "to what is left: to abstraction."

There are a number of similarities between "The Ebony Tower" and "The Cloud," the first and last of the fictions of *The Ebony Tower*, and one is surely meant to compare David's surrender to the ebony tower with Catherine's surrender to the black hole. While both places are horrific, it is for John Fowles more distinctively human, and therefore preferable, to be buried in the pit of the Nemo than to be self-emasculated in the shiny blackness of non-mystery and non-freedom.

III

For such a lengthy novel (656 pages in the revised edition I shall cite), especially a novel so full of mysteries and extraordinary incidents, the story line of *The Magus* is unusually straightforward. Nicholas Urfe, an upper middle class Oxford graduate in his mid-twenties, is the first person narrator and central character. In a few places in the text there are instances of retrospective narration, of Urfe's commenting after the fact on what he has earlier experienced. But in these places a false note is struck, for unlike the case of Pip in *Great Expectations* (which Fowles retrospectively claimed was an important influence on *The Magus*) there are no important distinctions between Urfe as character and Urfe as narrator; there is rather a linear chronicling of the events of little more than a single year and of Urfe's reaction to them as they happen.

The novel's first forty-eight pages sketch in Urfe's background and character – he is a womanizer, an egotist, something of an aesthete, rather a snob, fashionably bored and disaffected – and detail his affair with Alison, a knock-about young Australian who comes to take their relationship much more seriously than he does. To Urfe's relief, their cohabitation ends when he embarks for Greece, where he has accepted a teaching position at a private boys school on the island of Phraxos. His reflections as he leaves London confirm one's impression that Urfe is not a likeable young man: "So on top of the excitement of the voyage into the unknown, the taking wing again, I had an agreeable feeling of emotional triumph. A dry feeling. But I liked things dry. I went towards Victoria [Station] as a hungry man goes towards a good dinner after a couple of glasses of Manzanilla." In the middle of *The Magus* the two are reunited for a week-end on mainland Greece during which they climb Mount Parnassus while Urfe's callous treatment of Alison also reaches new heights. In its last eighty pages Urfe is back in London, shaken to his roots by what he has experienced on Phraxos, trying to understand what has happened to him and hoping that Alison, whose human worth he now realizes, will choose to see him again.

The rest of *The Magus* – upwards of five hundred pages – describes the mysterious happenings at the Bourani estate on Phraxos of Maurice Conchis, a rich old man who seemingly befriends Urfe but is actually a self-appointed reality instructor with a taste for the theatrical, the arcane, and the labyrinthine. The principal ingredients of the incredibly elaborate show he puts on for Urfe are the serial instalments of his life story, which epitomize the grimmer historical realities of the twentieth century; the special effects, tableaux, masques, and so on which enhance these recitations; "Julie" a beautiful, cultured English girl who plays under Conchis's direction a number of roles (as does her twin sister) and to whom Urfe becomes attracted; the elaborate ruse through which Urfe is persuaded that Alison has taken her own life; and the climactic mock courtroom scene in which judges enter in astrological costume, disrobe, and announce themselves as an international group of psychoanalysts conducting an experiment on Urfe, who is at one point invited to lash Julie with a cat-o'-nine-tails, and at another made to watch a blue movie of which she is the star.

While it was the seemingly endless, elaborately detailed stages of Conchis's "god game" that were responsible for the coolness of most of the original reviewers of the novel (Angus Wilson and Brian Moore among them), it is these same episodes that have been the prime target of the academic exegetes who have written on *The Magus*. This is perfectly understandable, for the Phraxos section of the novel invites (even demands) interpretative commentary in a way that the London and Parnassus sections do not. Indeed, as we shall see, it is precisely the stance of a critic confronting a difficult text that Urfe himself adopts in attempting to understand Conchis's fictions. One may nevertheless feel that this critical emphasis is misleading: for from the point of view, not of interpretative difficulty, but of qualitative discrimination, it is the London and Parnassus sections that are the finest things in *The Magus*. Its best realized character is Alison, who never sets foot on Phraxos, and the best realized strand in a novel that Fowles eventually came to see "tried to say too much" and was "altogether too full of mystery" is Urfe's contrasting relationships with Alison and her antithesis, Julie. It is through this contrast that the social theme of *The Magus* is articulated: Urfe's progression from an initial state of intense egotism and a sense of class and national superiority, to the classless and "speciesless" state (with attendant stirrings of the capacity to love) at which he has arrived at the end of *The Magus*.

At its beginning, Alison is shown to be demotic, offbeat, a bit of a tramp, good in bed, and mixed-up. But she also possesses an unself-conscious natural sexuality and a salty directness and candour; as Urfe reflects, she is "crude but alive." And although she is uncultured, he later realizes during their floral lovemaking in Greece that she possesses a natural poetry to which his fastidious aesthetic sense can respond. Indeed, when he is lonely and feeling sorry for himself, Alison can even come to represent for him "human warmth, normality, [a] standard to go by" and "a magnificent quotidianeity." But when things are going well for him or when his refined tastes are whetted, Urfe can treat her with great callousness. Embarrassed to meet an Oxford friend while in her company, he mumbles that she is "Cheaper than central heating." To Julie he mendaciously explains that he met Alison in Athens only out of "some sort of kindness to dumb animals" and insists that their relationship was temporary. How could it not be, for "You know what Australians are like ... They're terribly half-baked culturally. They don't really know who they are, where they belong. Part of her was very ... gauche. Anti-British ... I suppose I felt sorry for her, basically."

While Alison lives in the real world, where one gets blisters, has an abortion, weeps, and earns a living, Julie exists only in the Bourani world as a figure of romance enveloped in a supernal glow of mystery, culture, wealth, and unattainability. Julie has "a breeding, a fastidiousness, a delicacy" that "fatally" attract Urfe; her accent is a product "of boarding school, university, the accent of what a sociologist once called the Dominant Hundred Thousand." She further seems to incarnate "the emotional depths and subtleties of the English attitude to life," to have, like himself, "an inborn sense of decency and an inborn sense of English irony." In short, a romance mode is appropriate to her presentation because Julie is less a real person than a personification of Urfe's own selfishness. As Robert Scholes puts it: "She represents a narcissistic gratification rather than a real engagement with another person."[48]

In Urfe's numerous comparisons between them, Alison invariably comes off a poor second. While at times he is selfish enough to want to possess both women, it is clear that if a choice has to be made Alison does not stand a chance: "I stood up and screwed out my promiscuity of mind with my cigarette. She was spilt milk; or spilt semen. I wanted Julie ten times more." The two extended sex scenes between Julie and Urfe are written up by Fowles in as delicious a manner as possible; there are even elements of the lubricity that Hemingway called erectile writing. Fowles's purpose in doing this is to make all the more startling the discovery of Julie's dissimulation, and all the more striking the contrast with her subsequent copulation with an American negro buck on a stage set in front of Urfe during his trial. As they approach orgasm, Urfe closes his eyes – but he does not think of England, for it is precisely his notions of English superiority that are finally extirpated in this scene, the climax of his "disintoxication."

In the last section of The Magus Urfe returns to London shriven of "all my social past, all my background" and determined never "to live and work with the middle-class English again." He realizes that in his loss of Englishness he must be feeling as Alison had so often felt in London, and that as an antidote to "my alienation from England and the English – I ought to find all that I needed in Alison." The "innate sense" that suggests this to him is the promptings of love for the absent Alison, for at the end of his story Urfe seems to have finally learned the difference between love and sex, and between both of them and narcissistic gratification. Other considerations – the existential theme of hazard and its aesthetic correlative –

demand that the ending of *The Magus* be open and indeterminate, that the meeting of Alison and Urfe in Regent's Park end with her remaining, like the flight of pigeons overhead (and like Sarah at the end of *The French Lieutenant's Woman*), "an anagram made flesh." But to the ending is appended the refrain of the "Pervigilium Veneris" – "Tomorrow may loveless, may lover tomorrow make love" (in Allen Tate's translation) – and the most important point about the ending of *The Magus* (in either of its versions) is that there remains for Urfe the possibility of a love based on a mutual need in the real world, with its "stinging smell of burning leaves."

The class-classlessness, loveless-love theme, which is focused by the contrast between the novel's two central female characters, is rooted in the realistically presented London scenes at the beginning and the end of *The Magus*, and the equally quotidian Parnassus interlude in the middle. But whenever Urfe is on Phraxos, as he is for the great majority of the novel, "it almost seems," as Brian Moore has said, "as though a new writer [has] taken over the narrative."[49] The primary thematic concerns of this writer, whose surrogate within *The Magus* is Conchis, are philosophical and psychological rather than social; his ambition is nothing less than to teach the reader (whose surrogate is Urfe) a full, existentialist, philosophy of life. The presentational mode Fowles adopts is not that of the traditional realistic novel, but of romance. In his famous distinction between the two, Nathaniel Hawthorne explained that while the novel aimed at "a very minute fidelity, not merely to the possible, but to the probable and ordinary sense of man's experience," the writer of a romance, whose deep subject was (like the novelist's) "the truth of the human heart," was allowed a greater freedom in the management of "his atmospherical medium" and "could present that truth under circumstances ... of [his] own choosing or creation."[50] The distinction serves equally well as a description of the difference between the London and Parnassus sections of *The Magus* and the Phraxos section. Indeed Fowles rather heavy-handedly arranges to have the distinction signalled very early on, when Conchis is made to speak dismissively of the novel's exhaustion as an art form. The reader's entry into the world of romance is further signposted by the several references to Prospero's magical island in *The Tempest*, by the frequent reference to classical myths, the stylized, blatantly symbolic characters and appurtenances of Conchis's metatheatre, and the repeated references (beginning with a quotation from Pound's *Canto* XLVII concerning Odysseus's descent to the underworld to see Tiresias) to a quest, an ordeal, a trial, a voyage into dark unknown regions that Urfe (Orpheus) must undergo.

Fowles has attempted to harmonize the realistic and romance elements of *The Magus* through a method he later said he learned from Alain-Fournier's *Le Grand Meaulnes*: "my own secret and perpetual motto on the wall during the writing of *The Magus* [was] 'I like the marvelous only when it is strictly enveloped in reality'."[51] In doing so, however, Fowles made two serious miscalculations, which go far towards explaining why – for all its fresh invention and imaginative daring – the Phraxos section of *The Magus* ultimately comes to seem tedious and forced. By enveloping in reality Conchis's marvellous effects, Fowles presumably meant describing every extraordinary occurrence in meticulous detail and eventually providing a plausible naturalistic explanation of how each event could have been staged. But providing this realistic envelope necessitates an enormous amount of descriptive writing and many explanatory conversations, and nothing is more destructive of a felt sense of the marvellous and the mysterious than duration. Conchis, for example, may seem a genuinely enigmatic and compelling hierophant in the early stages of Urfe's ordeal; but at times later on it is hard not to agree with Brian Moore's observation that he "sometimes seems a mixture of Somerset Maugham and Dr Fu Manchu."[52] In *Le Grand Meaulnes*, a work of under 200 pages, only a small percentage of which describes the marvellous *domaine perdu*, the arresting fusion of romance and realism is finely sustained, as it is in the 100 pages of the title novella of *The Ebony Tower* (a deliberate variation on *The Magus*, as we have seen). But this fusion is inevitably dissipated in the over 600 pages of *The Magus*, and by the time Urfe leaves Phraxos much of Conchis's magic has come to seem machinery.

It has also come to seem programmatic, just as the intellectual stages of Urfe's voyage towards self-knowledge have come to seem too schematic and merely notional. Concerning the former: Fowles seems to have thought it essential to his existential beliefs in hazard and the absence of certainty in human existence to have Urfe undergo an endless succession of deceptions and frustrations in his attempts to understand what is happening to him. But just as duration is destructive of a sense of the marvellous, so the very repetition and eventual predictability of the episodes in which Urfe rends one veil of deception only to find another behind it comes to dull the reader's sense of involvement in his story. Concerning the overly schematic elements: one may observe that there are rather too many ideas and generalizations offered to the reader and that it would have been better if Fowles had made Conchis less preceptorial and didactic, and not allowed him to punctuate his romance with *sententiae*. For like duration, explanation is also destructive of a sense of the marvellous. To cite Hawthorne again: "When romances do really teach anything, or produce any effective operation, it is usually through a far more subtile process than the ostensible one."[53]

There is, however, one "subtile process" at work in the Phraxos section of *The Magus* which I want to draw out a little because it has been insufficiently appreciated, because it is Fowles's most sustained exploration of the reader's active contribution to the realization of a work of literary art, and because it is a most effective coupling of the existential theme and the aesthetic theme. Like John Fowles, Conchis is more interesting as a creative artist than he is as a reality instructor. *The Magus* is full of references to and descriptions of works of art, accounts of the impressions they make and of their meanings. There are the French existentialist novels Urfe had read at Oxford; Carné's film *Quai des Brumes*; the allusions to *The Tempest*, Pound's *Cantos*, Eliot's *Four Quartets*, *Great Expectations*, and *The Three Hearts* (a modern Greek novel); the poetry Urfe himself writes; the Modigliani and the two Bonnards at Bourani; the objets d'art there and at the de Deukans chateau; the stone head Conchis shows Urfe; the copy of the ancient statue of Poseidon; and the "little epistemological fable" of the prince and the magician. Of most importance in *The Magus*, of course, are Conchis's fictionalized autobiography and his various metatheatrical productions. In sum, there are even more works of art than there are ideas in the novel.

After its first sixth, almost every page of *The Magus* reflects Urfe's difficulties as he seeks to discover the meanings of Conchis's artistic productions. Since Urfe is a first person narrator and the reader is restricted to his limited point of view, the same interpretative difficulties that confront him also confront the reader. This being the case, an important thematic motif in *The Magus* is epistemological/aesthetic: the reflexive concern with the status and efficacy of a work of art, with the relationship of its affective qualities to its meaning, and with the interpretative processes by which meaning is discovered. Fowles signals his novel's reflexive concerns in its opening pages, when he has Urfe recall the serious error he and his Oxford crowd made in reading French existentialist novels: not realizing these texts were "not supposed to be realistic," they mistook "metaphorical descriptions of complex modes of feeling for straightforward prescriptions of behaviour." Urfe is beset with similar interpretative difficulties from the very beginning of his experiences at Bourani (when he hears a bird's song and reflects that "it was difficult not to think of it as meaningful") to their termination, when he realizes that in attempting to understand the summer's events by reading them as a detective story he has made another serious critical error involving recognition of genre. And in between, he several times explicitly refers to the experience he is undergoing at Conchis's hands as a book to be read – a text which is identical with the one the reader of *The Magus* holds in his hands.

The novel's concern with the meaning of an art work and with the reader-text relationship is epitomized in Urfe's attempts to interpret a particular two-part "text": the masque of Apollo presented on the lawn at Bourani, and Conchis's story of de Deukans, into which it is interpolated. Like most readers, Urfe desires to understand the text before him because "I'd enjoy it all the more if I knew what it meant." But he realizes that his task is difficult, for the text is "like an obscure poem" and Conchis, its author, "was evidently like certain modern poets: he tried to kill ten meanings with one symbol." In his struggle to find the meaning Urfe tries out different interpretative techniques (some of which anticipate the methodologies later used by critics in their attempts to supply authoritative accounts of the meanings of *The Magus*).

His first approach to the de Deukans story is impressionistic and self-regarding – like the bird in Robert Frost's "The Wood-Pile" Urfe takes everything said as personal to himself: "I thought I had grasped, during Conchis's telling, the point of the *caractère* of de Deukans. He had been talking of himself and me – the parallels were too close for it to mean anything else." But he soon moves on to more sophisticated strategies. One is a psychological theory of loss and symbolic repair: "that Conchis was trying to recreate some lost world of his own." Another is the source-hunting that leads to the kind of myth criticism in which features in a text are explained in terms of their archetypal referents. (Back in London at the end of *The Magus* Urfe uses the same technique in attempting to find the meaning of other incidents in Conchis's god game; and at one point in between – when he does not see the point of something Conchis has arranged – Julie suggests he adopt the similar critical strategy of finding meaning through discovery of the antecedent work to which the text at hand alludes.) A third strategy that Urfe implicitly considers is a kind of genre criticism, but this proves as unrewarding as his other techniques, for what Urfe says about the larger masque of Conchis's grand design is equally true of the particular texts of which it is composed: "there were no limits in this masque, no normal social laws or conventions."

Because he lacks the key that will unlock its meaning, Urfe comes to suspect the authenticity of the de Deukans story, a line of thought which, if pursued, would presumably come to relieve him of the need or the desire to discover the story's meaning. But this, too, proves of no avail, for works of art are not only self-authenticating; they also have affective power even when their meanings remain obscure, and Urfe continues to be "hooked" by the story, as he is by all of Conchis's fictions. So the question remains: what is the meaning of the text and how can it be discovered? The answer that *The Magus* seems to suggest – I am here extrapolating – is that this is a wrong question to pose, or at least a question posed in the wrong way. Suppose one asked instead what is it that hooks Urfe, what affects him to such a degree that he spends considerable mental effort in trying to understand? The question seems essentially answered when Urfe – pondering Conchis's insistence that "Why everything is, including you, including me is a matter of hazard. Nothing else. Pure hazard" – suddenly "grasps dimly, somewhere, that my ignorance, my nature, my vices and virtues were somehow necessary in his masque." It would follow from this that the meaning of the masque would be something in the production of which Urfe was himself intimately involved and to which he contributed. The meaning would not be a quality embedded in the text but the result of an active collaboration of reader and work of art. This is nothing like the impressionistic, subjective response in which the text becomes the mirror of the reader's egotism; it is rather the reader's imaginative apprehension of the text through his discovery of complementarities between it and himself. Such a process of growing phenomenological congruence (as one might call it) would not issue in an authoritative interpretation, but neither would it lead to the dissipation of the energy of the work of art, for what Conchis says of mysteries is equally true of works of art: they are important to mankind because they have energy and "pour energy into whoever seeks an answer to it." That is, it is the existence of mysteries and works of art that man needs, "not their solution." This view of the aesthetic act of reading is pluralist and indeterminate, and emphasizes emotional authenticity in place of authority. That is to say it is (in Fowles's terminology) existentialist, and as such it restates and reinforces the existential lessons concerning hazard, unknowing, freedom, and the unconditioned that elsewhere in *The Magus* Conchis drives home to Urfe less subtly and as a result less effectively.

IV

Like *The Magus*, Fowles's next novel had some important ideas to communicate. But *The Collector* is a much more successful artistic communication because it does not try to say too much, because its much shorter compass makes for compression and intensity, and because telling is replaced by showing. Goethe said that it was above all in the act of limitation that the master showed himself, and while one would want to save the adjective masterly for Fowles's third novel, one may certainly say that the act of limitation that is *The Collector* is a most impressive performance. Its comparative brevity, its austerity and impersonality all suggest an authorial recoil from the "egotistical sublime" and the luxuriance of imagination of *The Magus*. Fowles has made the subsidiary class theme of his first novel (which lent itself to realistic treatment) the principal tenor of *The Collector*, and the method of narrative presentation is thoroughly quotidian – deliberately so: "I tried to write in terms of the strictest realism; to go straight back to that supreme master of the fake biography, Defoe, for the surface 'feel' of the book."[54] In *The Collector* Fowles has become "the chameleon poet": there are no traces of self-consciousness, no reflexive questioning of the status of the text; and there is nothing indeterminate about the ending, which is not open but firmly closed. In his own terminology, Fowles is concerned only with sounding true, not with coming clean.[55]

Compared with its predecessor, *The Collector* not only manifests greater technical maturity but also a more mature vision of human life. In *The Magus*, for example, the references to Shakespeare's *Tempest* were part of the romance décor of Conchis's island kingdom. In *The Collector*, the allusions to the same play underline the novel's preoccupation with the fundamental questions of nature versus nurture, good versus evil. There had been manifestations of evil in *The Magus* – in Conchis's accounts of his experiences in the trenches of the western front in the First World War and on Phraxos during the German occupation in the Second. But these spectacular eruptions of evil were impressive largely for quantitative reasons; and one also noted that they were, so to speak, extramural; for when Urfe reflected on the "distance, enormous, between a Europe that could breed such monsters [the Nazis] and an England that could not," the reader could not be confident that his words were to be taken ironically. In *The Collector*, on the other hand, evil is shown to be ordinary and home-grown. Its personification is not, as in *The Magus*, the sadistic ss officer of popular mythology but an unexceptional clerk in a Town Hall Annexe who is set apart from his peers only through having won a fortune on the football pools. The evil he embodies is all the more horrific for being so ordinary and unspectacular. Unlike her creator in his first novel, Miranda in *The Collector* comes to realize the unimportance of quantitative distinctions when the subject is evil: "All the evil in the world's made up of little drops. It's silly talking about the unimportance of the little drops. The little drops and the ocean are the same thing."

In *The Collector*, Fowles has contrived an exemplary situation which makes possible a sustained and uninterrupted confrontation of two persons from opposite ends of the spectrum of class, intelligence, sensitivity, imagination, and the possibility of growth. In doing so he set himself a difficult artistic challenge, for it is essential to the novel's success that its two representatives be sharply individualized and realistically credible on the one hand, and on the other broadly representative and emblematic. Too little of the latter qualities would turn *The Collector* into a documentary-style horror story; too little of the former and the novel would weaken into allegory and expose the dubiousness of the premise that, as Clegg puts it, "there'd be a blooming lot more of this if more people had the money and the time to do it."

At the same time, in order to keep his novel from simplifying into melodrama and to make its two constituent parts function synergistically, it is necessary for Fowles convincingly to suggest (but no more than suggest) the existence of hidden affinities and interdependencies between Clegg and Miranda – to make the reader realize that, in the latter's phrase, theirs is a "linked destiny." This Fowles has effectively done. For all the differences in their attitudes to sex and love, both Clegg and Miranda are virgins and both are in their different ways untested by interpersonal experience. For all Clegg's power over his captive, one comes to see the point of Miranda's saying "You're the one imprisoned in a cellar." And while on the first page of her diary she insists that "I feel the deepest contempt and loathing for him," she must also admit "A strange thing. He fascinates me." She also comes to see how the reverse is true: "I am his madness." And while it was because of his hopeless love that Clegg has kidnapped and imprisoned Miranda, he has come to reciprocate her loathing well before her hideous death.

The key to the power and artistic success of *The Collector* is the way in which the novel is narrated. Clegg's first person account of events occupies the first 113 pages and is followed by a slightly longer section in which, via her diary, the reader is given Miranda's account of the same events. In the concluding twenty pages Clegg is again the narrator. As with the thief and the man of letters in "Poor Koko," one of the basic differences between Clegg and Miranda is language, a fact of which both are sharply aware. "She often went on about how she hated class distinction," Clegg reports, "but she never took me in. It's the way people speak that gives them away, not what they say … There was always class between us." As for Miranda, "What irritates me most about him is his way of speaking. Cliché after cliché after cliché." "Why," she exclaims at one point, "do you keep on using these stupid words – nasty, nice, proper, right?" At one extraordinary moment Clegg's response to Miranda's beauty is so intense as to bring out of him a rough eloquence: "I could sit there all night watching her, just the shape of her head and the way the hair fell from it with a special curve, so graceful it was, like the shape of a swallow-tail. It was like a veil or a cloud ..." But in the very next paragraph he is back in the world of stale expression he customarily inhabits: Miranda "always smelled sweet and fresh, *unlike some women I could mention*"; "several times she tried to escape, *which just showed*" (italics mine). In one of her most suggestive images Miranda finely encapsulates the dreariness of Clegg's way of speaking: "You know what you do? You know how rain takes the colour out of everything? That's what you do to the English language. You blur it every time you open your mouth." The difference between their ways of speaking is so fundamental to *The Collector* that one recalls what Osip Mandelstam said in 1921: "social distinctions and class oppositions pale before the present division of people into friends and enemies of the word."[56] Through allowing Clegg and Miranda to narrate the story of their relationship in his or her own words Fowles is not only able to characterize both of them in an exceptionally vivid way. Through the fusing of tenor and vehicle, of the novel's concern with words with the words of the novel, he is also able to have *The Collector* enact much of its meaning.

Clegg's social background is lower middle class (his Nonconformist roots are seen in his censoriousness concerning art and sex). Miranda calls him "the most perfect specimen of petit bourgeois squareness I've ever met"; but she later confides to her diary a fuller social profile of her abductor: "he's a victim of a miserable Nonconformist suburban world and a miserable social class, the horrid timid copycatting genteel in-between class," an example of "the blindness, deadness, out-of-dateness, stodginess and, yes, sheer jealous malice of the great bulk of England." Fowles has said that through the character of Clegg he wanted to attack "the contemporary idea that there is something noble about the inarticulate hero,"[57] and in *The Collector* – it is one of the novel's very few forced moments – he has Miranda read Alan Sillitoe's *Saturday Night and Sunday Morning* so that she can point out that there is in Clegg, "only ... turned upside down," something of Arthur Seaton, that novel's central character. One can see Miranda's point and still feel that, whatever the author's intention, such a reference is not particularly helpful. I would myself say that, socially speaking, the fictional character Clegg most resembles is Dickens's Uriah Heep; and in any event, after a point it is more interesting to consider Clegg not as a sociological portrait of the Many but as a psychological study of evil. In the latter regard, the fictional character he most resembles is the speaker of Browning's "Porphyria's Lover," who also has a fetishistic fascination with his beloved's hair and desires total possession of her more than her love ("Having her was enough," Clegg says). In both cases the fulfilment of this desire leads to the beloved's murder and to chilling rationalizations revealing a degree of inhumanity and a moral numbness that can only be explained by reference to the concepts of madness or evil.

What makes Clegg's evil so appalling is its very banality and small-mindedness, for just as his language takes the colour out of everything, the self-justifying secretions of his consciousness are a blur of little drops which ultimately corrode all wholesome and potentially ennobling human qualities. Thus, Clegg can feel "very happy" when he has successfully kidnapped and incarcerated Miranda "because my intentions were of the best. It was what she never understood." And his depriving her of any news from the outside world – a procedure he learns from reading *Secrets of the Gestapo* – he comes to think of as "almost a kindness, as you might say." When Miranda, *in extremis*, tries to seduce Clegg, he is revulsed: "She was like all women, she had a one-track mind"; and on the same page on which he alludes to his masturbating with the help of the obscene photographs he has taken of her while she was drugged, he can reflect that through offering him her body Miranda had "killed all the romance, she had made herself like any other woman, I didn't respect her any more." Finally his petrified moral sensibility can even find ways of asserting that the results of his actions are Miranda's "fault." The second time he takes pornographic pictures of her he can say that "it was her own fault" if the cords and gag were tight for, even though ill, she had put up "a bit of a struggle." And after her death, when he gets to "thinking perhaps it was my fault after all that she did what she did and lost my respect," another thought immediately follows: "it was her fault, she asked for everything she got."

While Fowles does not put a foot wrong in his depiction of Clegg, it is the characterization of Miranda that is perhaps the more impressive achievement, for while the captor's personality is fixed, incapable of change or growth, that of the captive must be convincingly shown to change during the course of the novel. Fowles's depiction of his heroine, however, has not always been deemed successful. Walter Allen's judgment, for example, is that "she seems ... merely a stereotype of a stereotype, of the contemporary middle-class girl of some education as we meet her on Sunday mornings in the *Observer*: frank, fearless, 'emancipated,' etc., decorously swinging."[58] This kind of assessment seems to me to be based on careless reading – on a first impression. At the beginning of *The Collector* Miranda certainly does answer to Fowles's own description of her (in the revised *Aristos*): "she was arrogant in her ideas, a prig, a liberal-humanist snob, like so many university students."[59] In fact, an index of Fowles's success in so characterizing her is the sharpness of the negative response to her in critics like Walter Allen. For there is no reason not to think that this is precisely the reaction Fowles wanted his readers to have. (One good reason for this is that it helps keep *The Collector* from being read as melodramatic confrontation of black and white.) But the cardinal point about Miranda is that she changes greatly during the course of the novel. Exposure to the evil of Clegg in the crucible of hazard that is her cellar prison leads to spiritual and moral growth; as the day of her death approaches she becomes ever more different from the trendy twenty-year-old whom Clegg kidnapped. She even has the purity of being to insist "I would not want this not to have happened ... It's like firing a pot [she characteristically uses an arty image]. You have to risk the cracking and the warping."

The particulars of the unbridgeable social and class differences between Miranda and Clegg – their opposing views on art, interior decoration, charity, the ban-the-bomb movement, and so on – are instanced on virtually every page of *The Collector*. But just as Clegg is ultimately more interesting on a psychological rather than a social level, so Miranda is ultimately more memorable as an embodiment of Good than as one of the sociological Few. She may read *Emma* and *Sense and Sensibility* during her imprisonment, and Fowles may assert that in his conception of her he was indebted to Jane Austen and Peacock.[60] But if one stands back from the immediate circumstances of her story, it becomes possible to see the young maiden imprisoned in a cellar room long ago used as a priest's secret chapel, as a freshly realized embodiment of the archetypal figure of the Protestant heroine, the secular saint – pure, noble, selfless, highminded, and assured of her own virtue – whose ancestors include the Lady in Milton's *Comus*, Richardson's Clarissa, Browning's Pompilia, George Eliot's Dorothea Brooke, and Shaw's Saint Joan. Just as Pompilia, dying at what should have been the beginning of her adult life, is assured that she will rise to Christ, her heavenly bridegroom, so Miranda is sustained by her assurance that she is "a representative" of the elect Few, the "band of people who have to stand against all the rest," and who are the twentieth-century descendants – their philosophy existentialist rather than positivist – of the "choir invisible" of George Eliot's post-Christian pantheon, "Whose music is the gladness of the world."

From the beginning to the end of her captivity Miranda's most passionate desire is to live. In her first diary entry she reflects that she "never knew how much I wanted to live before" and that "If I get out of this, I shall never be the same." And she later reflects: "I'm growing up so quickly down here. Like a mushroom." There are three principal *termini a quo* in reference to which her growth can be charted: first, she moves beyond the assumptions and values of her class (affluent upper middle) as represented by Ladymont, the posh school she had attended, with its "silly ones ... snobbish ones ... would-be debutantes ... daddy's darlings ... horsophiles, and ... sex cats" and its "suffocating atmosphere of the 'done' thing and the 'right' people and the 'nice' behaviour" (for no more than Clegg's is her own class without its linguistic indicators of asphyxiation). Second, she moves beyond her own theoretical notions of moral and sexual behaviour, for she comes to regret not having taken the "risk" of giving herself unreservedly to G.P., who is old enough to be her father. Finally, there is a metaphysical dimension to her growth: when early on Clegg had asked her if she believed in God, Miranda had answered: "Of course I do. I'm a human being." Later she had reflected that while she no longer knew if she believed in God, "praying makes things easier." But as her end approaches she comes to see that it is necessary "to live as if there is no God," and although in her final diary entry she deliriously writes: "Oh God oh God do not let me die," she has sometime before won through to the realization of "the black truth. God is impotent."

Miranda's last days are wrenching and deeply affecting; since her final hours are seen through Clegg's leaded eyes sentimentality is totally avoided while the ghastliness of her plight is intensified. As her end approaches – for the cold she has caught turns into pneumonia and Clegg cannot risk medical intervention – Miranda becomes acutely aware of her "terrible, utter loneliness" and of her claustrophobia, as if "the weight of the whole earth" were pressing on her dank underground room. She comes to long most of all for the sight of the sky and for sunlight, at first, perhaps, because she is a painter with sharpened visual perceptions, but finally because she is a human being longing for transcendence. In her terminal delirium, in which at one point "her coughing stopped her screaming," her thoughts turn outwards – to the needy children on whose behalf she had earlier worked, and finally to Clegg himself for like Christ from the cross "The last thing she said was 'I forgive you'." And at the moment of her death, Clegg, having brought her to an upper room, reports that "her eyes were staring white like she'd tried to see out of the window one last time."

V

In Fowles's next novel, *The French Lieutenant's Woman*, there is an echo of *The Collector's* concern with language when its protagonist, Charles Smithson, reflects that the "true inconsistency" between him and the title character is in the way they speak. On the whole, however, the differences between the two novels are more noticeable than the similarities. One of them is that in the later novel Fowles is concerned to give expression to both of what he considers the novelist's basic desires: to sound true and to come clean – to create a believable world on the one hand and on the other hand to make the reader aware of the hypothetical nature of the fictional construct, of the fact that the novel is "first cousin to a lie." He is also concerned to show his characters existing and interacting in the real social world of conflicting pressures and interests, rather than in the laboratory conditions of Clegg's basement room. Finally, there is in *The French Lieutenant's Woman* an historical dimension, for Fowles is not only concerned to show how character is shaped by society and class; he also wants to show at work the larger historical forces which impinge on human freedom – to show that "the vast pressures of his age" are "the great hidden enemy of all [the] deepest yearnings" of Charles Smithson. Such a creative undertaking is decidedly ambitious, and the fact that Fowles has succeeded so brilliantly in both sounding true and coming clean, and in embodying his views on the human condition in such a fresh and compelling invention, makes the novel a major achievement.

The French Lieutenant's Woman is an historical novel: it is set in the late mid-Victorian England of 1867 and is full of period detail. The novel rests on a firm but unobtrusive documentary base, and as instructors in Victorian literature courses at North American colleges and universities were quick to realize, it contains a good deal of palatable information and insightful generalization about the time: about shifting class relationships, about the difference between those who are gentlemen by birth and those who achieve that status through wealth; about the social position of women, from prostitutes to the daughters of the well-to-do who were educated in nothing save conventional good taste; about attitudes to sex, love, duty, and religion; about the impact of evolutionary ideas; about the Victorian fear of death; and about their "fatal dichotomy ... which led them to see the 'soul' as more real than the body ... indeed hardly connected with the body at all." "The fact that every Victorian had two minds," Fowles's narrator says, "is the one piece of equipment we must always take with us on our travels back to the nineteenth century."

The French Lieutenant's Woman is not only set in the England of a century ago; its principal subject matter and thematic concerns are those of much of the literature of the Victorians. As the many chapter epigraphs from the poetry of Tennyson, Arnold, and Clough remind the reader, Charles Smithson's rite of passage largely fits the paradigm of Victorian spiritual crisis in which, usually triggered by loss of faith, the individual is thrust from the passive security of traditional beliefs and moral and social sanctions into an abyss of self-consciousness and a sense of the chaotic flux of human existence, from which he eventually emerges with a new, more thisworldly and selfless faith. (Teufelsdröckh in Book II of *Sartor Resartus*, the speaker of Browning's *Pauline*, the Tennyson of *In Memoriam*, and Dorothea Brooke in *Middlemarch* all exemplify the pattern.) The fact that the terminus of Charles's dark night of the soul is existential (realization that the dark night is the human condition) rather than typically Victorian (the dawn of a new sun) is in itself not unprecedented in nineteenth-century literature, as the poetry of Arnold and Clough illustrates.

Another example of the Victorian subject matter of *The French Lieutenant's Woman* is the concern with showing the ways in which characters struggle against existing social conditions – from Sam and Mary's progression up the social ladder from below stairs to lower middle class respectability, to Charles's attempts (at a rung near the upper end of the ladder) to bear the weight of society's crushing dictates. The Victorian novelist whom this concern most calls to mind is George Eliot, whose narrator in *Felix Holt* succinctly voices one of her creator's deepest beliefs when she says that "there is no private life which has not been determined by a wider public life." In fact, were one so disposed, it would not be difficult to argue that a source for the basic situation of Fowles's novel (the triangle of the pretty, conventional Ernestina, the privileged Charles, the *déraciné*, unstable Sarah) is the third and final part of Eliot's *The Mill on the Floss* – Ernestina being a type of Lucy Deane; Charles resembling the cultivated but shallow Stephen Guest, who discovers unsuspected depths in his being through his destabilizing passion for Maggie; and Sarah being a version of Maggie Tulliver, whose exacerbated sensibilities and passionate nature lead to her becoming a social outcast. Indeed, Sarah is essentially a mixture of two common Victorian fictional types – the fallen woman and the socially displaced person, educated above her station and often found employed as a governess. And her predicament, on which the plot of *The French Lieutenant's Woman* turns, is wholly Victorian. To quote once more from *Felix Holt*: "After all, she was a woman, and could not make her own lot ... Her lot is made for her by the love she accepts."

But *The French Lieutenant's Woman* is Victorian in more than setting and subject; its most striking feature and the essential constituent of its success is that the novel utilizes some of the characteristic presentational methods of Victorian fiction. By making his 1969 novel a variation not only on his previous work but also on certain themes and methods of narrative presentation in English novels of a century ago, Fowles has been able to write an engrossing traditional novel which more than satisfies the demands of common readers in the wider audience he seeks to address, and at the same time to communicate his severe existential philosophy, which offers the reader not the shared richness of the traditional novel's sense of life, but the "cruel but necessary ... freedom" of the empty stretches of "the unplumb'd, salt, estranging sea."

The chapter epigraphs in *The French Lieutenant's Woman*, its digressions, generalizations, stylistic fullness, leisurely pace, and make-'em-wait chapter endings are all examples of the presentational décor of Victorian fiction. But by far the most important Victorian technique Fowles adopts is that of the omniscient narrator who feels free to intrude himself into the story he is telling, to address the reader directly, and to make comparisons between then and now. For while the novel is set in 1867 it is narrated from the point of view and the knowledge available in 1967, just as George Eliot's *Middlemarch*, set in the early 1830s, is narrated from the point of view and the knowledge available in 1867. The convention of the intrusive omniscient narrator was of course much disparaged by Henry James (among others) and its supersession by more sophisticated narrational devices was a key element in the development of the modern novel. That such modernist criteria are still in the ascendant was indicated by the fact that when it was first published some reviewers of *The French Lieutenant's Woman* quite embarrassed themselves by describing as experimental such features as the narrator's hindsight (the references to Henry Moore, Marshall McLuhan, the Nazis, and so on) and the breaking of the fictional illusion through direct addresses to the reader and reflexive comments on how the story is being told. For both these features are all thoroughly old-fashioned. Concerning the latter, for example, consider the following: "I know that the tune I am piping is a very mild one ..." says Thackeray's narrator at the beginning of the sixth chapter of *Vanity Fair*; "here, perhaps, it may be allowed to the novelist to explain his views on a very important point in the art of telling tales," says Trollope's narrator in the fifteenth chapter of *Barchester Towers*; and in the seventeenth chapter of *Adam Bede*, "In Which the Story Pauses a Little," George Eliot's narrator feels free to give a lengthy explanation of the kind of work she is writing and of how she would like the reader to respond to certain characters.

Narrators can be omniscient in three directions: spatially, in knowing what is going on in different places; temporally, in knowing what the future holds for characters and being able to place their actions and quandries in historical perspective; and psychologically, in knowing a character's innermost being and being able to report authoritatively on his thoughts (conscious and unconscious), emotions, and motivations (however complex). Of the first two directions, Fowles more fully exploits the second. The then-now, they-we contrasts made possible by a century of hindsight provide an excellent outlet for his didactic and preceptorial impulses – allowing him, for example, to point out the diminution of sexual pleasure in the contemporary world because of the loss of mystery. More importantly, temporal omniscience enables Fowles to place the stories of his characters in an historical, not just a social context, to show them struggling to adapt themselves to their changing historical situations and to evolve in order to survive (Charles is an amateur paleontologist and the narrator of his story often uses evolutionary metaphors). Fowles also uses the temporal perspective to help control the reader's response to his characters, who tend to be sympathetic to the extent to which they are moving, however gropingly, into the future (the world which we readers inhabit) and unsympathetic – like Ernestina or Mrs Poulteney – to the degree that they are fossilized in the nineteenth-century present. In addition, the then-now contrasts help to secure reader involvement, for while the chronological gap between setting and the reader's present time is sufficiently great to allow for the recognition of determining historical forces, it is sufficiently narrow to allow the reader to see how the past bears upon and prefigures the present – to make him feel that his own present-day situation would be, so to speak, the subject of the unwritten chapters which the narrator has chosen not to include at the end of his text.

It is in the presentation of Charles Smithson that the narrator of *The French Lieutenant's Woman* makes most use of the power of psychological omniscience. The course which Charles sails in the novel is charted with abundant psychological notation. There is no need to analyse this journey, for it is essentially the same route as that traversed by David Williams and Nicholas Urfe. (Indeed, when at the end of his novel Charles is left with tears in his eyes on the Chelsea embankment, he is in exactly the same situation as Urfe in Regent's Park at the end of *The Magus*.) More importantly, until his omniscience wanes in the final two chapters, the narrator of *The French Lieutenant's Woman* does a great deal of the reader's work for him, providing authoritative glosses for the stages of Charles's voyage from the security of the known into the refining fire of hazard.

But the path to these two final chapters leads through the title character of *The French Lieutenant's Woman* and it is necessary to say something about the source of Sarah Woodruff's fascination for Charles Smithson (and for the reader), for it is she who embodies the energizing mystery that is such an important part of Fowles's existential and aesthetic premises. The technical key to her mystery and magnetism lies in the fact that the narrator is only selectively omniscient concerning her; for most of the novel he forgoes his powers of psychological penetration and insists on seeing Sarah strictly from the outside, and usually from a certain distance. Near the beginning of the novel the reader is given some information about Sarah that only an omniscient narrator could provide: that she possesses an "instinctual profundity of insight" and that her essence was "that fused rare power ... understanding and emotion." And at the end of the twelfth chapter the reader is again taken inside her mind when he is told that she is standing at her open window in the middle of the night because she is contemplating jumping from it. At the very beginning of the next chapter, however, the narrator has changed his tune, for in the first of his digressions concerning his creative difficulties he insists that he does not know and cannot report what is going on in Sarah's mind as she stands at the window. There is, of course, a substantial discrepancy between the end of the one chapter and the beginning of the next, for the psychological datum that Sarah was on the brink of committing suicide is hardly an "outward fact." Few readers, however, have seemed to notice, let alone be bothered by, this inconsistency and it is not the first time we have seen Fowles having his cake and eating it too.

The quality of Sarah's mysteriousness is enhanced by suggestions of a certain intimacy, a special bond, between her and the narrator. They are, for example, the only central characters in the novel who possess imagination, and in the deception she practises on Charles it is hard not to regard her as the narrator's surrogate. And on no fewer than three occasions the narrator is close enough to Sarah to allow him to give close-up views of her peacefully-sleeping face. This sense of intimacy is most effectively conveyed in the novel's single most luminous detail, a moment of exceptional delicacy. When we are shown Sarah in the Exeter hotel unwrapping the modest purchases she has made, the narrative point of view is strictly that of the camera eye. But when she unwraps a Toby jug she has bought, the narrator pauses to note that it "was cracked, and was to be recracked in the course of time, as I can testify, having bought it myself a year or two ago for a good deal more than the three pennies Sarah was charged." The temporal omniscience that allows the narrator to say that the great-great-granddaughter of the servant Mary is "one of the more celebrated younger English film actresses" is used to make a socio-historical point; but its employment in the matter of the Toby jug has a quite different effect; without making Sarah one iota more explicable, it does suggest a shared taste and sensitivity between her and the narrator, a special affinity that helps convey, despite all the talk of her mental instability, a sense of her essential wholesomeness. It is this rare blend of intimacy and mystery that helps to make Sarah a more energizing fictional creation than Julie or the Mouse, or even than Conchis, for all his extravagant apparatus.

The reason Fowles offers only a strictly outside view of Sarah for all but the first chapters of his novel is obvious: her enigmatic quality is the source of her magnetizing energy, which would be dissipated if she were to become comprehensible to Charles or to the reader. Through a careful rereading one can deduce *what* Sarah did to Charles in the hotel at Exeter – for in addition to the Toby jug she had bought a nightgown and dark-green shawl to make her look seductive, and a roll of bandage to help her simulate a swollen ankle. But no amount of rereading will shed any light on *why* she has done so. As with Conchis's masque, any explanation of Sarah must be considered non-authoritative and reductive (even that of the perceptive Dr Grogan). The task of Charles and the reader is therefore not to interpret Sarah, for one is denied the wherewithal to do so, but to establish a state of phenomenological congruence with her – that is, to enter into an acceptance of unknowing and mystery.

This brings us to the notorious matter of the two different endings that have been provided for *The French Lieutenant's Woman*, a presentational device for which there is no precedent in Victorian fiction (with the exception of Froude's *The Lieutenant's Daughter* and the partial exception of *Great Expectations*). Fowles's narrator explains that he has chosen to provide alternative endings because at the conclusion of his novel it is no longer possible to use the fictional techniques of an earlier age in writing a novel based on existential principles: "the conventions of Victorian fiction allow, allowed no place for the open, the inconclusive ending; and I preached earlier of the freedom characters must be given." The conclusive endings of Victorian fiction were a reflection of the nineteenth-century belief that, as Conchis puts it in *The Magus*, "we were fulfilling some end, serving some plan – that all would come out well in the end, because there was some great plan over all." At the beginning of the "Finale" to *Middlemarch* George Eliot's narrator says that "Every limit is a beginning as well as an ending," but this remark does not keep one from seeing that the various threads that make up the complex web of that novel's world are all comprehensible and tied together and that its fictional time is *kairos* (in which each event is "charged with a meaning derived from its relation to the end"), not *chronos* ("mere successiveness" or "one damn thing after another").[61] Even when the ending of a Victorian novel is tragic there tends to be found the sense of a greater order and harmony, like the "Unseen Pity" at the close of *The Mill on the Floss* which invests the end of Maggie Tulliver's story with a sense of providential finality. In the twentieth century, however, there is (to quote Conchis again) "no plan. All is hazard. And the only thing that will preserve us is ourselves."

The two endings of *The French Lieutenant's Woman* are, then, an attempt to provide an appropriate close both for the novel's vehicle and for its tenor. But this does not mean that they have equal weight and authority. The second ending, the modern one, is clearly the right ending not only because it comes last – though that is an undeniable advantage – but because it is clearly the fitting conclusion to the subtle process of instruction and illustration to which the reader has been so willingly subjected during the course of the novel. In addition, the first – the Victorian – ending tends to invalidate itself; for it is not simply a happy ending: it is also a gushily sentimental one – with its Chopin mazurka on the sound-track; its cloying final tableau, in which Sarah's two-year-old daughter, an underaged *dea ex machina*, engagingly bangs her rag-doll against the cheek of her new-found father; and its magic wand evaporation of mystery ("And he comprehended: it had been in God's hands, in His forgiveness of their sins"; God is not a good novelist, as Jean-Paul Sartre has said). In the second ending there is no intervening god or surrogate thereof. As Charles Smithson walks away from the house in which Sarah has once again inexplicably rejected his love, he walks out of the world of Victorian society and Victorian fiction into a twentieth-century reality where not even fictional narrators can pretend to omniscience. The narrator can, however, report with confidence that "there are tears in his eyes." But as for Sarah (it is the last glimpse the reader is given of her): "There are tears in her eyes? She is too far away for me to tell."

VI

During the eight years between *The French Lieutenant's Woman* and the publication of his next novel, John Fowles's thinking about the nature of creative activity and the function of the novel underwent a significant shift in emphasis – from product to process, from audience to artist, from literature as a communicative act to literature as an expressive act. In a number of places Fowles has spoken about his late-blooming views on the psychopathology of the creative artist, particularly on patterns of what post-Freudian ego psychology calls loss and symbolic repair. The most succinct statement of his views occurs in a 1977 interview:

I think writers are made genetically. You have to have a certain natural gift in your brain (with words) obviously. I think you also have to have a sense of loss implanted when you are very young. In other words, I think writers are quite literally born, therefore, I do not believe in creative writing. The Freudian theory of this, that I would apply to all artists, is that some people have had a very peculiar experience after the loss of their mother and the discovery of their own separate identity. Young infants really don't have clear frontiers between themselves and their mother. With some people it's the kind of fluidity of this experience, the changing of shape and the supreme happiness from the sort of union with mother that probably dominates their adult lives, unconsciously of course. All this goes into the unconscious. Although I am not a total Freudian, I find this very convincing because I think what is interesting about the novel is the obsessive repetitive need in true novelists to go on telling stories. We always have to be telling legends, myths, which very often try in some way to make the world more perfect. Obviously, there is some dim memory of a more perfect, happier, magical state and we are all trying to get to that. It's very obvious in novelists like Thomas Hardy who was totally fixed on his mother. All the women he fell in love with all through his life even had his mother's physical features.[62]

In an article published in the same year, Fowles not only elaborated his views on Hardy's mother fixation; he also added to the critical commentary on his own work by offering readings of the endings of *The Collector* and *The French Lieutenant's Woman* in the light of his latter-day views on "the writer's secret and deepest joy [being] to search for an unrecoverable experience."[63] In *Daniel Martin* Fowles continued his exploration of these concerns, which are unquestionably among the novel's most interesting features. At the same time, however, it is hard not to regard them as the principal reason why *Daniel Martin* is Fowles's least satisfactory fictional performance.

Essentially, *Daniel Martin* is another ambitious variation on its creator's informing fictional concerns and paradigmatic methods of narrative presentation. At the novel's centre is a male character who is placed in a situation of stress through which he becomes aware of a deprivation, senses an inauthenticity and lack of freedom in his present existence ("as if he ... was an idea in someone else's mind, not his own") and is moved in the direction of the dark, existential unknown. The novel's Arnoldian epigraph (it is in fact from Gramsci's *Prison Notebooks*) – "The crisis consists precisely in the fact that the old is dying and the new cannot be born: in this interregnum a great variety of morbid symptoms appears" – could have served equally well for any of Fowles's earlier novels.

The central figure in *Daniel Martin* is the title character and narrator, a playwright and commercially successful screen writer in his mid-forties who near the novel's beginning is called from Los Angeles and the arms of his nubile mistress Jenny, a budding film star young enough to be his daughter, to England and a series of events that leads him simultaneously back into his past and forward into the uncertain future. Elsewhere in Fowles, as we have seen, the stimulus of crisis and possible transformation is a mysterious female, sexually exciting and enigmatic, possibly dissimulating, and associated with an older male preceptorial figure of creative gifts who is a member of an elect. In *Daniel Martin*, the central female figure is Jane, Dan's contemporary, who once took him to bed during their student days at Oxford, an *acte gratuit* which, like Sarah's seduction of Charles Smithson in the Exeter hotel, seems in retrospect increasingly puzzling: Dan feels he has been manipulated but cannot understand why. In the present time of the novel the recently widowed Jane is even more perplexing. Like Sarah (or Catherine in "The Cloud") she seems pathologically disturbed, on the brink of the void. But as Dan attempts to draw Jane back to a fulfilling life, as her husband from his deathbed had asked of him, the reader, again reminded of Charles Smithson and Sarah, and of David Williams and the Mouse, comes to see that it is actually Jane, with her insistence on keeping her selfhood unviolated and her "tenacity of right feeling – that strangest of all intransigences, both humanity's trap and its ultimate freedom," who is drawing Dan out of the prison of the present into the liberating possibilities of the recovered past and the unknown future.

There is, of course, a difference between the thematic profile of fictional characters and their actual characterization, and a major shortcoming of *Daniel Martin* lies precisely in the discrepancy between the thematic strength and felt weakness of its two central characters. Dan is treated by his creator with an indulgence most glaringly instanced in the prolix, meandering pace at which he is allowed to tell his story and elaborate his feelings and thoughts. There is no irony, no distance, between reader and central character, as there was in *The Magus* (where an epigraph from de Sade – "Un débauché de profession est rarement un homme pitoyable" – established a critical attitude to Nicholas Urfe even before he began to speak) and in *The French Lieutenant's Woman* (where it soon became clear that the twentieth-century narrator did not much care for his Victorian protagonist).

One reason for this crucial lack of distance is that Fowles has given Daniel Martin two roles to play: he is both the central male character and the older preceptorial figure. It is true that in the long closing section of the novel, which describes in interminable detail Dan and Jane's touring in Egypt, an old German Egyptologist is introduced who explains the ancient concepts of *qadim, kayf,* and *ka*, the last of which had also been referred to in *The Magus*. For the most part, however, Dan must be his own menopausal magus. (Indeed, his conversations and relations with Jenny closely resemble those of G.P. with Miranda in *The Collector*.) The trouble with Daniel Martin being his own wise man is that he does not yet possess the credentials for the role. As Conchis explains in *The Magus*: "Hazard makes you elect. You cannot elect yourself." If Dan were elect he would not be in a state of perplexed becoming; indeed the crisis situation in which his renewed involvement with Jane places him is precisely the hazard that may make him elect. Fowles might have handled the difficulty of his central character's dual role by developing a distinction between Dan the narrator (recounting after the fact) and Dan the character in the novel's present and past time. Such a distinction would perhaps have made the flashbacks into Dan's childhood, adolescence, and young manhood somewhat more difficult to handle, but that Fowles toyed with the distinction is indicated by the random switchings in the text from first person to third person narration. Such a distinction would have helped to provide that essential distance between character/narrator and reader which is unfortunately absent from Fowles's apparently too autobiographical, certainly too self-indulgent, novel.

The major weakness in the characterization of Jane seems similarly connected with the fact that she is middle-aged. Her mystery and the fascination of her wounded otherness are repeatedly insisted upon by Dan but only notionally realized; they remain largely unfelt by the reader. The principal reason for this is that Jane – no longer young, with grown children having affairs and problems of their own – cannot generate that erotic glow, that fundamental association with "the great alchemy of sex" which is so important a part – for the central male character and for the reader – of the fascination of earlier Fowles women. In Dan's case it is largely the very repetitiveness and staleness of the sexual present (finely shown in the novel's second chapter, an intimate scene between him and Jenny) from which Jane offers deliverance: "She was also some kind of emblem of a redemption from a life devoted to heterogamy and adultery, the modern errant ploughman's final reward; and Dan saw, or felt, abruptly, for the first time in his life, the true difference between Eros and Agape." Indeed, what is most interesting about Jane – it is a striking adaptation of Fowles's thematic and presentational paradigm – is that she is an emblem not of possible transformation through sexuality but of possible renewal through imaginative repossession of the past; a Wordsworthian, not a Lawrencian figure. I shall shortly return to this most interesting development; my present point, however, is that John Fowles does not seem to have fully realized the presentational and characterizing implications for his fiction of what should perhaps be thought of as his mid-life withering into the truth.

A final presentational feature of Fowles's fictional paradigm is the "secret place," a mystery-laden setting that becomes the crucible of possible trans-formation. In *Daniel Martin* there are several such places: Tsankawi, one of New Mexico's abandoned mesa sites, "haunted by loss and mystery, by a sense of some magical relationship," where Dan takes Jenny and is disturbed to note her obliviousness to the place's uniqueness; Kitchener's Island at Aswan, which Dan and Jane visit; and most important (because they are associated with a personal past) "the green and closed, dense with retreat" places of Dan's Devon youth: the combe he helped harvest in the lyrical sense (Tolstoyan, not Hardyesque) with which the novel opens; the land-scapes, "all Ceres and simplicity," of his sexual initiation; and Thorncombe, the farm visited in his youth, now owned and periodically returned to in his middle age. In the context of Fowles's oeuvre, what is most interesting about the secret places of *Daniel Martin* is that while in the earlier novels such places were primarily associated with mysterious females and erotic alchemy they are now, like the central female figure, associated with loss, the mysteries of the past, and the sources of creativity (for "You create out of what you lack. Not what you have"). In Jane, Dan finds "some old charge of curiosity about existence, of irony, enigma, secret purpose," a "re-entry into the past [which] had answered some previously unseen lack," and "some clue ... that might be central to what I wanted to write myself." Similarly it is at Tsankawi that Dan senses in himself the longing for "a totality of consciousness that fragmented modern man has completely lost" and has dropped into his mind "the tiny first seed of what this book is trying to be."

These secret places are splendidly evoked through Fowles's considerable powers of natural description, and it is with regret that one must say they are more interpolated into, than integrated with, the narrative and that there is something rather too stagy and set-piece about them (indeed, during his visit there Dan considers using Kitchener's Island for a scene in a film script about its eponym). Even the poetically written, prelapsarian opening scene, though it is clearly meant to, does not stay in one's mind throughout the novel as a reference point and/or emotional undertow, as does, for example, the thematically and stylistically similar "The Hot Summer of 1911" pro-logue to Angus Wilson's more suitably proportioned *Late Call*. And one must further regret that the Devon secret places are associated not only with the narrator's past but with his and the author's peculiar notions about essential Englishness (as opposed to Britishness and Americanness). This Robin-Hoodism business is something of an idée fixe with Fowles (it was first broached in 1964 in "On Being English but not British," an article published in, of all places, the *Texas Quarterly*). Certainly Daniel Martin, like John Fowles, is an intelligent man and interesting conceptualizer, but there is far too much cerebrating in *Daniel Martin* and one finds particularly trying the attempt to impose a personal fantasy on the national psyche.

The linkages of unknown/known, past/present, creativity/quotidian, freedom/inauthenticity, loss/repair are further developed in the novel through Dan's reflections on the art of the film versus the art of the novel. Through Jane and through the seed planted at Tsankawi Dan comes to resolve to attempt a novel, to leave "the sanctuary of a medium he knew for the mysteries and complexities of one he didn't." He reflects that "Film excludes all but now; permits no glances away to past and future; is therefore the safest dream. That was why I had given so much of my time and ingenuity to it." In another place he speaks of "the prime alienation of the cinema ... the final cut allows no choice, no more than the one angle; no creative response, no walking around, no time for one's own thought. In the very act of creating its own past, the past of the scenario and the past of the shooting, it destroys the past of the mind of each spectator." In short, the medium of film serves to further the fragmentation of modern man, to chain him to the present. The novel, on the other hand, offers an approach to the possibility of wholeness, of the experiential totality of past, present, and future.

This complex of thematic material suggests that *Daniel Martin* is fundamentally a novel of self-expression whose principal subjects are reflexive and self-regarding: the artist-narrator's personal quest and the workings of his own imaginative processes. (This of course accounts for the lack of distance between Dan and the reader.) So considered, it is interesting to note that the novel is open to the same charges that Fowles had earlier made against much modern art in *The Aristos*, where he had denied that the proper function of art was self-expression, a doctrine he regarded as tyrannizing the modern artist and leading to depreciation of the craft of the art, even to " 'insincere' and 'commercial' craftsmanship." Alas, one is forced to wonder whether Fowles has not forgotten his own salutary admonitions, for *Daniel Martin* contains not only presentational variations on his own earlier fictions, but also a number of rather slick and cumulatively debilitating variations on the presentational devices of others, which it is hard to regard as other than "insincere" attempts to sugar-coat the pill of self-expression.

There are for one thing the Iris Murdoch touches: the North Oxford ambiance of Jane and her husband (he is a philosopher, a Roman Catholic, a suicide); Dan's daughter's affair with her boss, an old friend and alter ego of Dan's; and other entanglements, one of which a character actually calls "one of those Iris Murdoch situations." Another example is found in those places where Dan talks about and analyses his generation, especially his Oxford peers and what they have done with their careers. These aspects of *Daniel Martin* are reminiscent of nothing so much as Frederic Raphael's *Glittering Prizes*! And then there are the utterly flat and long-winded passages of banal circumstantial detail, which read as if lifted verbatim, with only the names changes, from a C.P. Snow novel:

She had been far more at ease the day before, when they had met to get their visas – only briefly, for she had gone off, once the formalities were completed, to meet Roz and do some last shopping; and later, when they had met again at Roz's for the family supper. It had gone well, Roz had put herself out to be nice to Caro, who had responded and perhaps learned from the brisk way her cousin handled her mother ... teased her over her still latent financial and other qualms. Indeed, she had been more at ease earlier that very morning, before the take-off. Roz had driven them to Heathrow, and kept the reality at bay.

One would have thought Fowles incapable of writing such inert prose, or of creating a character as lifeless and unfocused as Dan's daughter Caro. Not for nothing does Dan at one point during the novel say of himself that "he had felt like someone locked up inside an adamantly middle-class novel; a smooth, too plausible Establishment fixer out of C.P. Snow."

In addition to these specific "commercial" variations there are a number of other features of *Daniel Martin* that seem variations on middlebrow best-seller fiction. Especially noticeable are the large number of more or less extraneous characters: Barney Dillon, the successful television intellectual, full of self-pity over having sold out; the two young Cockney sisters, "actresses" whom Dan alternately beds during the time of their frictionless *ménage à trois*; Fenwick, the Tory MP of stock manners and views; Andrew, the landed aristocrat of supercilious manner; Malevich, the American film producer; Abe and Mildred, Dan's Jewish-Hollywood friends; the American couple of predictable behaviour who are travelling in Egypt; Jimmy Assad, who knows how to get things done in Cairo and reminds one of a contact man in a James Bond novel; Ahmed Sabry, the Egyptian "satirical play-wright" met at a dinner party; and so on. To be sure, most of these are well-done sketches, but they are by and large decorative vignettes, unorig-inal in conception and facilely executed in a way that adds little to the novel's reflexive concerns.

Since one wants to conclude on a positive note, let us consider how Fowles has contrived to conclude his novel positively. The climactic scene of *Daniel Martin* is in its penultimate chapter. It involves Dan, Jane, a raw day, the ruins of Palmyra in Syria among which they are walking, two dun-coloured puppies at the mouth of a crevice formed by some ruins, and their mother, a starving mangy bitch who offers her own body to be hunted and shot, thereby distracting attention from her young and leaving them unharmed. In both *The French Lieutenant's Woman* and *The Magus* Fowles had flaunted the openness and indeterminacy of his endings, a vehicular parallel to the existential (no absolutes, no intervening god) tenor. In the middle of *Daniel Martin*, however, the Fowlesian narrator complains (in a way surprisingly reminiscent of Saul Bellow's repeated complaints about the terminal negations of the existential vision) about "a received idea of the age: that only a tragic, absurdist, black-comic view (with even the agnosticism of the 'open' ending suspect) of human destiny could be counted as truly representative and 'serious'." In the scene among the Palmyra ruins – a secret, mystery-laden place but one without a trace of green or a hint of the erotic – Fowles has provided a superb withering-into-the-truth image of desolation that at the same time contains the seed of the recognition of a biological agape that makes Jane's void begin to grow luminious, obscurely but convincingly prompting her finally to open herself to Dan's love, and thereby allowing the novel to end with a "serious" positive affirmation of the strength in what remains behind, in the primal sympathy which having been will ever be, in the soothing thoughts that spring out of human suffering.

VII

In *Daniel Martin* John Fowles attempted with imperfect success to press methods of narrative presentation developed for primarily communicative purposes into the service of a primarily expressive concern with the psychology of the creative artist (of himself) and his sense of loss. However unsatisfactory the result, the attempt was impressive, even inspiriting, for it showed a novelist of considerable talent and proven achievement striking out in important new directions. There can be no question that a sense of loss and a longing for what Rimbaud called the true life which is absent is a fundamentally important theme in nineteenth- and twentieth-century literature (it even figures centrally in writers as committed to the novel's mimetic and communicative functions as Brian Moore and V.S. Naipaul). Certainly one hopes that Fowles will continue to probe his sense of loss and longing for the unrecoverable; indeed one hopes that he will come to do so more deeply and directly – for while he has said that for the creative artist everything hinges on the parental bond, one thing there is virtually no trace of in any of his prose fiction is a sense of parental or familial ties, of the recognition (in Brian Moore's phrase) that parents form the grammar of our emotions. At the same time one hopes that Fowles will find a way of communicating through narrative his expressive concerns – his late-blooming belief that "the deepest benefit of any art ... is self-expression and self-discovery."[64] For Fowles rightly regards his talent for narrative as his greatest natural gift as a writer, and it is this gift, together with his commitment to the traditional communicative functions of the novel, that has been at the root of his success in engaging the attention of a large audience on which to work the magic of his art.

Chapter Four

V.S. Naipaul:
Clear-Sightedness and Sensibility

I

V.S. Naipaul's copious and varied canon may be divided into three chronological parts. To the 1950s belongs his apprentice work, the three astringent comedies set in his native Trinidad: *Miguel Street* (1959), his first written but third published book, and the novels of 1957 and 1958, *The Mystic Masseur* and *The Suffrage of Elvira*. There is no journeyman period in Naipaul's development, for the first phase of his career closes in 1961 with the publication of the masterly *A House for Mr Biswas*. The subject is once again East Indian life in Trinidad, but the qualitative difference between it and the first three works is great enough to justify the atomic analogy of the quantum leap.

The 1960s, the second phase of Naipaul's career, saw the publication of no fewer than six books, including three remarkable non-fictional works. *The Middle Passage* (1962) offered impressions of five societies of the New World's Third World – Trinidad, British Guiana, Surinam, Martinique, and Jamaica. *An Area of Darkness* (1964) described the author's shattering yearlong sojourn in India, the land of his ancestors, "a journey that ought not to have been made; it had broken my life in two."[1] And in 1969 Naipaul answered two questions posed in *The Middle Passage* – "How can the history of this West Indian futility be written? What tone shall the historian adopt?" – with *The Loss of El Dorado*. This work supplied a past for Trinidad through recounting two unmitigatedly grim historical episodes (the end of the Spanish search for El Dorado in the late sixteenth century and the early years of British rule two centuries later), and is written in what is for Naipaul an unusually obscure and portentous style which, as Graham Greene has said, falls "like a curtain between author and reader."[2] In the fictional works of the 1960s Naipaul successfully extended his range as a novelist. The title novella of *A Flag on the Island* (1967), which employs a first person American narrator, is a comic entertainment containing some home truths about the post-war Caribbean, but *Mr Stone and the Knights Companion* (1963), which is set in south London and has an entirely English cast of characters, and *The Mimic Men* (1967), the confessions of a colonial politician "shipwrecked" first on his native island and then in England, are impressive expropriations of new fictional territory and impressive works of art.

During the 1970s, the most recent phase of his career, Naipaul again published three non-fictional works: *India: A Wounded Civilization* (1977) is the result of another long visit to the subcontinent, and *The Overcrowded Barracoon and Other Articles* (1972) and *The Return of Eva Perón, with The*

Killings in Trinidad (1980) are collections of his journalism. Three works of fiction, which manifest a major extension of range, were also published during the decade. The title novella of *In a Free State* (1971) and *A Bend in the River* (1979) are both set in newly independent African countries; and while the setting of *Guerrillas* (1975) is an unnamed Caribbean island that resembles Trinidad, one of its most striking features is the deliberate exteriorization of the depiction of the one place on earth Naipaul knows intimately from the inside.

Indeed, a measure of the great distance he has travelled since he began writing fiction in the mid-1950s (and of the sustained creative labour that made it possible) is that representatives of Trinidad's East Indian community, the subject of his first three novels, appear only in passing in one scene of *Guerrillas*, and the novel's three principal foci – race, sex, and a white outside point of view – are the very elements which in his 1958 article, "The Regional Barrier," Naipaul lamented he was unable to use in making his Trinidadian subject matter more appealing to the non-West Indian reader. (Concerning sex, he said that he lacked sufficiently wide experience, disarmingly adding that his friends would laugh and his mother be shocked.) In "The Regional Barrier" Naipaul had analysed what appeared to be a serious creative impasse: his regional fictions tended to elicit responses from his English audience that were "not literary judgments at all"; and the three ways of increasing that audience's interest in such subject matter were closed to him for reasons of artistic integrity. The only way out was "to cease being a regional writer." But in order to write Naipaul's kind of social fiction it was "necessary to know so much: we are not all brothers under the skin."[3]

In this analysis, as in some other places in his periodical writing, the young Naipaul was perhaps guilty of a certain amount of special pleading and overstatement concerning the difficulties and disadvantages of a writer coming from a cultural backwater, a place at the edge of the world with no society, no culture, no past, and no future – to echo some of his repeatedly voiced designations of Trinidad. For one thing, the power of *A House for Mr Biswas* rests on the reader's sympathetic identification with the title character: that is, on the fact that the reader and Mr Biswas are "brothers under the skin." For another, it is hardly self-evident that a background like Naipaul's is necessarily a disadvantage for a novelist; the examples of Conrad, Joyce, and Jean Rhys (a writer whom Naipaul came to rate very highly) suggest that such a condition can be a stimulus rather than a hindrance to creative fulfilment and major achievement. Indeed, as the years have passed, Naipaul has come more and more to seem a central writer precisely because he is so uniquely qualified – by his Indian ancestry, Trinidad childhood, British base, and temperamental inability to stay in one place for long – to bring into fictional focus the important subject of the social and political reality of Third World societies – "to bring us news," as John Updike puts it, "of one of the contemporary world's great subjects – the mingling of its peoples."[4] For novelists like François Mauriac or Brian Moore, the door may close at twenty; but for V.S. Naipaul, fictional doors were to be set open long after he left Trinidad at the age of eighteen to attend Oxford on a scholarship.

Moreover, the themes that inform Naipaul's later fiction – homelessness, the absence of society or community, the sense of inauthenticity and loss, the mingled anxiety and acedia – are hardly peculiar to him or to those of similarly marginal cultural and social backgrounds. They are rather representative aspects of the condition of modern man: "Who ain't a slave?" as Melville's Ishmael asked over a century ago. By the 1970s Naipaul had come to realize this and consequently to change the terms of his analysis of his situation as a writer. He now saw that to be a colonial was "in a way, to know a total kind of security," in that all major decisions were taken out of one's hands. As he had become more aware of his own insecurity and begun to reflect it in his novels he had become less colonial; at the same time, with their power and influence in permanent decline, "the people of England [had] become more colonial themselves."[5] Naipaul does not go on to say that as a result English society had become less representative of the condition of contemporary man. But if one were to pursue his line of thinking, a novelist of society and of traditional liberal values like Angus Wilson could come to be seen as the chronicler of a marginal society and its parochial concerns, while the *déraciné* Naipaul, constantly on the move and seeing everything with a stranger's eye and through a sensibility continually exacerbated by its having no point of rest, could be seen as a novelist of the unholding centre of the contemporary world (a realm that Wilson belatedly tried to engage effectively in his 1973 novel, *As If by Magic*).

Naipaul's work can hardly be called undernoticed, but the six books, and the evergrowing number of theses and articles devoted to his fiction have not said all that they might about his development and achievement as a novelist. One reason is their understandable concentration on the content of his work, on its post-colonial subject matter and its distinctively Third World or Commonwealth elements.[6] Naipaul himself has complained about the Procrustean bed of Commonwealth literature topoi – particularly the search for identity – into which some critics have tried to make him and his work fit. In 1965 he noted that students of Commonwealth writing (one of the growth industries in English studies) were already preparing theses on his work and that they "write or even telephone to say that they get the impression from my books that I am engaged in a search for identity. How is it going?" He further insisted – the maturation of his views since "The Regional Barrier" of 1958 is striking – that "the problems of Commonwealth writing are really no more than the problems of writing."[7]

A corollary of the Commonwealth approach has been a similar over-emphasis on considerations like the presence or absence of warm human sympathy or the degree of positive commitment to emerging societies. This has led to many observations which, Naipaul complained as early as 1958, "are not literary judgments at all." For example, in a twice-reprinted article, Gordon Rohlehr has argued that the early Naipaul was at times an "irre-sponsible ironist" because he lacked "a sensitive participation in the life he anatomizes"; and while William Walsh waxed eloquent in Leavistic tones over the "essential humanity," "comprehensive humanity," and "fullness of human sympathy" of *A House for Mr Biswas*, he lamented as a weakness of *In a Free State* "something I can only call an overdeveloped, on occasion even an overwrought, sense of human offensiveness ... some radical horror of human flesh."[8] Such observations are different only in degree from the hypothetical Trinidad critic whom Naipaul imagined as writing of *Vile Bodies*: "Mr Evelyn Waugh's whole purpose is to show how funny English people are. He looks down his nose at the land of his birth. We hope that in future he writes of his native land with warm affection."[9]

Certainly no one would deny that his congenital fastidiousness, the Brahmin cast of his sensibility, is an important determinant of Naipaul's fiction. He has himself insisted that it is not style, technique, or plot that should draw one to a novelist: "What is it that we look for when we go to the work of a favourite writer? It is, I feel, a peculiar type of adventure – an adventure with a mind, a sensibility, that appeals to us. A certain way of looking and feeling, which we think amusing or illuminating. We do not go for char-acters or for language so much as *for the writer himself*. A writer stands or falls by his sensibility and our assessment of his work depends on our response to his sensibility."[10] Naipaul's sensitivity to sights, sounds, and smells is acute, and when the object of his attention is the physical world or the appearance of persons the result has been some superb descriptive writing. Some of his finest effects have been achieved through the precise notation of externals, like the atmosphere of tension and danger that is gradually built up in *In a Free State*. For example, all of the menace of the anonymous African to whom Bobby and Linda give a lift is seminally present in his initial description:

The African was dressed like those labourers they had seen that morning being marshalled into the lorries. But his clothes looked more personal and less like cast-offs. His striped brown jacket was stained in many places and the bloated tips of the wide lapels curled; but the jacket fitted. The pullover, rough with little burrs of dirt, fitted; and the shirt, oily black around the collar, with two or three old tidemarks of sweat, was like a second skin.

When the object of Naipaul's scrutiny is the human body and its functions, especially the female body and its sexual functions, this sensitivity can intensify into something close to revulsion and make one recall the chilling comment in *A House for Mr Biswas* concerning Anand, Naipaul's only self-portrait of the artist as a young man: "contempt, quick, deep, inclusive, became part of his nature. It led to inadequacies, to self awareness and a lasting loneliness. But it made him unassailable." There can be no doubt that Naipaul's degree of "human sympathy" more resembles that of Jonathan Swift or Céline, say, than that of Browning's Fra Lippo Lippi or Dostoevsky's Father Zossima; but it is hard to see what per se this has to do with qualitative judgments on individual novels. More importantly, such observations can keep one from appreciating the nature and the intensity of Naipaul's "passion" as a novelist. He has himself insisted that the passion of a great artist like Chekhov or Dickens did not rest on doctrine, especially not on "the rigid principles of liberalism" or the "doctrinaire Romanticism" that denies there are "differences between classes, races, continents." Their passion – and Naipaul's – rather "begins with ... direct vision and compassion"; it "comes from the heart" and is based on "a recognition of difference and an abhorrence of it. Dickens was horrified by the low."[11]

While certain themes and certain questions concerning human sympathy have been too exclusively dwelt on by commentators, insufficient attention has been given to the development of Naipaul's technical and formal skills as a novelist, to his appropriation and adaptation of different fictional forms and styles as he struggles to give artistic shape to his vision and expressive shape to his sensibility. One of Northrop Frye's best known dicta is that poems can only be made out of other poems; it seems no less true to say that novels can only be made out of other novels. Certainly one of the most preposterous statements ever made about Naipaul's work is Paul Theroux's: that "he has no literary ancestors" and "wholly original, he may be the only writer today in whom there are no echoes of influences."[12] As E.H. Gombrich has argued in *Art and Illusion* and elsewhere, any artist renders his vision of reality through schemata, which he has inherited from earlier artists (or learned from contemporaries): "The original genius who paints 'what he sees' and creates new forms out of nothing is a Romantic myth." An artist can "re-fashion" what he has learned from tradition, "adapt it to his task, assimilate it to his needs and change it beyond recognition, but he [cannot] represent what is in front of his eyes without a pre-existing stock of acquired images."[13] At the same time, surprisingly little attention has been paid to Naipaul's extremely interesting views on the function of the novel, the state of contemporary fiction, and his method as a novelist for whom artistic vocation is a way of life. It is with a collation and extrapolation of his scattered comments on these subjects that a critical consideration of his fiction may properly begin.

II

While the themes and the sensibility of his fiction may be distinctly con-temporary and while he is in the vanguard of fictional exploration of im-portant new territory (both Third World places and "free state" psychological spaces), Naipaul's conception of the vocation of the creative writer – its responsibilities, excruciations, and rewards – is squarely in the central Ro-mantic tradition of nineteenth- and twentieth-century literature, and his views on the nature and function of the novel are decidedly conservative and traditional. His assessment of most major contemporary fictional modes is sharply negative: he has even gone so far as to claim that Borges's greatness as a writer has nothing to do with the "very short, and very mysterious stories," the famous puzzles and "intellectual jokes," on which his "inflated and bogus" Anglo-American reputation is based.[14]

For Naipaul, "The Novel is of the West. It is part of that Western concern with the condition of man, a response to the here and now."[15] What is important in a novelist is his "analysis of ... human relationships, the depth of [his] insight, and whether [his] work is in some way illuminating of ... aspects of the human predicament."[16] A concern with the condition of man can of course take many forms; Naipaul's concern is primarily with man's social being and with the novel as "a form of social inquiry." He has admitted to difficulty in entering into the mood of "ironic acceptance" in R.K. Narayan's novels and in relishing their comedy, for to do so was "to ignore too much of what could be seen" (the "cruel and overwhelming" reality of small town life in southern India), and "to shed too much of myself: my sense of ... even the simplest ideas of human possibility."[17] And his "sense of history" as well, for in Naipaul's conception of the novel's social function historical perspective is an important element. "What is history, what is civilization, what is disaster?" Naipaul insists that "these are important questions" for the contemporary novelist, as is "the psychic damage of historical upheaval."[18]

But while the novelist must be concerned with social and historical realities, it should not be thought that his function is remedial. It is wrong for readers to expect from novelists philosophies, ideologies, or partisan commitments. The good novelist is concerned not with nostrums but with diagnosis, with the painful and difficult work of understanding the social and historical reality he examines. His goal is "a clear vision of the world"; for novels to last "they must have a certain clear-sightedness."[19] As for Conrad, so for Naipaul, the novelist's task is above all to make you see. For "the world we inhabit, which is always new, goes by unexamined, made ordinary by the camera, unmeditated on; and there is no one to awaken the sense of true wonder. That is perhaps a fair definition of the novelist's purpose, in all ages."[20] But Naipaul's reaffirmation of the novel's traditional functions and his assertion of the similarity of novelistic purpose "in all ages" hardly implies that he thinks it possible to reproduce the achievements of the great novels of the last hundred years, which were able to bring us "to terms with ourselves."[21] The societies today's novelists examine are very different from those of the past, and their fictional representations and interpretations of them must be correspondingly different.

Social inquiry, historical imagination, unsentimental concern, and clear-sightedness: these are the hallmarks of Naipaul's conception of the novelist's purpose and the explanation of his antipathy to a novelist like Hemingway. One should ask of the twentieth-century writer: "How much of the modern world does his work contain? You should be able to see the lineaments of today's society in the work of a good [modern] writer. That is why Hemingway is not good. There's not a drop of 1976 in him."[22] To read Hemingway is "to enter a kind of a fairyland." He suffers from a "moral blindness" and will "never tell you what is going on in the streets outside. He reduces the whole of Paris in the 1920s ... to someone trying to write."[23] In Hemingway (as Ralph Ellison has similarly complained), social inquiry or moral concern count for less than style and technical perfection. In Naipaul the latter qualities count for relatively little, and much of his criticism of contemporary writers concerns the overemphasis on style and technique that is the result of their having forgotten the basic responsibilities of the novelist. For Naipaul the novelist's function is interpretative and his primary aim is always to communicate. Today, however, uncertainty about the function of the novel has led to "over-sophisticated taste" and the mistaken "conviction that the novel as we know it has done all that it can do and new forms must be found."[24]

The results of these false views have been various: chief among them is that the subordinate place of expression has been forgotten. Displays of overt technique are symptoms of the novelist's lost sense of purpose, for "true technique consists in a number of unnoticeable things"; its purpose is to facilitate communication between writer and reader, for the novelist's "aim is always to communicate."[25] The novelist with purpose has no need of pyrotechnics. As Naipaul has said of his own later work: "What I am doing is sufficiently painful and novel to have no need of structural deformations."[26] Naipaul is even more adamant concerning displays of style (by which he means the opposite of proper words in proper places): "Stylists! I hate style ... The more natural the writing, the better it is. Language should be transparent."[27]

Other symptoms of the fiction writer's malaise – of deflection from concern with the condition of man and response to the here and now – are the self-consciousness and self-absorption of novelists; their "retelling of myths" ("Why retell stories? What's the point?");[28] the employment of allegory ("Allegory can prove everything and nothing. Hermann Hesse works out his conclusions very neatly, but I wonder whether these really needed the novel form");[29] the concern with "difficult philosophy" and with abstractions like "Good and Evil and God";[30] the taste for Borges-like fantastications. At the other extreme, there is what Naipaul has called "the documentary heresy." A commitment to social inquiry and to the traditional mimetic forms of presentation is quite different from the aim of the writer who seeks only to record. In its anonymity, the documentary is a "denial of art":

The artist who, for political or humanitarian reasons, seeks only to record abandons half his responsibility. He becomes a participant; he becomes anonymous. He does not impose a vision on the world. He accepts ... but he invariably ends by assessing men at their own valuation. The time comes when he is content to communicate the egoism of the brute.

George Moore's exactitude, Hemingway's Harry Morgan, Visconti's Sicilian peasants: each represents a deeper documentary sounding, a progressive contraction of the artistic vision. The concept of the artist alters. He is now a man with news or new techniques ... So, at the end of the documentary approach, the personality and the spirit are abandoned.[31]

A key difference between the documentary writer and the Naipaulian novelist is the method employed and the role of sensibility. The documentary writer or social analyst presumably knows what he is going to say before the act of composition begins, but the method of a novelist is to work "towards conclusions of which he is often unaware."[32] This is not the method of all novelists, of course. Conrad, for example, seems to have begun with general truths and then worked out their demonstration. And the method of Joyce Cary was to work out everything beforehand, perhaps writing the ending first. This accounts "for the static quality of some of Cary's books: everything has been settled, there is only to be explanation, no exploration, no chance discovery ... Some quickening element is missing. It seems to me that Cary ... denied himself the full use of his novelist's gifts."[33] According to Naipaul, most imaginative writers, certainly himself, "discover themselves, and their world, through their work"; "In the experience of most writers the imaginative realizing of a story constantly modifies the writer's original concept of it." Events, ideas, and attitudes are tested and changed in the novelist's dramatic imagination. It is this engagement that helps to give a novelist's work life and authority. Most importantly, this method enables the novelist to "say more than he knows" and "to convey the inner truth of the things observed."[34]

The key transforming element in a novelist's imagination is sensibility, which is "not a quality of intelligence but a quality of feeling."[35] He would agree with Thomas Hardy that the business of the creative writer is to record impressions, not convictions. Naipaul has distinguished between his private values, which he regards as "liberal and humane" and which may be thought of as qualities of his intelligence, and what is the *sine qua non* for a novelist: "a particular kind of sensibility, a particular way of looking at the world – a kind of morbidity."[36] An illustration of this difference between intelligence and sensibility is found in Naipaul's two differing responses to the events that provided the story line for his 1975 novel *Guerrillas*. The novel is closely based on the circumstances (including two murders) surrounding the break-up in 1972 of the Trinidad "commune" of Michael de Freitas (also known as Michael X and Michael Abdul Malik), a black power leader who had attained a certain notoriety during his years in England. In two long magazine articles Naipaul recounted in detail the history of de Freitas and his associates, who included the daughter of a Conservative member of the British Parliament, and analysed its implications.[37] The two conclusions distilled from his analysis were insightful and humane, and each was focused by a literary reference (one to O'Neill's *The Emperor Jones*, the other to Conrad's "An Outpost of Progress"). But when these same events and personalities were placed in the crucible of Naipaul's imagination and shaped by his sensibility, the "conclusion" was something quite different. *Guerrillas* is the only one of his novels that has an epigraph, but it is not from O'Neill's play or Conrad's story. It is a quotation from the manuscript of a novel being written within the novel *Guerrillas* by Jimmy Ahmed (the de Freitas figure): "When everybody wants to fight there's nothing to fight for. Everybody wants to fight his own little war, everybody is a guerrilla." It is not clear whether this epigraph should be read ironically (Jimmy's novel is a tissue of banalities and absurd fantasies) or psychologically (as a statement about resentment); what is clear, as we shall see, is that the vision of *Guerrillas* is different from, and darker than, that of the magazine articles.

And as we shall also see, the disjunction between intelligence and sensibility, what is being said and what is being shown, can sometimes be found within a novel. While concerned social inquiry aspires to clear-sightedness and constructivity through the medium of realistic presentation, negating intensities of sensibility may simultaneously be seeking expression through the distortion of realistic surface – as in *The Mimic Men*. And in *A Bend in the River* there is an analogous discontinuity between the novel's private and public vision.

The last major aspect of Naipaul's aesthetic is his conception of the novelist's vocation. Underpinning his fictional method and his commitment to the novel's representational and interpretative functions is his Romantic view of the nature of creative vocation. For Naipaul, it is the activity of the creative imagination that gives meaning and value to human existence. As for Balzac and Proust, so for him: commitment to "the creative activity of the mind" and through that to "self-fulfillment and truth to the self" is nothing less than their *dharma*.[38] Most of the hallmarks of the Romantic artist are found in Naipaul's comments on his calling: the novelist, who writes out of the sense of duty to himself and to his vision, is set apart from other men and engaged in a lonely struggle. Because of the honesty and dedication his calling demands he is unprotected, terribly insecure, even a *poète maudit*: "writing is just a sort of disease, a sickness. It's a form of incompleteness, it's a form of anguish, it's despair."[39] But it is not without its unpredictable satisfactions: the "miracle" of the moments of inspiration; the "slow magic" of working towards unexpected conclusions; the "great experience" of discovering "depths of responses that one never knew existed before."[40] Finally there is the great Romantic doctrine of recompense for loss through the symbolic repair of imaginative creation. As John Fowles puts it, the artist creates out of what he lacks, not what he has; as Naipaul has said: it was "the sense of loss and defeat that made me want to be a writer."[41]

The beneficial power of the mind's creative activity is not only an essential aspect of Naipaul's method; it is also a theme in three of his novels, in which to different degrees the creative process and its rewards become a subject of the creation. In *A House for Mr Biswas*, the title character's skill as a sign painter is both an outlet for his suppressed longings and an indication of his superior sensitivity to the crude materialist society of rural Trinidad. When he "worked late into the night by the light of a gas lamp, excitement and the light transforming the hut," the activity of sign painting could even make Mr Biswas "persuade himself that he lived in a land where romance was possible." As an adult he also discovers a talent for writing, but when he tries to nourish it through correspondence courses the result is preposterous compositions in a genteel idiom on the English seasons (he has never been off his tropical island); and when he tries to write fiction the result is absurd wish-fulfilment fantasies. But when his mother dies Mr Biswas becomes "oppressed by a sense of loss: not of present loss, but of something missed in the past ... that part of him which yet remained purely himself, that part which had for long been submerged and was now to disappear." It is to heal this wound, to gain relief from this acute discomfort, that he involuntarily finds himself writing a poem about his mother, in which romance, fantasies, and "cheating abstract words" are replaced by the simple concrete particulars of memory: black earth cut by a spade, a journey, hunger, welcome, food. Through writing this poem, his one authentic creative act, Mr Biswas's self-consciousness is "violated" and the wound of loss repaired: "he was whole again."

In *Mr Stone and the Knights Companion* the title character, feeling the pressure of mortality and the futility of his life of sterile habit, with no emotional outlet and no recompense for adolescent loss, similarly experiences through creative activity one liberating moment of gain, which changes his life (for a time). Finally, *The Mimic Men* may be viewed as the story of Ralph Singh's learning to tell his story – his attempt to clarify and order his life and to repair through literary creation his abiding sense of loss and inauthenticity. For Singh's sense of "shipwreck" and dispossession is not simply owing to his colonial upbringing, and any attempt to explain his malaise solely in terms of the topoi of Commonwealth literature would be grossly reductive. Singh's loss is a universal human deprivation which is felt especially sharply by persons of creative potential, whose creative acts are in fact responses to loss. For Ralph Singh, as for V.S. Naipaul, the analysis of Wallace Stevens in "Notes toward a Supreme Fiction" holds true: "From this the poem [the creative activity of the mind] springs":

> that we live in a place
> That is not our own and, much more, not ourselves
> And hard it is in spite of blazoned days.

We are the mimics.

But to begin to speak of the novels of the 1960s is to get ahead of ourselves. A consideration of the creative products of the confluence of Naipaul's intelligence, sensibility, method, and sense of *dharma* should begin at the beginning of his career.

III

Naipaul's first three books – he has himself referred to them as an apprenticeship – need not detain us long. *Miguel Street* is a series of local colour sketches of the inhabitants – most of them poor but dishonest – of a Port of Spain slum street. They include Hat, who "always read the papers. He read them from about ten in the morning until about six in the evening"; Popo the carpenter, who "was always busy hammering and sawing and planing" but who never finished anything; Bogart, "the most bored man I ever knew," who did everything "with a captivating langour"; B. Wordsworth, a failed poet, who "did everything as though he were doing some church rite"; Elias, whose inability to pass examinations caused his occupational ambitions to dwindle from medical doctor to sanitary inspector to driving a scavenging cart; Titus Hoyt, who had pedagogic ambitions and founded the short-lived Miguel Street Literary and Social Club; and Laura, whose eight children had seven different fathers. These and other local characters are recalled by a first person narrator who is looking back on the world of his childhood and adolescence. His reminiscences end with an account of the day he left Miguel Street to take up a scholarship in England. Despite the pretentious closing sentence concerning the "dancing dwarf" of his shadow on the airport tarmac, the narrator never becomes a felt presence in the book; and the device of retrospective narration is used for no serious artistic purpose – it simply serves as a portfolio for the young author's amusing sketches.

The subject of both *The Mystic Masseur* and *The Suffrage of Elvira* is East Indian rural life in Trinidad, in particular the effects of the advent of democracy in the early post-war years. In *The Middle Passage*, Naipaul describes "the squalor of the politics that came to Trinidad in 1946 when, after no popular agitation, universal adult suffrage was declared. The priv-

ilege took the population by surprise. Old attitudes persisted: the government was something removed, the local eminence was despised. The new
politics were reserved for the enterprising, who had seen their prodigious
commercial possibilities. There were no parties, only individuals. Corruption, not unexpected, aroused only amusement and even mild approval."[42]
Corruption, together with ignorance and superstition, are key ingredients
in the stories of the rise of Ganesh Ramsumair from masseur, to pundit, to
"mystic," to successful island politician, to "G. Ramsey Muir, Esq. MBE,"
colonial stateman, and of the electoral machinations in the town of Elvira,
during which Mrs Baksh's prediction comes true: "Everybody just washing
their foot and jumping in this democracy business. But I promising you,
for all the sweet it begin sweet, it going to end damn sour." Both novels
are low-key comedies; their energy level has been succinctly described by
Kingsley Amis:

the humour [is] subdued and kind, concerned with small-scale stratagems between
neighbours, in-laws or rivals. It gradually dawns upon one that this humour, conducted throughout with the utmost stylistic quietude, is completely original. The
characters are trapped in a web of inefficiency and bewilderment which is always
on the point of nullifying their crafty pursuit of prestige, making them helpless but
vociferously protesting victims of chance and untraceable whim. When Surujpat
Harbans finally gets elected to the Legislative Council, nobody can possibly say
how it happened. "Is this modern age" and "this Trinidad backward to hell, you
hear" – somewhere between the two Harbans has slipped in.[43]

The subdued humour and the quietude are, however, only achieved at
a certain cost; for in the interests of entertainment the author has stylized
and simplified the society he depicts. Naipaul has compared the "lesser
world" of his Trinidad childhood to the southern India town that is the
subject of R.K. Narayan's novels, and just as he complains of Narayan's
omission of "much of what could be seen" in his society, so one may
complain of similar omissions in *The Mystic Masseur* and *The Suffrage of
Elvira*.[44] There are also presentational similarities (the understatement, the
deadpan description of farcical situations) between these novels and Narayan's.
At least in Naipaul's case, such devices make the reader aware of a distance
between the droll denizens of the novelist's world and the sophisticated
narrator. This is registered in the contrast between the pungent ungram-
matical lilt of much of the dialogue and the crisp spareness of the educated
narrative voice, which is sometimes tinged with condescending overtones.
Certainly some West Indian commentators were much vexed by Naipaul's

manner. At the end of *The Pleasures of Exile* (1960) for example, George Lamming went out of his way to charge that in these works Naipaul was "ashamed of his cultural background and striving like mad to prove himself through promotion to the peaks of a 'superior' culture."[45] Para-critical though the judgment may be, Lamming did have a point – which as late as 1976 Naipaul was reluctant to grant. In the foreword to a collection of his father's stories, he emphasized that there was nothing in them "that implies an outside audience; the barbs are all turned inwards." Naipaul went on to add that in his early works "this way of looking" became his own, a claim which seems disingenuous and with which few will agree.[46] For is not an outside audience addressed in the prefatory note to *The Mystic Masseur*, which explains that "Trinidad is a small island, no bigger than Lancashire, with a population somewhat smaller than Nottingham's"? And in *The Suffrage of Elvira* is not an outside audience implied in authorial asides like the following: "Many of [the children] were half-dressed according to the curious rural prudery which dictated that the top should be covered, not the bottom"; "He took half a *roti*, a dry unimaginative sort of pancake ..." In short, though it seems heavyhanded to deal so severely with such un-pretentious and entertaining works, one may say of *Miguel Street*, *The Mystic Masseur*, and *The Suffrage of Elvira* what Naipaul said in *The Middle Passage* of much West Indian writing: that the works are not diagnostic of the society they depict and do not have "universal appeal" because they invite the reader to witness, not to participate.[47]

Naipaul was certainly right, however, in saying that the greatest influence on his early work was his father. Seepersad Naipaul, who died in 1953, was a journalist for most of his working life. He also wrote stories of Hindu life in Trinidad, the only society he knew; his son describes these stories as groundbreaking attempts to write about a community that had not been written about before. In *V.S. Naipaul: A Critical Introduction*, Landeg White has an excellent discussion of the young Naipaul's indebtedness to these stories, showing how they supplied the son with a way of artistically rendering Trinidad society. But Seepersad Naipaul's influence on his son's development as a writer goes beyond the filial adaptation of paternal schemata. Naipaul has spoken of his intimacy with his father as "the big relationship in my life,"[48] and it was during the major creative impasse of his early career, described in "The Regional Barrier" of 1958 (the same year that the last of his apprentice works was published), that the father's greatest benefaction to his son's creative life was realized. Seepersad had once spoken better than he could have known when he told his son that "if you are at a loss for a theme, take me for it";[49] for the subject of Naipaul's fourth novel is the life of his father, and the piety, warmth, and human sympathy (always under full artistic control) that inform *A House for Mr Biswas* enabled Naipaul to break entirely out of the mould of his early books, to put behind him the minor key of colonial social comedy, and to produce a major novel which does have universal appeal because the reader is made to participate, not merely to witness.[50] It is hard not to feel that Naipaul indirectly dramatized the effect on himself of this liberating act of the imagination in *Mr Stone and the Knights Companion*, the novel he published two years after *A House for Mr Biswas* (we have already noted something of the parable of artistic creation contained in both novels). For just as Mr Stone was raised from the droll passivity of his Pooter-like existence through the creative act of realizing in words his project for the protection of the old (his one act of sympathetic concern for the lives of others) so through the writing of *A House for Mr Biswas* V.S. Naipaul raised himself from the rut of a regional writer of social comedies and thereby found release for his enormous creative gifts.

A House for Mr Biswas is the life story of an unexceptional man different from the other members of his community only in his dissatisfaction with the conditions of his life and his longing for something better. The events in his life are framed by the domiciles of others in which he has to live, and the focus of his longing is simply a house of his own. The world into which Mohun Biswas is born is the Hindu community of Trinidad, the claustrophobic nature of which is described in *The Middle Passage*:

Living by themselves in villages, the [Hindu] Indians were able to have a complete community life ... [It was a] money-minded community, spiritually static because cut off from its roots, its religion reduced to rites without philosophy ... It was a world eaten up with jealousies and family feuds and village feuds; but it was a world of its own, a community within the colonial society, without responsibility, with authority doubly and trebly removed. Loyalties were narrow: to the family, the village ... family organization [was] an enclosing self-sufficient world absorbed with its quarrels and jealousies, as difficult for the outsider to penetrate as for one of its members to escape. It protected and imprisoned, a static world, awaiting decay.[51]

The fictional recreation of this world is marvellously done. It is rendered with a memorable fullness and sharpness, an attitude neither sentimental nor judgmental, and a passion authenticated by the quality of the prose. One fictional schema which Naipaul has utilized in presenting his world is that of the old-fashioned family saga novel. *A House for Mr Biswas* chronicles the fortunes of two families through almost three generations. One is the affluent Tulsi family, into which Mr Biswas is married, the epitome of the East Indian "complete community life" offering a stagnant security. Here, for example, is what as a young woman Mr Biswas's wife Shama expects from life:

to be taken through every stage, to fulfil every function, to have her share of the established emotions: joy at a birth or marriage, distress during illness and hardship, grief at a death. Life, to be full, had to be this established pattern of sensation. Grief and joy, both equally awaited, were one. For Shama and her sisters and women like them, ambition, if the word could be used, was a series of negatives: not to be unmarried, not to be childless, not to be an undutiful daughter, sister, wife, mother, widow.

In the second half of *Mr Biswas*, the Tulsi family moves from the rural security of Hanuman House to Port of Spain, "a new world" in which everybody "had to fight for himself" and in which the awaited decay of their way of life begins. The other family is that of Mr Biswas. The reader is taken from the mud huts of the rural village of Hindi-speaking agricultural labourers where at the beginning of the novel Mr Biswas is born to Bipti and Raghu, through the forty-six years of his life, to a college library "in a northern land" where the marbled endpaper of a dusty leatherbound book reminds Anand, the son of Mr Biswas, of "the marbled patterns of old-fashioned balloons powdered with a rubbery dust in a shallow white box" which during his childhood he would see at Christmas time at the Tulsi store in Arwacas.

But more important than the chronicle motif to the fullness and authority of the novel is its expansive method of presentation. As with the Christmas balloons remembered by Anand, every rift in *A House for Mr Biswas* is loaded with the ore of vivid descriptive detail. In a comment that suggests something of the creative exuberance that must have sustained him during the composition of his novel, Naipaul has described his method and the reasons for its employment: "In a way it's like a sleight of hand; you mention a chair and it's shadowy; you say it's stained with wedding saffron, and suddenly that chair is there, palpable. In fact, I got so fascinated with my method I even give it away at one point, when I describe a character telling a story with all those inconsequential details which give verisimilitude."[52] (The reference is to Jagdat's mendacious account during a Sunday lunch of how he had spent his morning – he had actually been drinking whiskey with Mr Biswas: "He said that he had been out on some business, described conversations and incidents with an abundance of inconsequential, credible detail ...")

It is hardly an easy thing to sustain this "luxuriance and expansiveness" of manner over a length of 500 pages without having it become programmatic and dwindle into either ornamental festooning or documentary fill; but Naipaul has done so with a vividness and amplitude that bring the world of the novel fully to life. There are the major geographical settings, including Port of Spain, The Chase, "a long, straggling settlement of mud huts in the heart of the sugarcane area," the estate at Shorthills (the hills beyond it a "coagulation of greenery"), and Green Vale, made "damp, shadowed and close" by its trees:

They were tall and straight, and so hung with long, drooping leaves that their trunks were hidden and appeared to be branchless. Half the leaves were dead; the others, at the top, were a dead green. It was as if all the trees had, at the same moment, been blighted in luxuriance, and death was spreading at the same place from all the roots. But death was forever held in check. The tonguelike leaves of dead green turned slowly to the brightest yellow, became brown and thin as if scorched, curled downwards over the other dead leaves and did not fall. And new leaves came, as sharp as daggers; but there was no freshness to them; they came into the world old, without a shine, and only grew longer before they too died.

There are the buildings, including the jerry-built house in which Mr Biswas is to die; the rumshop in Pagotes; Pundit Jairam's "bare, spacious, unpainted wooden house smelling of blue soap and incense, its floors white and smooth from constant scrubbing, its cleanliness and sanctity maintained by regulations awkward to everyone except himself"; the rudimentary dwelling the negro carpenter George Maclean builds for Mr Biswas at Green Vale; the appalling Port of Spain slum where Bhandat lives; the decaying house at Shorthills; the holiday cottage at Sans Souci; and Hanuman House, where the saffron-stained chair is found:

The most important piece of furniture in the hall was a long unvarnished pitchpine table, hard-grained and chipped. A hammock made of sugarsacks hung across one corner of the room. An old sewingmachine, a babychair and a black biscuit-drum occupied another corner. Scattered about were a number of unrelated chairs, stools and benches, one of which, low and carved with rough ornamentation from a solid block of cyp wood, still had the saffron colour which told that it had been used at a wedding ceremony. More elegant pieces – a dresser, a desk, a piano so buried among papers and baskets and other things that it was unlikely it was ever used – choked the staircase landing.

Finally there are the characters: among them Lal, the Presbyterian convert who teaches at the Canadian mission school; F.Z. Ghany, the Muslim solicitor; Mongroo, the village stick fighter; Mr Biswas's Aunt Tara, her husband Ajodha, and their sons Rabidat and Jagdat; his sister Dahoti and her low caste husband Ramchand; the old men in Arwacas who gather in the evening to smoke their *cheelums* and talk of returning to India; the journalist colleagues of Mr Biswas in Port of Spain, neither over forty, "who considered their careers closed and rested their ambitions on the achievements of their children"; the many members of the grotesquely extended Tulsi family – the matriarchal Mrs Tulsi, her brother-in-law Seth, her sons Shekhar and Owad, her fourteen daughters and their children, her sons-in-law, including Govind, Hari, W.C. Tuttle, Sharma, and Mr Biswas himself.

It is important not to exaggerate the differences between Mr Biswas and the community with which he is at odds. To do so would lead to an oversimplified and possibly sentimental response to him. In many ways Mr Biswas is the epitome rather than the obverse of his community's manners and mores. He is no less drolly venal and ignoble than his brothers-in-law, for example, and while Hanuman House lies like an incubus on his spirit he more than once welcomes the security that comes with his dependence on the Tulsis, and it is in their bosom that he is restored to health after his nervous breakdown at Green Vale. He is a subject of the novel's comedy not because he is a naïf stumbling in a fallen world but because he is no less irresponsible, querulous, jealous, and philistine than the other characters. But Mr Biswas does have a sense of loss and the consequent longing for something absent from him, and a desire, if not for something so abstract as individual freedom, then at least to be undependent. These give the story of his life a more than comic or documentary dimension and make his eventual attainment of a house, however foolish the purchase, a victory for the sense of human possibility.

Near the beginning of the novel Mr Biswas's predicament is defined:

He stayed in the back trace and read Samuel Smiles. He had bought one of his books in the belief that it was a novel, and had become an addict. Samuel Smiles was as romantic and satisfying as any novelist, and Mr Biswas saw himself in many Samuel Smiles heroes: he was young, he was poor, and he fancied he was struggling. But there always came a point when resemblance ceased. The heroes had rigid ambitions and lived in countries where ambitions could be pursued and had a meaning. He had no ambition, and in this hot land, apart from opening a shop or buying a motorbus, what could he do?

It is not that Mr Biswas is in conflict with his society or that he is struggling with the problem of vocation – the themes of hundreds of nineteenth- and twentieth-century novels and plays. It is rather that his society is "so incoherent and rudimentary that he cannot begin to define himself against it,"[53] nor find in it any real vocations to choose among. This early realization, however, does not still the hunger of Mr Biswas's imagination, which continues to prey intermittently upon life. When he arrives at The Chase, where he is to manage a Tulsi store, he reflects that his removal there is merely "a pause, a preparation" and that "Real life was to begin for [him and Shama] soon, and elsewhere." After six years of failure and tedium there he has given up reading Samuel Smiles but still feels "that some nobler purpose awaited him, even in this limiting society." At Green Vale, where he works as a sub-overseer, Mr Biswas tries to fight an "exhausting vacancy that left him with the feeling that he had drunk gallons of stale, lukewarm water." He makes his first attempt to have his own house built, but this and other pressures bring on a prolonged breakdown, the desolating sense of being "in a place that was nowhere, a dot on the map of the island, which was a dot on the map of the world," and the feeling of descent into the void, of which the eerie dead greenness of the place's trees is the emblem.

When at the novel's midpoint Mr Biswas leaves Hanuman House at the age of thirty-one to search for a job in Port of Spain, he is still able to persuade himself that "The past was counterfeit, a series of cheating accidents. Real life, and its especial sweetness, awaited; he was still beginning." The truth of the matter, however, for him as for other Naipaul characters, is precisely the opposite. This he first comes to see shortly after his arrival in the capital: "The past could not be ignored; it was never counterfeit; he carried it within himself. If there was a place for him, it was one that had already been hollowed out by time, by everything he had lived through, however imperfect, makeshift and cheating." This realization coincides with a change in fortune: a job as a reporter, relatively decent lodgings for his family (though in a Tulsi house) and four good years later epitomized in his memory by the freshness and expectation of morning. This freshness begins to fade, as does his insight concerning determination by the past, when Owad, Mrs Tulsi's intolerable son, leaves for study in England, and Mr Biswas begins to feel that "there ... was surely where life was to be found." A sense of despair and of the void begins to return night after night, "visions of the future [become] only visions of his son's future," and after the failure of his second attempt to build a house he even comes to lose his oldest vision, first voiced to his mother when years before he had left her mud hut to seek his future: "And I am going to get my own house too."

Then, suddenly, the return of Owad from England sets in motion a series of events that leads to the purchase of his house, after which the novel comes quickly to its end, passing over the last five years of Mr Biswas's life and closing with a resumé of his illness and death. The ending is very low key, but one does not forget what had been said hundreds of pages before in the novel's post mortem prologue: that during his final months of illness and despair Mr Biswas "was struck again and again by the wonder of being in his own house, the audacity of it"; and that for him "to have died among the Tulsis, amid the squalor of that large, disintegrating and indifferent family" would have been terrible, would have been to die as he was born, "unnecessary and unaccommodated."

While it is a consistently engaging work, *A House for Mr. Biswas* is not a flawless novel. Its imperfections are owing to a certain discontinuity between content and form. Just as Mr Biswas's problem is that his society provides no channels for ambition or opportunities for self-definition, the same society provides Naipaul with none of the themes and conflicts that are the meat and drink of the traditional kind of novel he is writing. Naipaul was himself aware of this difficulty and has commented on his early attempts to find a "centre" for his writing and its approach to "truth":

For me the problem may have been especially difficult, because all the novels I had read were about settled and organised societies, and I was aware of a slight fraudulence in applying a form created by that type of society to the squalor, disorder and shallowness of my own. The novel is such a civilised, sophisticated and complex thing – an imaginative attempt at realising the world: and there seemed such a gap between this attempt and an inarticulate society bounded by a few simple parasitic professions.[54]

Evidence of Naipaul's problem is found in the opening scenes of *Mr Biswas* – in the uncertainties of tone and traces of condescension which bespeak his difficulties in putting behind him the manner and presentational style of his first two novels. A more serious difficulty is that, because of the rudimentary nature of his society and the culturally conditioned passivity of his character, Mr Biswas's life necessarily has little shape or direction. This gives to the novel an episodic quality and to the reader the sense of moving on rather than moving forward. This is surely one of the major reasons Naipaul added to his novel the prologue describing Mr Biswas's death and his last days in his house: to supply at the beginning the sense of an ending that could not have been sensed in the chronological narrative of events in his life. But while the prologue is a fine touch, it is arguably insufficient by itself. And Naipaul will tolerate no other piece of artifice to help him organize his enormous slice of life into a work of art. A final difficulty, found in the latter part of the novel, concerns the key relationship between Mr Biswas and his son Anand, on whom the father begins to rest his own frustrated ambitions. "I don't want you to be like me," he once tells his son: "Anand understood. Father and son, each saw the other as weak and vulnerable, and each felt a responsibility for the other, a responsibility which, in times of particular pain, was disguised by exaggerated authority on the one hand, exaggerated respect on the other." The difficulty is that this relationship is insufficiently developed; having a number of scenes narrated from Anand's point of view does nothing to remedy the matter. In retrospect one understands that Anand is a version of the young V.S. Naipaul and that it is he who has grown up to become the author of his father's life. But this reflexive aspect of the novel ought to have either been made more explicit or been pruned.

These imperfections are, however, relatively minor matters and I mention them only because *A House for Mr Biswas* has in some quarters been rather too indiscriminately praised. If not a masterpiece, the novel is unquestionably a major achievement, of which one may say what E.M. Forster said of Lampedusa's *The Leopard*, another luminous portrait of a static marginal society: "Reading and rereading it has made me realize how many ways there are of being alive, how many doors there are, close to one, which someone else's touch may open."[55]

IV

From the point of view of comprehensive humanity and extension of the reader's sympathies, *A House for Mr Biswas* is the high-water mark of Naipaul's career; in everything after it a progressive narrowing of his sympathies may be observed. At the same time his "passion" as a novelist has intensified, his sensibility has become more acute, and his vision of human possibility has darkened, as may be seen by comparing the brutal endings of the novels of the 1970s to that of *Mr Biswas*. A less expansive sympathy and the determination to colonize new fictional territory finds it presentational corollary in the adaptation of different schemata and in a narrowing of focus, for none of Naipaul's later novels attempts the inclusiveness or panoramic breadth of *A House for Mr Biswas*.

Concentration of focus and freshness of subject matter are the most obvious features of the short novel Naipaul published in 1964. He has described *Mr Stone and the Knights Companion* as a reaction against the "luxuriance and expansiveness" of *Mr Biswas*: "I set out ... to write a compressionist novel pared to the bone ... I determined to put in nothing inessential, however alluring; no more dialogue than was absolutely necessary, no picturesque description, nothing."[56] The novel is a serio-comic *tranche de vie* set in one of the southern suburbs of London. Within its 160 pages is packed a wealth of sharply observed, freshly described circumstantial detail – of characters' appearances, manners and habits, of buildings, streets, backyards, dinner parties, office routine, and so on – that gives the novel a convincing solidity of specification. All of the characters are English, and even the narrative eye is white: notation of the "Europeans Only" card below the bell of the private hotel in Earl's Court where Mr Stone's future wife lives does not indicate an outside, hypersensitive-to-race narrator. It rather registers exactly the defensive gentility of the hotel, a refuge of seedy respectability in an area now inhabited by "young-people in art-student dress and foreigners of every colour."

As V.S. Pritchett and Walter Allen have both noted, the setting and the central character, a thoroughly unexceptional lower middle class office worker, suggest an obvious type: the 'little man' of English fiction, especially its turn-of-the-century incarnations in the title character of Wells's *History of Mr Polly* and the Pooter of the Grossmiths' *Diary of a Nobody*. There can be little doubt that in bringing his English subject into focus Naipaul made use of such schemata. Pritchett thinks (as I do) that Naipaul has successfully revivified the type because "he has begun from scratch and built up brick by brick."[57] But Allen feels that Naipaul has approached his scene too much "through memories of its Edwardian laureates" and that "a feeling of the actuality of the present" is not registered.[58] Both V.S. Pritchett and Walter Allen have been for many years distinguished critics of English fiction; both are in addition professional fictional recorders of English lower middle class social life; so they should know.

The subject of *Mr Stone and the Knights Companion* is a crisis point in the life of its title character, who is sixty-two when the novel opens and about to enter his climacteric, his *crise de soixante*. The centre of interest is kept strictly on Mr Stone's consciousness and its ripples; everything in this excellently integrated novel is seen either through his eyes or in relation to him. Even Whymper, the vulgarly trendy public relations man on his way up, a splendid characterization who threatens at moments to monopolize the reader's interest, is kept in place through several suggestions of a hidden affinity between him and Mr Stone. Three thematic motifs may be discerned in the account of Mr Stone's crisis; one has to do with the state of contemporary England, for just as Mr Biswas was a synecdoche for East Indian life in Trinidad, Mr Stone may be seen to epitomize Naipaul's view of England as a society that is "closing up," falling into a pattern of empty rituals and into the false security of the colonial, for whom all important decisions are made elsewhere. "The whole structure of society," Naipaul said in 1968, "seems to pull people down."[59] Another motif, already instanced, has to do with "the creative activity of the mind." This is a subordinate part of the novel's central theme, which is what may be said to give universal appeal to its parochial subject. I speak of the Romantic pattern (found, *inter alia*, in Wordsworth's "Resolution and Independence" and Eliot's *Four Quartets*) of recognition of the emptiness of one's present life and of the inevitability of death; crisis; and the eventual passage from darkness to some measure of light through creative activity and an awakened sense of human sympathy.

The novel opens with a moment of premonitory terror for Mr Stone: as he unlocks the front door of his house, a neighbour's cat leaps at him from the darkness. The cat interrupts the "soothing pattern" of Mr Stone's habitual existence which has sustained him for many years and is symbolized by the tree seen from his window, the seasonal transformation of which speaks to him not of a process of growth and decay or of "the running out of his life" but of "the even flowing of time." For Mr Stone, life is "something to be moved through" and experiences are something to enjoy only retrospectively, when they have been "docketed and put away in the file of the past." If one reads carefully and does a little subtraction, one can infer that Mr Stone's state of emotional entropy is rooted in the trauma of a primal loss unrepaired after forty-five years: the death of his mother when he was seventeen. As the weeks pass, a number of minor occurrences, like the leap of the cat, evoke in Mr Stone sensations of threat and "an awareness of his own acute unhappiness," and he begins to have visions of the insubstantiality and corruptibility of all things. He unexpectedly marries, but his union with Margaret – the quality of their relationship is indicated by their mutual term of endearment: "Doggie" – hardly provides nourishment for his little understood hungers and does nothing to allay the sense of time speeding on, drawing him ever nearer to "retirement, inactivity, corruption."

It is during an early spring holiday in Cornwall that these apprehensions are intensified to the point of crisis. Tired and a little lost at the end of an outing, Mr Stone has a strange experience. He asks directions of an ominous looking farm labourer who is watching a brush fire burn across a field. The man does not answer but instead walks into the field, disappearing into the smoke of the fire, which continues to burn until it reaches the wall where Mr Stone is standing. Once the smoke has dissipated it is for Mr Stone "as if there had been no fire, and all that had happened a hallucination." The unreal quality of the moment, "when earth and life and senses had been suspended, remained with him." As with his earlier visions of transience, but much more disturbingly, "It was like an experience of nothingness, an experience of death." The next scene is thoroughly quotidian and unmysterious, but equally disturbing. In a Cornish teashop, Mr Stone comes to see himself in the mirror of a recent pensioner. "Forty years with the same firm," the man says joylessly and querulously, while "rolling his wrinkled cigarette between his lips." Mr Stone stares with horrible fascination at the man and his companions, two fat women of custodial manner whose shiny new handbags suggest a "cosy grossness."

It is at the end of the same day that the idea of the Knights Companion – a fraternal organization for pensioners of Excal, the company for which he has worked for years – comes to Mr Stone. He labours to put his idea into written form, and when the company's president decides to implement it, his life begins to brighten. His unexpected success leads to the refurbishment of his dingy house, every domestic sensation seems heightened, he has some social successes, is lionized a little, and even comes to think of himself as urbane. And one particularly delightful dinner party he comes to regard as "the climax of his life."

But Mr Stone's Indian summer is short-lived. Autumnal realities intrude: his oldest friend dies; the cat from the opening scene, with whom he had come to feel a sympathetic affinity, is put away by its owners; Miss Millington, his cleaning woman of many years, becomes senile and has to be put out to pasture; and the activities of the Knights Companion turn up some grisly stories of mistreatment of the elderly. Worst of all, like Anthony Maloney's Great Victorian Collection in Brian Moore's novel, the Knights Companion scheme, the one creative act of Mr Stone's life, begins to pass from his control, to be credited to the uncouth and self-serving Whymper and put to meretricious uses. Mr Stone comes to feel that "his passion and anguish had gone for nothing," that "the only pure moments, the only true moments" of his life were those he had spent in his study creating his scheme, writing – like the Naipaulian novelist – "out of a feeling whose depth he realized only as he wrote." Mr Stone's spiritual nadir comes when he wishes his scheme had never been realized, for "All action, all creation was a betrayal of feeling and truth." And on the novel's penultimate page his vision of the insubstantiality of matter returns.

If one views Mr Stone's negative conclusions in the context of his creator's views on "the creative activity of the mind," it becomes possible to say that Mr Stone is an imperfect or incomplete creative artist. For he does not realize that creative activity is its own reward, that for the true artist, in Robert Frost's memorable phrase, strongly spent is synonymous with kept, or in the words of Mr Biswas, speaking to Anand shortly before his own authentic creative act: "no true effort is ever wasted." In addition, Mr Stone fails to realize that the ideal of detachment cannot be that of the creative artist, for "it is impossible to think of a writer, a novelist, as being anything but attached."[60] But all is not lost for Mr Stone, for on the novel's last page his negations are superseded by a diminished but palpable assertion of the humanity and sympathy of *A House for Mr Biswas*. Returning home and unlocking his front door, Mr Stone is again surprised by the leap of a black cat, the offspring of the one encountered at the beginning of his story. But this time – it is an indication, however minimal, even droll, that Mr Stone has learned something of human value from what has transpired during his novel – "his fear blended into guilt, guilt into love. 'Pussy'."

Much as one admires Naipaul's achievement in *Mr Stone and the Knights Companion* – its intelligence, economy of means, freshness of invention and description – it is true to say that compared with *A House for Mr Biswas* the novel possesses little resonance. This is because *Mr Stone* is rather too schematic, and its prose style a little too mannered, too lacquered. While superbly thought out, the novel does not seem to be as deeply felt. To use Naipaul's own terms, there is abundant intelligence but relatively little sensibility. It is as if there were a *cordon sanitaire* between the narrator and his subject, as there was never felt to be between the narrator and subject of *Mr Biswas*. One suspects that Naipaul himself may have come to see this, for in his next novel he dispenses with objective and dispassionate third person narration, employing a first person narrator and a confessional mode which ensures that the acute sensibility of the central character – an East Indian living in London, like his creator – will be to the fore.

The Mimic Men (1967) is the story of Ranjit Kripalsingh (or Ralph Singh), in present time a forty-year-old post-colonial West Indian politician living in exile in a suburban London hotel, where he is writing his memoirs in the attempt to impose order and intelligibility on the events of his life. His narrative, a non-chronological *Bildungsroman*, moves backward and forward over his life and its two island termini – "Isabella" and Britain – as he tries to make connection between past and present, colonial life and London, childhood and adult life, while telling how he rose from humble origins to complete disaster (though this designation does not suggest the unrelieved seriousness, even solemnity, of Singh's self-examination).

Like its predecessor, *The Mimic Men* was a major new departure for Naipaul. In addition to the first person narration, there is the fact that the novel has a sophisticated political perspective. It sees the post-colonial cultural and political realities of West Indian society from the outside, from a generic viewpoint which shows Singh's public career to be typical of the "colonial politician" and events in Isabella to be exemplary of what has happened "in twenty places, twenty countries, islands, colonies, territories." In addition, *The Mimic Men* is a novel of ideas, for as he broods in the solitude of his hotel room Ralph Singh has all the time in the world for reflections on big questions concerning politics, the meaning of history, the value of writing, authenticity, and identity. Finally, for the first time in Naipaul's fiction, the central character is what the central characters of all of his subsequent fictions will be: uprooted and homeless, existing "in a free state." The more *déraciné* the characters, the more unfit they become for serio-comic treatment and – this is a key Naipaulian rule of thumb – the more they are defined by and presented in terms of their sexuality, a quality of sensibility rather than intelligence and an essential constituent of the atmosphere, characterization, and theme of *The Mimic Men* and the novels that have followed it.

It is hard not to think that one of the models Naipaul utilized in creating *The Mimic Men* was Ralph Ellison's celebrated 1952 novel *Invisible Man*, the *Bildungsroman* of an American black, also narrated retrospectively in the first person. Even if not a direct influence, *Invisible Man* is similar enough – despite its greater technical, formal, and stylistic sophistication – to make for an illuminating comparison. Both novels are about a talented young man who comes to biological maturity in a marginal society and to the beginnings of emotional and intellectual maturity in the anonymity of a cosmopolitan metropolis. While we are once told what he is called, Ralph Singh is for all practical purposes as nameless as the protagonist of Ellison's novel. Like the titles of both novels, this points to a similar lack of identity and to the false roles both assume on their journeys to self-discovery within the determining context of larger historical and racial patterns.

Both embark on political careers in constituencies wracked by racial tension and both careers are brought to an end by bloody race riots – East Indian versus Negro in Isabella, Negro versus White in New York. Disillusioned with the active life and no longer able to see how they can function positively in society, both withdraw from the world to brood upon their past and its inauthentic roles and to try to understand what has happened to them, who they are, and what the larger meaning of their stories is through writing their own histories – that is through "the creative activity of the mind." Both come to discover that their end is in their beginning and both struggle to conclude their accounts on an optimistic note and to assert gain. But they do so in ways that seem theoretical and are so qualified by other elements in their stories as to make the endings of *Invisible Man* and *The Mimic Men* distinctly indeterminate. Finally, Ellison has insisted that his work is not basically about race, politics, or even a particular society, but about identity, freedom, and becoming human. The same may also be said of Naipaul's novel, for while one can understand why Angus Wilson and others have complained about the fuzziness of its political parts, one also feels that such criticisms are not to the point. Politics and race are the subject matter of much of the novel, which does offer a thoughtful commentary on a Third World society. But *The Mimic Men* is not essentially a political novel; it is rather a novel of character and sensibility.

The first of its three sections opens in London shortly after the Second World War, when Singh is a student at an unnamed institution resembling the London School of Economics. Having no authentic character, unable to discover the thread on which his unrelated adventures and encounters are strung, he describes how he created the role of an extravagant colonial dandy. Around the time that cracks, caused by a renewed sense of not knowing who he is, begin to appear in this facade, Singh marries Sandra, a London girl in a situation like his own (it is one of the reasons they are sexually compatible): "She had no community, no group, and had rejected her family." He returns with her to Isabella where husband and wife assume the preposterous roles of West Indian bright young things. While Singh amasses a fortune from real estate development, his marriage sours and Sandra eventually leaves him.

In the long second section of *The Mimic Men* Singh describes his boyhood and adolescence on the island in the attempt to uncover the roots of his sense that – in words Naipaul has used of himself – "the world I was born in was not real."[61] Singh presents his younger self, his family (except for his father, whose ultimate solution to inauthenticity is withdrawal from the world) and his school friends as all being "mimic men" of the new world, born in the wrong place – in his favourite image, "shipwrecked" on the island. The novel's final section describes Singh's political career during the early days of the island's independence; his relationship with Browne, a black politician who plays Forbes Burnham to Singh's Cheddi Jagan (to use a Guyanese analogy); his realization of the unreality of political power ("in a society like ours, fragmented, inorganic ... a society not held together by common interests ... no power was real which did not come from the outside") and that he is, as ever, "imprisoned in pretence"; and finally his withdrawal and eventual exile in "the greater disorder, the final emptiness: London and the home counties." It is there that Singh, like Mr Stone in Cornwall, reaches his spiritual nadir. He experiences "a moment of total helplessness" that is "the limit of desolation. The moment linked to nothing. I felt I had no past." Through the act of writing his memoirs, Singh begins to come back from this brink and through the repossession of his past to begin to understand himself.

The pattern he comes to discover in his life is loss and constant yearning for what Rimbaud called the true life which is absent. There is the initial shipwreck of the primal loss, expressed through dreams "that I was a baby again and at my mother's breast"; there is the longing during childhood for what is beyond: "the clear air of adulthood and responsibility, where everything was comprehensible"; there is the "secret life" of adolescent fantasy – the dream of leadership of the knights and horsemen of an Aryan homeland of high plains, mountains, and snow; there is the "feeling of shipwreck and wrongness among crowds" and the conscious holding back of himself "for the reality which lay elsewhere"; and there is the political fantasy of young manhood, the "longing for freedom and what we considered the truth of our personalities."

In *The Mimic Men* two antidotes for Singh's consuming sense of loss and of the unreality of the present are suggested. One is acceptance of the reality principle: the recognition that "Where you born, man, you born," as Mr. Deschampsneufs tells him; as Singh himself puts it, "We cannot keep ourselves back for some tract of life ahead. We are made by everything; by action, by withdrawal." The other antidote is the creative activity of the mind: at the end of his narration Singh is able to say that "writing, for all its initial distortion, clarifies, and even becomes a process of life"; and he had earlier averred that through writing the story of his life he had come to feel that its events were not "aberrations, whimsical arbitrary acts," but that "the personality hangs together. It is one and indivisible."

These are, however, only adumbrations, more asserted than shown; and their constructive implications are severely qualified throughout the novel, especially in its concluding chapter, by the negating actuality of Singh's sensibility, especially the detailed notations of his attitude to sexuality, and its Naipaulian surrogate, food.[62] That this sensibility is a crucial determinant of his story is suggested in tableau form on both the first and last pages of the novel, where in each case Singh is positioned between distasteful sexual emblems. In the novel's opening paragraph we are told that his room in Mr Shylock's boardinghouse is bounded by "pleasure and its penalty": at one end the attic room with a mattress on the floor where Mr Shylock is serviced by his mistresses; at the other the basement where Lieni, the Maltese housekeeper, lives with her illegitimate child. In the concluding paragraph of *The Mimic Men* 300 pages later, Singh, at his table in his hotel's dining room, has on one side the man he calls Garbage, to whose repellent eating habits a full page of description has been devoted, and on the other his former bedmate Lady Stella, who is characterized solely by her dual fondness for the *Oxford Nursery Rhyme Book* and daily sexual gymnastics, to participation in which Singh proved unequal – his physical shrinkage miming his emotional distaste.

Between these tableaux, the intensity of Singh's attraction/repulsion to female sexuality is several times underlined. His distaste for the promiscuity of his student days in London intensifies into self-disgust when in a post-coitum mood he catches "sight of the prostitute's supper, peasant food, on a bare table in a back room." He cannot reciprocate the affection of Lieni because of his abhorrence of physical intimacy:

I could have stayed forever at a woman's breasts, if they were full and had a hint of a weight that required support. But there was the skin, there was the smell of skin. There were bumps and scratches, there were a dozen little things that could positively enrage me. I was capable of the act required, but frequently it was in the way that I was capable of getting drunk or eating two dinners. Intimacy: it was violation and self violation.

If we read carefully, we discover over a hundred pages later that Singh's fondness for weight in a woman's breasts is radically connected to his sense of loss, for it is owing to his memory of the "consoling weight, the closeness of soft smooth flesh," of his mother's breast. This also explains why Sandra's generous breasts, which have much more than a hint of weight about them, so appeal to him. Indeed, they become so magnified through Singh's concentration on them as to become grotesque and recall Darl's description in Faulkner's *As I Lay Dying* of his sister's "mammalian ludicrosities." Breasts again loom large in the most extraordinary scene in *The Mimic Men*: Singh's hours, during an intransit stopover in a foreign city, with an enormously fat black prostitute, whose naked appearance and professional activities are described in obsessive, revulsed detail. As she undresses, for example, her "breasts were released. They cascaded heavily down. They were enormous, they were grotesque, empty starved sacks which yet contained some substance at their tips, where alone they had some shape ... Below those breasts, wide flabby scabbards which hung down to the middle, her dimpled, loose belly collapsed; flesh hung in liquid folds about her legs which quivered like risen dough."

This scene, like other places in *The Mimic Men* where Singh's more than fastidious sensibility is dominant, has given trouble to commentators offering constructive thematic accounts of the novel. In her *Colonial Encounter*, for example, Molly Mahood ignores the scene's appalling palpability, denaturing it by making it into a symbol of something abstract: "the total failure of all relationship." She performs a similar act of conceptual transference and sanitation on Garbage's meal, which becomes simply a "ludicrous ... emblem" of Singh's life which "disinfects but does not destroy our sense of an ending" (whatever that means).[63] Landeg White says something similar about the obese prostitute and goes on to assert wrongly that the novel "concludes on a note of optimism."[64] Its penultimate paragraph concludes in this way (writing as a "process of life") and in the antepenultimate paragraph Singh does assert that he has cleared the decks and prepared himself for what will be the action of a free man. But the novel's last paragraph ends not with positive assertion (which we might call a quality of intelligence) but with the fixations of sensibility: Lady Stella and then Garbage, who concludes the novel by "bringing his two-pronged knife down on the struggling cheese. *Dixi.*"

In *The Mimic Men*, then, there are two distinctive strands – conceptual and perceptual, intellectual and emotional, constructive and demoralizing – which even at its conclusion are not reconciled. This may be said to make *The Mimic Men* an imperfect work of art compared with *Mr Stone and the Knights Companion*, which is fully controlled by Naipaul's intelligence, or the title novella of *In a Free State*, in which sensibility dominates. But this may hardly be said to make *The Mimic Men* a less interesting or less engaging work, any more than a similar discontinuity makes Naipaul's 1979 novel, *A Bend in the River*, in which after two novels dominated by a desolating sensibility he again attempted the presentation of a constructive, humane theme.

V

By the end of the 1960s, with three impressive and distinctly different novels to his credit, Naipaul had put far behind him the "regional barrier" difficulties which had troubled him a decade before, and was about to enter a new phase of his career as a novelist, a phase which was to be again characterized by an impressive extension of range and the development of new presentational devices. One reason for this mutation was Naipaul's deepening sense of global dislocation and his deepening pessimism concerning the Third World. The final section of *The Overcrowded Barracoon* (1972), for example, contains first person accounts of the pathetic syndrome of small colonies of "the Third World's third world" – British Honduras, St Kitts, Anguilla, Trinidad, Mauritius – attempting to realize an independent identity but being "condemned ... to an inferiority of skill and achievement" (a barracoon is a barrack for the confinement of slaves).[65] In *India: A Wounded Civilization* (1975) Naipaul described the land of his ancestors as suffering from a crippling limitation of vision and response caused by traditions that left "no ideas, only obsessions, no discussion, only disingenuous complaint and an invitation to the wallow, the sweet surrender to tragedy."[66] And *The Return of Eva Perón* (1980) contained even more gloomy reports on Argentina and Zaire.

Another reason for the mutation was a change in Naipaul's conception of himself as a writer. In 1971, for example, he spoke of his growing awareness of his own insecurity, of the sense that "I am always peripheral" and of no longer having a society of his own to write about.[67] Like the *déracinés* of his 1971 collection, he had come to exist "in a free state" of placelessness. In two articles from the early 1970s one can see Naipaul further redefining his sense of himself as a writer, and identifying his new subject matter, through the discovery of two precursors. One of them is Jean Rhys, who like Naipaul had come from the West Indies to England, and whose achievement as a novelist Naipaul regards as "very grand": "Out of her fidelity to her experience, and her purity as a novelist, Jean Rhys thirty to forty years ago identified many of the themes that engage us today: isolation, an absence of society or community, the sense of things falling apart, dependence, loss ... Her books may serve current causes but she is above causes."[68] The other precursor is Joseph Conrad, to whose work it had taken Naipaul "a long time to come round" and to realize that three-quarters of a century ago the elder novelist had "meditated on my world, a world I recognize today." Conrad "had been everywhere before me. Not as a man with a cause, but a man offering ... a vision of the world's half-made societies as places which continuously made and unmade themselves, where there was no goal ... His achievement derives from the honesty which is part of his difficulty, that 'scrupulous fidelity to the truth of my own sensations'."[69]

The novels Naipaul published during the 1970s have so many features in common that they may be regarded as isomers, compounds which have the same ingredients but different structures. The title novella of *In a Free State*, *Guerrillas*, and *A Bend in the River* are all set in newly independent nations of the Third World, two of them African, one West Indian. In each case heat, sweat, dirt, repugnant sights and smells, abandoned industrial estates, ugly corrugated buildings, and colonial relics are the backdrop to violent political eruptions which are obliquely glimpsed by the foreign central characters in the foreground. These characters exist in a free state of non-alignment ("It's not your business or mine," says Bobby in *In a Free State*, "They have to sort these things out for themselves") but are nevertheless tested by events, and found wanting. Political destabilization follows the same pattern in each novel: racial strife among the principal ethnic factions, demagogy, exploitation of non-white minority groups (mainly Indian), and (in two of the three) evidence of American intervention. In each case the fear and anxiety of the central characters are counterpointed by the rage and hate of blacks consumed with a sense of injury. This is epitomized in the most shocking and disturbing scene in Naipaul's entire canon – the climactic episode in *Guerrillas* in which Jimmy Ahmed brutally sodomizes Jane before bringing her to Bryant, his male lover, who hacks Jane to death with his cutlass and hastily buries her corpse in a shallow pit near the commune latrines. Finally, a key aspect of all three novels is the interplay of foreground and background, private and public: Bobby's journey into the heart of the darkness both within and without; in *Guerrillas* Jimmy Ahmed's notion that "everyone is a guerrilla" and Roche's "two failures," personal and professional, which "were linked and ran together"; in *A Bend in the River* the president's insistence on his subjects' achieving African authenticity, which counterpoints Salim's search for personal authenticity. But while the constituent parts are largely the same, each novel is a distinct entity with different properties because each has a different form and employs a different schema.

Naipaul has described *In a Free State* as both "a book about journeys, unhappy journeys, by people switching countries, switching cultures" and a book "properly about power and powerlessness."[70] It consists of five parts: a prologue and an epilogue, both excerpts from a journal in which Naipaul, "looking with my stranger's eyes," recounts telling incidents from two of his own journeys; "One Out of Many," a story about an Indian servant and his destabilizing passage from the sidewalks of Bombay to marriage to a repellently fat negress in Washington, DC; "Tell Me Who to Kill," a grim story about two West Indian brothers who emigrate to Britain; and the superb title novella, to which over half the book's pages are devoted and to which I shall refer exclusively in the following discussion.

In the foreground of *In a Free State* are two white characters, the countryside and towns they pass, and the people they encounter during a two-day journey by car through an East African country. The country is unnamed, but its topography and politics suggest an amalgam of Uganda, Kenya, Tanzania, and Buganda. The characters are Bobby and Linda, one a civil servant of the country's government, the other the wife of a man similarly employed. As Naipaul has elsewhere described them, both are "English people who go to Africa in search of some sort of personal fulfilment, and are lost."[71] One may add that they are also losers. In the novel's background are the bloody politics of present-day Africa: the strife between the country's president and the king of one of its constituent tribes, which the president – the country's army dominated by members of his own tribe – has begun to move against as the novel opens. But this struggle is only one aspect of the novel's larger background: the primitive Africa of latent savagery and horror that lies just below the surface décor of independence and progress and is sensed more sharply by Linda than by Bobby, until in the novel's climactic scene the brutal truth is painfully brought home to him.

In technique, *In a Free State* is a striking mixture of descriptive writing and dialogue. There is only a little psychological notation, and the very spareness of the narrative helps sustain the single emotional key (the steadily increasing sense of fear) and the "parabolic drift" (to appropriate an excellent phrase of Tennyson's) which are characteristic features of the novella form (the generic schema of *In a Free State*) and make not inapposite comparison with Conrad's *Heart of Darkness*, a work alluded to by Bobby and Linda. In bringing his work off so successfully Naipaul has used to good advantage two dominant characteristics of his new self-definition as a writer: his sensibility and his being "always on the periphery" with no society of his own to write about. The acutely registered perceptions of the fastidious narrative eye of *In a Free State* help to create the atmosphere of menace which suffuses the story, as in the description of the drain of the sink in Bobby's hotel room: "The brown water gurgled away past the black brass outlet into the dark hole, past the flowing strands of slime that were like the ferns at the bottom of a brook; it sent up a rotting smell." And while looking with a "stranger's eye" may be a disadvantage for certain kinds of fiction, in *In a Free State* a reportorial, travelogue technique is superbly used for the economical evocation of place: the capital city which "owed nothing to African skill ... Africa here was décor"; the bar of the New Shropshire in which Bobby, a homosexual, is spat upon by the Zulu he is trying to seduce; the fat, menacing Africans encountered on the road; the derelict resort town and the derelict colonel, the proprietor of its hotel; the isolated Indian home where Linda finds shelter; and the landscapes, like the valley Bobby and Linda pass through on the second day of their trip:

Again there were fields, terraced hills, huts. In the rain the day before the colours had been soft, green and grey; the paths had meandered into mist; the fields had been empty. Now in the dead sunlight the colours were harsher. Mud was black, vegetation was shining green. The huts that yesterday in the rain had looked such comforting shelters were now seen to be rough structures of grass standing in fenced yards of trampled black mud. Women and children in bright clothes were at work with simple implements in little patches of wet black earth. The women maintained a fixed stoop on straight, firm legs, their broad hips rigid, exaggeratedly humped; so, doubled up, flexible and curving only from waist to head, they hoed and weeded and stepped along their row. All over the valley, among the women and the children, there were little smoking bonfires of damp weedings. It was the immemorial life of the forest. The paths were simple forest paths, leading to nothing else.

The single thematic thread of *In a Free State* is the tension between Bobby's sentimental idealism and theoretical liberalism and the dark reality of the Africa about him and of his inner self. The incidents in the novella and its other characters, chiefly Linda, serve as stepping stones for Bobby's rite of passage, his journey towards a Naipaulian perception of Africa's desolation and the discovery (made at least by the reader; Bobby seems a loser even in his journey towards self-knowledge) that evil and brutality are within him as well as without. In his conversations with the Zulu and with Linda, and in the narrator's comments about him, one sees that Bobby has come to Africa because of the "safe adventure" it offers him, the frisson of sexual contact with black males, the sweet melancholy of exhaustion after long fatiguing drives on open roads, and the gratifying feeling – he cites Somerset Maugham – that "we can always do what we really want to do." "Africa saved my life," he tells Linda: " 'I feel all this' – he indicated the great valley – 'belongs to me.' " Twice he insists "My life is here," and several times he reiterates his optimistic views on how well the Africans are handling their post-colonial responsibilities.

A third of the way through the novel Bobby can still act out in his mind "a make-believe of danger and escape on the empty African road." But as the journey progresses a growing "sense of hazard" and "the sense of nightmare" begin to replace his indulgent fantasies. We notice that over and over again in their conversations it is Bobby who turns out to be wrong and Linda, who loathes Africa, who is either proved right or who we feel sure is right: about the weather, about who is in charge at a roadblock, about the rightness of the colonel's harsh treatment of his black steward, about the murder of the king by the president's men. Not for nothing does Bobby dream of being in a car quarrelling with a woman: "Everything she said was accurate; everything was wounding ... he couldn't explain himself." Linda's rightness is all the more galling to Bobby and all the more striking because she is in her way every bit as unattractive as he. Her reactionary opinions of Africans are as programmatic as Bobby's enlightened ones. No longer young, with a reputation as a "man-eater," she is "hardly good-looking" and her body, its functions and accessories – including a vaginal deodorant – are repeatedly made to seem repugnant, as when she is stung by an insect and Bobby, in an absurd gesture, leans over to kiss the "rising red bump" just below her ribs. But over and over again it is Linda who is correct in her assessment of events and when he can stand it no longer Bobby viciously denounces her, concluding "You're nothing. You're nothing but rotting cunt."

The savagery of Bobby's attack is not simply the result of homosexual revulsion for the female; it is an index of the evil within Bobby, the suppressed anger and violence that lie below the surface décor of his romantic and liberal sentiments and which twice before during their journey had almost erupted into violence: once when his attempts to seduce Carolus, the barboy at the colonel's hotel, had been frustrated; once in the filling station at Esher when the pathetic ineptitude of an attendant had resulted in damage to his car. The attendant's small size, the fineness of his features, and the dead blackness of his skin had identified him as a member of the king's tribe, then being persecuted offstage by the president's army. It was only the intervention of Linda that prevented a small-scale repetition of this violence on the tarmac of the filling station.

The climax of Bobby's journey into the desolation of African reality (as Naipaul perceives it) comes in a white-washed stone building, a police post around which are the bound, naked bodies of members of the king's tribe: "All showed the liver-coloured marks of blood and beatings. One or two looked dead." Here Bobby becomes the object of hatred and violence when he is mocked and gratuitously beaten by the fat soldiers of the president's army. Like this encounter, all of the events in *In a Free State* are very unpleasant indeed; even the one positive image of human possibility in the book is chilling: the terminal fortitude of the exasperated colonel, waiting to be killed by his black employees in his deteriorating hotel in the derelict resort town where Africans recreate the ways of the bush in ruined villas and packs of wild dogs roam the streets at night. But the novel's grimmest and most negating moment is its last, when it becomes clear that Bobby, restored to the safety of the white compound, has learned nothing from his adventures. In the concluding paragraph, Bobby's reflection that he will have to leave Africa is immediately superseded by the more congenial thought that he will have to fire Luke, his houseboy. Luke's periodic drunkenness, alternating with churchgoing and the reading of devotional and educational primers, is an epitome of debased African reality, and his epicene appearance – for he too belongs to the king's tribe – recalls the filling station attendant and the beaten prisoners and suggests that in coldly enjoying his power over his servant, Bobby is enacting what he was kept from doing at Esher, thus perpetuating the very cycle of violence of which he was the victim at the white-washed police post.

The climax and the ending of Naipaul's next novel are even more unpleasant than those of *In a Free State* and the hopeless nature of the situation diagnosed even more insistently underlined. There are three central characters in *Guerrillas*: Jimmy Ahmed, a black power leader of half-negro, half-Chinese descent, who has been deported from England to his native West Indian island, where he has established, presumably as a cover for guerrilla activity, an unsuccessful agricultural commune; Roche, a white liberal who has suffered for his beliefs in South Africa, written a highly regarded book about his experiences there, and come to the island to do what he can for the forces of progress; and Jane, an Englishwoman who is living with Roche but becomes involved with Jimmy. Naipaul is as pitiless concerning these characters and their interrelationships as he is tireless in his notation of the sweat, dirt, heat, and ugliness that surround them. All are pathetically limited and inauthentic; each misunderstands and misinterprets the others and wrongly thinks he or she figures largely in the others' thoughts and fantasies. All mime gestures appropriate to their received ideas of either revolution, humanitarian concern, or romance, but do so with an awkwardness that ill conceals their inadequacies and essential hollowness. All are emotionally, spiritually, and intellectually impoverished, burnt-out cases like the drought-stricken, sun-scorched landscapes and like the island itself, which seems to Jane (nothing in the novel gainsays her view) "a place at the end of the world, a place that had exhausted its possibilities." A fourth character tells Jane and Roche that they will never change, that the life they have led is the life they will lead: "The setting may change, but no one will make a fresh start or do anything new." The analysis is as true of Jimmy as it is of the two other dead souls. In *A House for Mr Biswas* and *The Mimic Men*, similar realizations by the central characters concerning the temporal determinants of their lives were signs of their positively coming to terms with their situations. But in *Guerrillas* – this is an index of the novel's pessimism and its shrunken sense of human possibility – the same insight is grimly deterministic and serves only to emphasize the hopelessness of the central characters' lives.

In the novel's opening scene, Roche and Jane drive out to Thrushcross Grange, Jimmy's absurdly named commune. The tropical setting, the exact description of the landscape, and their disagreement during the drive bring to mind the African journey of Bobby and Linda. Indeed, the two sets of characters have so many features in common that the reader occasionally experiences a sense of *déjà vu*. Roche is an older, heterosexual Bobby, whose conventional liberal attitudes are shown to be as inadequate as Bobby's similar ones to the political and social realities of the countries in which they are working, though Roche, being older, is less self-deceived concerning his ineffectuality. Jane and Linda resemble each other even more. Both are promiscuous, insincere, utterly without commitment, less liberal than the men they are associated with, and usually more accurate in their assessment of events. Linda's vaginal deodorant becomes Jane's tampon, her swift insertion of which is smartly described. Linda is called "rotting cunt" in her story; Jane "rotten meat" and "dirty cunt" in hers, and in each case the physical detail, like the repeated emphasis on the overtanned, coarsened skin between Jane's breasts, suggests authorial agreement.

While the ingredients of the two novels are similar, their schemata are different. *In a Free State* has the spareness, intensity, and clarity of thematic outline characteristic of the novella form. *Guerrillas*, on the other hand, has affinities with those novels of Graham Greene in which *déraciné* white characters are placed in violent Third World settings. There are telling similarities between Greene and Naipaul which have been insufficiently remarked by the latter's commentators: the exact understated prose with its dispassionate registration of the distasteful, sordid, and ugly; self-exile and its attendant peregrinations; the preoccupation with failure – both individual failure and the failed cultures of the decaying parts of the world both writers compulsively seek out. In *Guerrillas*, generic similarities to novels like *The Quiet American*, *The Comedians*, and *The Honorary Consul* underscore temperamental affinities.

Recognition of differences in schemata facilitates an understanding of why *Guerrillas*, for all the fine things in it, is a less successful fiction than *In a Free State*. In the first place, Naipaul has unsuccessfully attempted to get into his novel the parabolic drift and the cumulative force of his novella. The novel's title and its epigraph indicate the intended larger dimension.

But this is only notionally realized because guerrilla activity, while often talked about by non-participants, is insufficiently concretized. "Guerrilla" remains an abstraction unrooted in the realistic surface of the novel. Similarly, while Naipaul tries very hard to have the landscapes of *Guerrillas* convey the heightened intensity of the landscapes of *In a Free State*, he is unable to do so successfully because the greater length of the novel form tends to dissipate effects that can be concentrated in a shorter form. While failing to adapt characteristic features of the novella form, Naipaul has at the same time failed to utilize effectively the elbow room that the longer form of *Guerrillas* affords. Extended inside views of all three central characters are offered, but only Jimmy's characterization is thereby enhanced. Despite copious psychological notation and background information, Roche is no more complexly realized than Bobby, and rather less well focused. And the characterization of Jane, the most compelling and original figure in the novel, is actually weakened by the inside views and the background information. It is Jane's externals, her speech, gestures, and actions, and what they are made to suggest about her inner being, that make her so memorable and disturbing.

At the same time, while a great many of the novel's pages are given over to talk about politics, violence, and revolutionary activities, little is done to dramatize them. Even Jimmy, a political force and a committed revolutionary, is characterized almost entirely in sexual terms, and his bold attempt to bend a mob to his political will – a key turning point in the novel – takes place off stage and is summarized in a few sentences. In short, Naipaul has chosen a genre requiring a strong story line, a certain amount of action and a sense of political and cultural place to explore an essentially static, even claustrophobic situation – the relations between Jimmy, Roche, and Jane. One reviewer of *Guerrillas* suggested that Naipaul was too interested in the historical mood and not enough in the human motive; but the opposite is surely the case. A great deal of time is spent in the creation of a mood appropriate to the psychological exploration of the central characters, but only in a few places – Bryant's night at the films, Roche's visit to Stephens's mother – is much attention paid to the creation of an historical mood.

Finally, one feels that another reason for the novel's imperfect success has to do with the very intensity of Naipaul's revulsed sensibility. I noted earlier how his intellectual assessment of the de Freitas affair was different from and more constructive than that of his sensibility. And while one can hardly complain that *Guerrillas* is weakened by an absence of remedial or constructive elements – their absence was after all essential to the impact of *In a Free State* – one may say that in *Guerrillas* Naipaul's negating sensibility is so intense as to result in "a contraction of the artistic vision" analogous to that which he had a decade before condemned in clinical and documentary works that, "like the obscene photograph," made "no statement beyond that of bodily pain and degradation."[72] Certainly it is significant that in his next novel Naipaul endows his first person narrator with a less morbid and less acute sensibility than that of the third person narrator of *Guerrillas* (though the difference is one of degree, not of kind) and attempts to mitigate his withering vision of Third World reality by the inclusion of a sympathetic central character who embodies at least some sense of human possibility.

A year after its publication Naipaul was led to exclaim: "I can't face any more books like *Guerrillas* ... I would like to write something more celebratory, a book of reconciliation and delight. I suppose in a very simple way I mean something with a happy ending."[73] It is by no means self-evident that *A Bend in the River* is a fulfilment of Naipaul's wish, even though its murders do occur offstage and its female lead is neither buggered nor hacked to death in her final appearance: she merely has her genitals repeatedly spat upon. What is apparent is that the novel's public subject is of at least equal weight with the private subject and that with its larger cast of characters and much more extended time scale it is more of a "social inquiry" informed by historical vision than were *Guerrillas* or *In a Free State*. It also contains a good many more ideas than the two preceding novels, though there is a price to be paid for their inclusion. Since the novel's narrator is not given the penetrating intelligence and taste for conceptualization of, say, Ralph Singh, Naipaul is forced to have a number of things said by means of long speeches by other characters, which in every case seem flat and contrived.

The public subject of *A Bend in the River* is Zaire (formerly the Belgian Congo), especially the period since Mobutu came to power. The setting is the town of Kisangani (formerly Stanleyville), a port on the Congo (now the Zaire) river a thousand miles upriver from the west coast of Africa. The country, its president, the town, and the river are all unnamed, but their originals will be clear to anyone who has read Naipaul's 1975 article, "A New King for the Congo." The town is explicitly said to be a smaller version of the country's downriver capital city, and it is clear that Naipaul also considers the town a synecdoche for Zaire as a whole, for all of central Africa and (as at the end of Conrad's *Heart of Darkness*) even for London, epitome of the civilized world.

The time scale is roughly a decade, from the mid-1960s when Salim, the narrator and central character, comes to the town to take over the store he has bought sight unseen, to the mid-1970s when he is fortunate enough to get out of jail and be able to leave the town for good. Early in the novel the town is shown coming back to life after the internecine wars of independence. Zabeth, half *marchande*, half magician, comes from her village in the bush to trade at Salim's store and eventually brings her son Ferdinand to live in the town and attend its *lycée*, a colonial leftover run by Father Huismans, a Belgian priest. There is a second rebellion, but it is an atavistic and hopeless affair: "The rage of the rebels was like a rage against metal, machinery, wires, everything that was not of the forest and Africa." Control by a central authority in the capital begins to be felt for the first time; business revives and eventually booms (owing to the area's mineral wealth) and signs of westernization – chief among them the Bigburger franchise – begin to appear. So do the grandiose buildings of the Domain, in the unreal atmosphere of which the "new Africa" is to be created. The Domain, a vast state enterprise including a polytechnical college, a model farm, and residences for intellectuals, is the brain-child of the country's president (the "Big Man"), whose vision of a new African consciousness and authenticity is shown to be rooted in demagogy and *Realpolitik* and eventually leads to the eruption of a fresh cycle of violence. The revolution becomes *"un pé pourrie*. A little rotten,"* as Salim is told by Citizen Théotime, the drunken incompetent who is given Salim's business when it is nationalized and who must immediately employ Salim to run it.

"*Un pé pourrie*" is to put it mildly, however, for over and over again one is made aware that all of the changes in the town are of the *plus ça change* variety – like the endemic harassment and extortion, and the rampant peculation of officials. Add slaves to the illicit traffic of army officers in ivory and gold and, says Salim, "it would have been like being back in oldest Africa. And these men would have dealt in slaves, if there was still a market." Salim repeatedly calls attention to the "old Africa" always visible beneath the surface décor of the new: the acres of shacks with mounds of garbage near the glassy modern buildings of the Domain; "the squatters cooking fires on the pavements in the centre of town"; the elaborate equipment of the capital's modern airport – reminiscent of those of London or Brussels until one notices that the baggage being checked is like "the cargo of a market jitney"; the land in daylight, when "you could believe in the vision of a future," as opposed to the land at night, "if you were on the river" (where Salim will be in the novel's ghastly concluding scene): then "you felt the land taking you back to what was there a hundred years ago, to what had been there always."

At the end of *A Bend in the River* Salim's disillusioning observations are underlined by Ferdinand, a representative figure whose birth and early years in the bush, schooling at the *lycée*, indoctrination at the Domain, and membership in the president's regime recapitulate the brief history of his nation: "We're all going to hell, and every man knows this in his bones. We're being killed. Nothing has any meaning. That is why everyone is so frantic. Everyone wants to make his money and run away. But where?" In the novel's last scene, this rhetorical flourish is given powerful symbolic expression. At several places in the novel, Salim's narrative eye had lingered on tangled clumps of water hyacinths, the tall, pale flowers, white in the moonlight, which began to appear in the upper Congo river during the mid-1950s and since then have spread downriver, even reaching the capital, "as if rain and river were tearing away bush from the heart of the continent and floating it down to the ocean, incalculable miles away." Although its rubbery vines and leaves clog up waterways, blocking the channels to villages and growing faster than villagers can destroy them, and although the mutilated body of Father Huismans, "his head cut off and spiked," had been found in its tangles, Salim had felt that the water hyacinths simply reflected the moods of their observers. At the beginning of his infatuation with Yvette, bathed in moonlight and the memory of Joan Baez's songs, they had even spoken to him of romance. But in the closing paragraph of *A Bend in the River* it is of the African reality of brutality and desolation that the hyacinths speak as, illuminated by a searchlight and to the crackle of gunfire, a drifting barge packed with Africans floats through the treacherous flowers while thousands of moths and flying insects swarm in the air.

The concluding tableau of *A Bend in the River* is as grimly negative as those of *In a Free State* and *Guerrillas*. How, then, can it be said that the novel contains a constructive alternative? The answer is intimated in a comment of Marlow's near the end of *Heart of Darkness*, Conrad's famous tale of the Congo: "The most you can hope for from [life] is some knowledge of yourself." The very first sentence of *A Bend in the River* indicates Salim's commitment to self-understanding at the same time as it lays down, so to speak, the ground rules for our judgment of his story: "The world is what it is; men who are nothing, who allow themselves to become nothing, have no place in it." Salim comes from a close-knit Muslim trading family on the east African coast, part of a long settled community of traditional values, customs, and pieties which is in the process of being broken up by the rising tide of African nationalism. Salim has turned his back on this world and early in the novel speaks of his sense of pessimism, insecurity, passivity, and placelessness. As he later puts it, he is "floating and lost." It is similarly early on that he brushes against that fundamental Naipaulian tenet: "I wondered about the nature of my aspirations, the very supports of my existence; and I began to feel that any life I might have anywhere ... would only be a version of the life I lived now."

As the novel progresses, three alternatives to Salim's mingled acedia and anxiety present themselves. All prove specious. His love affair with Yvette seems to offer the possibility of renovation through "the true life of the senses"; the sexual act seems full of wonder, and simultaneously brings both awareness of "my immense previous deprivation" and its rapturous repair. But Yvette proves to be as promiscuous, mendacious, and restless ("My life is still fluid. I must do something") as Linda or Jane, and Salim's anointing of her genitals with, so to speak, the chrism of the Naipaulian sexual sensibility confirms the impossibility of fulfilment through the flesh. The opposite temptation is another alternative: evaporation of the problems of authenticity and living in the world through the Eastern vision of life and pain as illusion. But this, Salim comes to realize, is part of a way of feeling that "comforted only to weaken and destroy." The third alternative is represented by Salim's boyhood friend Indar, whose philosophy of life is a cross between Dr Tamkin's in Saul Bellow's *Seize the Day* and Rinehart's in Ellison's *Invisible Man*. Indar says he has learned to exist positively in the here and now of the present, to extirpate the sense of loss and homesickness and of longing for the "good place" through trampling on the past: for "the past can only cause pain." One of Indar's principal aids to living in the present is the airplane, "a wonderful thing [that] is faster than the heart. You arrive quickly you leave quickly. You don't grieve too much." Indar's undoing begins when he comes to leave the Domain, where he has been helping to spin the fantasies of the new Africa. The plane servicing the town has been requisitioned by the Big Man and Indar has to endure the repugnant reality of African life on a days' long steamer trip downriver (his embarkation is the novel's most vividly realized scene). He reaches the bottom of the barrel offstage in London where, spirit broken, "he does the lowest kind of job. He knows he is equipped for better things, but he doesn't want to do them."

In contrast to these false alternatives is the intermittently glimpsed but discernible change that Salim undergoes. He comes to have a more informed and involved awareness of the nature of the African society of which he is a part. He realizes that Mahesh, corrupted by the *égoïsme à deux* of his life with Shoba, and other of the town's expatriate businessmen have "cut themselves off [and] begun to rot" and recognizes that he must act if he is not to become like them, or like Metty, a family retainer who comes to lose all contact with the traditional values of his Muslim past. Salim's action is to go to London to see Nazruddin – the most attractive character in the novel, who knows how to survive, how to function positively in alien societies, and how not to take himself too seriously – and to become engaged to Nazruddin's daughter to whom long ago on the coast he had given his "unspoken commitment" to wed. For while Salim has come to see that "one had to live in the world as it existed," part of the world that exists for him is a sense of cultural traditions, responsibilities, and pieties – so different from the bogus antidotes of sexuality, mystical visions, or living in the present. In what remains within him of his past Salim finds some strength and direction.

It is not, however, as easy as the above redaction suggests to follow the thread of Salim's development, for especially near the end of the novel it almost seems as if Naipaul is embarrassed by the positive implications of his character's evolution. He has Salim assert – it is not shown – that he became engaged to Kareisha "in a state of indifference and irresponsibility" and he even interpolates a session with a fat prostitute during an in-transit stopover in a foreign city, a gratuitous and ineffective attempt to transfer to the end of *A Bend in the River* something of the deconstructive energy of the end of *The Mimic Men*. What might account for Naipaul's attempt to undercut the constructive implications of Salim's development? Perhaps he has become dishabituated to endings containing positive notes; or perhaps the exacting novelist was unhappy with the fact that his work contained a discontinuity between its private and public worlds. For whatever hopeful possibilities are suggested by the conclusion of Salim's personal history, he has after all put the dark continent behind him for good, and there is absolutely no suggestion of an analogously hopeful possibility for Africa (as Naipaul bluntly put it in 1979: "Africa has no future").[74] Salim's renewal can do nothing to stem the growth of the choking blotches of water hyacinths.

VI

The size and scope of Naipaul's canon, and the scale of his achievement as a novelist, can make one forget that he is, actuarially speaking, still only in mid-career. While it would be foolish to attempt predictions concerning the next phase of his development, it is very difficult to imagine that a "book of reconciliation and delight" is in the cards, or a return to the "comprehensive humanity" of *A House for Mr Biswas*. It would be equally misleading to use terms like human sympathy or pessimism to chart Naipaul's development or to assess his achievement. Commentators who are tempted to do so should recall Thomas Hardy's comment on his critics: "That these impressions have been condemned as 'pessimistic' – as if that were a very wicked adjective – shows a curious muddle-headedness. It must be obvious that there is a higher characteristic of philosophy than pessimism, or than meliorism, or even than the optimism of these critics – which is truth."[75] One is nevertheless tempted to hope that Naipaul's future work will continue to be informed by a sense of human possibility and of the constructive power of the creative activity of the mind. Coming from a writer of such severe clear-sightedness and discriminating sensibility such a recognition would be inspiriting. For as we have seen, Naipaul makes no appeal to simplifying abstractions and has no ideology, belief, or partisan viewpoint from which to derive support. Nor has his sense of the excruciations of contemporary life made him turn from social inquiry to futuristic visions or "inner space" explorations, as a similar sense has made Doris Lessing. Nor does he fantasticate or attempt to escape into aesthetics as did the *déraciné* Nabokov. Nor does he luxuriate in the creative conundrums of the *crise de roman*. To sustain himself and support himself in his work Naipaul has nothing but his intelligence and sensibility, his passion for clear-sightedness, and his sense of *dharma*. One may say of him what he said of Jean Rhys: "what a stoic thing [he] makes the act of writing appear."[76]

Conclusion

Contemporary novelists are not alone in having become increasingly self-conscious and increasingly aware of the problematic nature of their enterprise. Literary critics have similarly become more reflexive about the nature of their work and more doubtful about its value. And just as there are those who speak of the novel's exhaustion as an art form, so there are those who speak of the exhaustion of the tradition of humane, constructive, and evaluative critical discourse. Few would deny that this new critical self-consciousness is salutary or that there is much that is tonic about the flowering in English studies of structuralist and deconstructive criticism, and the varieties of reader-response criticism. Of particular interest is the increased emphasis given to the writer-reader relationship; and it is also inspiriting to find these new methods putting to rout the idealizings and moralizings, and the mechanical demonstrations of unity that are still the meat and drink of many academic critics.

But the new critical methods are not an unmixed blessing. One ominous development is that the critic has tended to replace the creative artist as the centre of attention. While certain kinds of deconstructive criticism reduce the man of creative imagination to a mere *bricoleur* (a handyman who assembles things out of odds and ends) the status of the critic is vastly inflated and his own intelligence, creativity, and excruciations hold centre-stage. As Gerald Graff has wittily remarked: "The day may not be far off when no first-rate literary critic will be able to purchase health insurance."[1] This inflation cannot but be troubling to those who regard the function of literary criticism as analogous to Newman's conception of the university as the great ordinary means to a great but ordinary end. While much of the new critical discourse becomes more and more esoteric and self-regarding, even solipsistic, the great ordinary work of literary criticism languishes: the mediation between reader and creative artist through the provision of relevant context, the witness of disinterested care and catholic sensibility, and the making of rigorously sympathetic qualitative discriminations. While the reader of a literary text, often forgotten in the older criticism, has become all-important, the audience for whom the critic writes is sometimes forgotten. One small example of this trend is found in the report of one appraiser of the manuscript version of this book, who complained of the absence of theorizing and found particularly bothersome my "programmatic evenhandedness," a quality I regard as a hard-won critical virtue, not a mechanical vice.

A more serious complaint is that much of this body of criticism seems essentially negative. Increasingly complex experiments are performed on fictional texts, but these operations tend to disregard the nature and undermine the health of the patient, and to render the novel permanently dependent on the latest critical technology. This, too, cannot but deeply trouble those who believe in the essential health and wholesomeness of fiction, who can sense what D.H. Lawrence meant when he called the novel "the one bright book of life," and who understand George Eliot's insistence that the greatest benefit we owe to the artist is the extension of our sympathies. As we have seen, the four subjects of my book share a belief in the essential health and fundamental importance of the novel form. Their work bears witness to the fact that even in the time of the *crise de roman* not all novelists need follow the examples of Nabokov, Beckett, Pynchon, Barth, et al. Their work shows that there is a place in serious contemporary fiction for a self-aware realism that combines in constructive and enriching ways the inevitable self-consciousness of the present day with the representational and communicative strengths of the traditional novel.

Notes

INTRODUCTION

1 Quoted in Mel Gussow, "Writer without Roots," *New York Times Magazine* (26 December 1976), p. 19
2 "Conrad's Darkness," *The Return of Eva Perón, with The Killings in Trinidad* (New York: Knopf 1980), p. 227
3 Paul Michael Gallagher, interview with Brian Moore, *Hibernia* (10 October 1969), p. 18
4 Donald Cameron, "Brian Moore: The Tragic Vein of the Ordinary," *Conversations with Canadian Novelists: Part II* (Toronto: Macmillan 1973), p. 75
5 "The Documentary Heresy," *Twentieth Century*, 173 (1964), p. 108
6 "The Dilemma of the Contemporary Novelist," in John Colmer, ed., *Approaches to the Novel* (Edinburgh: Oliver & Boyd 1967), pp. 115-22
7 "Is the Novel Dead?" *Books* (Autumn 1970), pp. 2-5
8 *The Situation of the Novel* (Harmondsworth: Penguin Books 1972), p. 11
9 "The Novelist V.S. Naipaul Talks about His Work to Ronald Bryden," *Listener* (22 March 1973), p. 368
10 "Brian Moore" in George Garrett, ed., *The Writer's Voice: Conversations with Contemporary Writers* (New York: Morrow 1973), p. 63
11 Foreword to *Poems* (New York: Ecco Press 1973), p. vii
12 "The Dilemma of the Contemporary Novelist," p. 125
13 "Writing Is Magic," interview with Francis Wyndham, (London) *Sunday Times* (10 November 1968), p. 57

CHAPTER ONE: ANGUS WILSON: DIVERSITY, DEPTH, AND OBSESSIVE ENERGY

Quotations from Angus Wilson's novels are from the following editions: *Hemlock and After* (London: Secker & Warburg 1952); *Anglo-Saxon Attitudes* (London: Secker & Warburg 1956); *The Middle Age of Mrs Eliot* (London: Secker & Warburg 1958); *The Old Men at the Zoo* (London: Secker & Warburg 1961); *Late Call* (London: Secker & Warburg 1964); *No Laughing Matter* (London: Secker & Warburg 1967); *As If by Magic* (London: Secker & Warburg 1973); *Setting the World on Fire* (London: Secker & Warburg 1980).

1 Quoted in Frank Kermode, "The House of Fiction: Interviews with Seven Novelists," in Malcolm Bradbury, ed. *The Novel Today: Contemporary Writers on Modern Fiction* (Manchester: Manchester University Press 1977), p. 122
2 For excellent summaries of these changes see Bradbury's introduction to

The Novel Today and his and David Palmer's preface to Bradbury and Palmer, eds, *The Contemporary English Novel*, Stratford-upon-Avon Studies 18 (New York: Holmes & Meier 1979).

3 "The Revolution in British Reading," *American Mercury* (December 1951), p. 52

4 Edmund Wilson, "Emergence of Angus Wilson," *The Bit between My Teeth: A Literary Chronicle of 1950–1960* (New York: Farrar, Straus 1965), p. 270; V.S. Naipaul, "Jasmine," *The Overcrowded Barracoon and Other Articles* (London: André Deutsch 1972), pp. 27-8

5 "A Clean Sweep" (review of *Hemlock and After*), *The Month* (October 1952), p. 239

6 For this passage I have cited the first American edition of *Hemlock and After* (New York: Viking 1952). The first British edition reads "elephant figure of Mabel Lucie Attwell chubbiness … "

7 *Angus Wilson: "Hemlock and After," A Study in Ambiguity* (Bern: Francke Verlag 1971), p. 56

8 Frederick P.W. McDowell, "An Interview with Angus Wilson," *Iowa Review*, 3 (1972), p. 82; Waugh, "A Clean Sweep," p. 238

9 "The Future of the English Novel," *Listener* (29 April 1954), p. 746; "Diversity and Depth," *TLS* (15 August 1958), p. viii; "Angus Wilson," in Malcolm Cowley, ed., *Writers at Work: The Paris Review Interviews* (New York: Viking 1959), pp. 253-66

10 *Paris Review* interview, pp. 263, 257, 258, 264

11 *The Wild Garden or Speaking of Writing* (London: Secker & Warburg 1963), p. 131

12 *The World of Charles Dickens* (London: Secker & Warburg 1970), pp. 241-2

13 K.W. Gransden, *Angus Wilson*, Writers and Their Work, No. 208 (London: Longmans, Green 1969), p. 21

14 "The Novelist and the Narrator," *English Studies Today*, second series, G.A. Bonnard, ed. (Bern: Francke Verlag 1961), p. 48

15 Introduction to Charles Dickens, *Little Dorrit* (Harmondsworth: Penguin Books 1967), p. 25

16 "The Novelist and the Narrator," p. 49

17 "The Significance of Jung," *TLS* (25 July 1975), p. 830

18 "Mr Wilson's People," *Puzzles and Epiphanies: Essays and Reviews 1958–1961* (London: Routledge & Kegan Paul 1962), p. 196

19 See my "The Later Doris Lessing," *Room of One's Own*, 4 (1979), pp. 46-53.

20 *The Wild Garden*, p. 138

21 *The Wild Garden*, p. 31

22 *The Wild Garden*, pp. 149-50

23 *The Wild Garden*, p. 33

24 "The Novelist and the Narrator," p. 44

25 "Evil in the English Novel" has been published twice, first in four instalments in the *Listener* (27 December 1962; 3 January 1963; 10 January 1963;
17 January 1963), subsequently in the *Kenyon Review* 29 (March 1967),
pp. 167-94. The Front Matter in this number of the *Kenyon Review* states
that "Evil in the English Novel" appears in its pages in "a substantially different form" from the version in the *Listener*. This is incorrect: the differences are almost entirely stylistic. Because the later version does mention *No
Laughing Matter* (then unpublished and called "Laughing Mirrors") I have
preferred to cite it.

26 "Evil in the English Novel," pp. 167, 192

27 "Evil in the English Novel," pp. 194, 190

28 *The Novels and Tales of Henry James*, New York Edition (New York: Scrib-
ner's 1908), 12, xxi

29 "The House of Fiction: Interviews with Seven Novelists," p. 122

30 Quoted in Rubin Rabinovitz, *The Reaction against Experiment in the English
Novel 1950-1960* (New York: Columbia University Press 1967), pp. 66-7n

31 Letter to *Spectator* (13 October 1961), p. 501

32 *The Novel Now* (London: Faber & Faber 1967), p. 104

33 "The Novelist and the Narrator," p. 45

34 "The Dilemma of the Contemporary Novelist," pp. 124-5

35 *Iowa Review* interview, pp. 81, 101

36 *Paris Review* interview, pp. 257, 259

37 Foreword to *Poems*, p. vii

38 *The Wild Garden*, p. 16

39 "Political Metaphors: 1. The Politics of the Family," *Listener* (10 January
1974), pp. 41-2

40 *High Windows* (London: Faber & Faber 1974), p. 30

41 See Herman Servotte, "A Note on the Formal Characteristics of Angus
Wilson's *No Laughing Matter*," *English Studies*, 50 (1969), pp. 58-64; Malcolm
Bradbury's "The Fiction of Pastiche: The Comic Mode of Angus Wilson,"
in his *Possibilities: Essays on the State of the Novel* (London: Oxford University
Press 1973), pp. 211-30; and Robert Burden, "The Novel Interrogates
Itself: Parody and Self-Consciousness in Contemporary English Fiction," in
Bradbury and Palmer, eds, *The Contemporary English Novel*, pp. 133-55.

42 This section is untitled in the English edition of the novel; the title does appear
in the American edition (New York: Viking 1967).

43 Bradbury, "The Fiction of Pastiche," p. 213

44 Burden, "The Novel Interrogates Itself," p. 146

45 I have borrowed the terminology of Robert Alter in his *Partial Magic: The Novel as a Self-Conscious Genre* (Berkeley: University of California Press 1975), pp. xi, ix

46 "Evil in the English Novel," p. 193

47 Shigehisa Narita, "A Reformer, Not a Revolutionary: Angus Wilson Talks on Novels and Novelists," *Eigo Sei Nen (The Rising Generation)* (Tokyo), 115 (1969), p. 758

48 "Letter to *The Amherst Student*," in Hyde Cox and Edward Connery Lathem, eds, *Selected Prose of Robert Frost* (New York: Collier Books 1968), p. 107

49 "Passengers to India" (review of Gita Mehta's *Karma Cola*), *Observer* (2 March 1980), p. 38

50 BBC 2 interview, broadcast 2 March 1976

51 Jonathan Raban, "Global Charades," *Encounter* (July 1973), p. 79; Angus Wilson, "*As If by Magic*: Angus Wilson on His Own Novel," *Dutch Quarterly Review*, 6 (1976), p. 266

52 "*As If by Magic*: Angus Wilson on His Own Novel," p. 265

53 Martin Price, "The Stuff of Fiction: Some Recent Novels," *Yale Review*, 63 (1974), p. 565

CHAPTER TWO: BRIAN MOORE'S GRAMMARS OF THE EMOTIONS

Quotations from Brian Moore's novels are from the following editions: *Judith Hearne* (London: André Deutsch 1955); *The Feast of Lupercal* (Boston: Little, Brown 1957); *The Luck of Ginger Coffey* (Boston: Little, Brown 1960); *An Answer from Limbo* (Boston: Little, Brown 1962); *The Emperor of Ice-Cream* (New York: Viking 1965); *I Am Mary Dunne* (New York: Viking 1968); *Fergus* (New York: Holt, Rinehart 1970); *Catholics* (New York: Holt, Rinehart 1972); *The Great Victorian Collection* (New York: Farrar, Straus 1975); *The Doctor's Wife* (New York: Farrar, Straus 1976); *The Mangan Inheritance* (New York: Farrar, Straus 1979); *The Temptation of Eileen Hughes* (New York: Farrar, Straus 1981).

1 "The Writer as Exile," *Canadian Journal of Irish Studies*, 2 (1976), p. 6

2 Philip French, review of *I Am Mary Dunne*, *New Statesman* (25 October 1968), p. 550

3 Unsigned review of *Fergus*, *TLS* (9 April 1971), p. 413

4 "The Simple Excellence of Brian Moore," *New Statesman* (18 February 1966), p. 227

5 Quoted on the dust-jacket of the American edition of *The Luck of Ginger Coffey*

6 Review of *The Luck of Ginger Coffey*, *New York Times Book Review* (4 September 1960), p. 16

7 "Brian Moore and the Fallacy of Realism," *Honest Ulsterman* (March–April 1970), pp. 11, 13

8 Review of Robertson Davies's *The Manticore, Washington Post Book World* (26 November 1972), p. 8

9 Richard B. Sale, "An Interview in London with Brian Moore," *Studies in the Novel* 1 (1969), p. 73

10 Gallagher, p. 18

11 Sale, pp. 71-2

12 Hallvard Dahlie, "Brian Moore: An Interview," *Tamarack Review*, 46 (1968), p. 14

13 Sale, p. 77. In a letter to me Brian Moore has commented on the suggestion that "there is something willed about my limiting assessment of Joyce's greatness. I realise this is perfectly justified given my comments on Joyce. But believe me it was the experimental and fantastic Joyce who so excited me long ago when I first read *Ulysses* and it was *Ulysses* and not *Dubliners* (not even the *Portrait*) which was my main influence when I wrote *Judith Hearne*. I think what happened is that I realised that the experimental Joyce was inimitable (and all the Barthian balderdash with which we have been visited in the past forty years doesn't seem to have proved me wrong) but that the Joyce who said his work was a celebration of the commonplace could continue to teach me a great deal."

14 "Too Much Hocus in the Pocus," review of *The Magus, New York Herald Tribune Book Week* (9 January 1966), pp. 4, 12

15 Dahlie, p. 22

16 Sale, p. 77

17 Gallagher, p. 18

18 Cameron, p. 75

19 Cameron, p. 66

20 Robert Fulford, interview with Brian Moore, *Tamarack Review*, 23 (1962), p. 15

21 "The Writer as Exile," pp. 8, 10

22 Quoted in Hugh Hebert, "Metaphor Concern," *Guardian* (13 October 1975), p. 8

23 Gallagher, p. 18

24 Quoted in Rochelle Girson, "Asphalt Is Bitter Soil," *Saturday Review* (13 October 1962), p. 20

25 "Reference Back" and "Dockery and Son," *The Whitsun Weddings* (London: Faber & Faber 1964), pp. 40, 38

26 Dahlie, p. 18

27 John Wilson Foster, *Forces and Themes in Ulster Fiction* (Totowa, New Jersey: Rowman & Littlefield 1974), p. 151

28 "Eveline," *Dubliners* (New York: Viking Compass Books, nd), p. 40

29 "Deception," *The Less Deceived* (London: Marvell Press 1973), p. 37

30 Dahlie, pp. 16-17

31 Dahlie, p. 18

32 Dahlie, p. 17

33 Sale, p. 74. See Dahlie, p. 17.

34 Fulford, p. 13

35 Fulford, p. 17

36 Fulford, p. 14

37 Sale, p. 73

38 Cameron, p. 83

39 Fulford, p. 18

40 Cameron, p. 81

41 The essential sameness of the Belfast of the post-1970 troubles and the city he lived in from his birth in 1921 until his early twenties is the subject of Moore's finest piece of non-fictional prose, "Now and Then" (*Threshold* [Belfast], 23 [1970]); also published in the *Atlantic* (September 1970) under the title "Bloody Ulster: An Irishman's Lament." In a review of Malcolm Cowley's *Exile's Return* ("The Crazy Boatloads," *Spectator* [29 September 1961], p. 430) Moore described the usual reaction of the returning expatriate to be "the terrifying realisation that the country of their boyhood is lost for ever." But in "Now and Then," when a 1970 visit to Belfast triggers childhood memories, the juxtaposition of past and present leads to the more terrifying realization that in the country of Moore's boyhood nothing has changed: "the same old, awful mess."

42 Hubert de Santana, "The Calligraphy of Pain," *Maclean's* (17 September 1979), p. 44

43 Dahlie, p. 23

44 "The Writer as Exile," p. 12

45 *Forces and Themes in Ulster Fiction*, p. 179

46 "The Albatross of Self," review of *Hear Us O Lord from Heaven Thy Dwelling Place, Spectator* (4 May 1962), p. 589

47 Gallagher, p. 18

48 "Brian Moore Talks about *I Am Mary Dunne*," *Literary Guild Magazine* (September 1968), p. 5

49 *Brian Moore* (Lewisberg: Bucknell University Press, 1974), p. 71

50 Dahlie, p. 20

51 This excerpt is Salingeresque: "My brother Rory, who was ten years older than I, heroed out when his parachute failed Somewhere Over Germany, back in 1945. My elder sister Sheila ran off to Australia with a feckless veterinarian and has been breeding like a rabbit in the outback ever since. My younger

sister Moira is wedded to Christ and poverty in a Manchester convent and my
father, Dr Charles Grattan Tierney, died four years ago after an illness which
destroyed his life's savings as surely as night unraveled Penelope's loom."
The following passage recalls Mailer: "For, all my life I have been a seeker:
no Hound of Destiny has pursued me down the nights and down the days. I
am the hunter, I seek the hound, yet, until today, no tracks have appeared
to show that he has indisputably passed my way, and the rumors of his presence which I have followed over the years have often seemed garbled, the
road empty, the spoor faked." And this last reads like an entry in the diary of
Bellow's Joseph: "I am obsessed by fears that I am insensitive to certain
nuances of life in New York. I was furious that it had not occurred to me that
Eddy's was what he said it was. Thinking of Gallery, whose favorite spot it
is, I was sure that Max was right. But the other side of me – a wiser, more
bitter self – was outraged at my own shallowness in being swayed by these
fraudulent equations of in and out, hip and square."

52 See DeWitt Henry's acute observation in his "The Novels of Brian Moore:
A Retrospective" (*Ploughshares*, 2 [1972], p. 18): "unlike Joyce's *Portrait*,
where the developing sensibility in the prose is proof itself of talent and calling
worth the human cost, as Moore separates Brendan's point of view from
that of the other characters, and contrasts its first person narration (Brendan's
'writing') to the third person 'inside' narration in which the rest of the book
is told, he contrasts Brendan's sensibility to his own[;] the resulting irony
lends credence to Brendan's worst self-doubts, for as narrator Brendan is fatuous and self-indulgent, his style self-consciously literary, and though it does
sober up and toughen towards the conclusion, still it retains this basic note of
affectation."

53 Cameron, p. 68

54 Philip French, "Dream Machinery," review of *The Great Victorian Collection*,
TLS (17 October 1975), p. 1225

55 Compare Philip Roth's comments (quoted in James Atlas, "A Visit with
Philip Roth," *New York Times Book Review* [2 September 1979],
pp. 12-13): "My obsession for the last seven or eight years has been the uses
to which literature is put in this country. The writer in his isolation publishes a
book, the book goes out into the world, and the strangest things begin to
happen. Some of them are wounding. Some of them are interesting. Some of
them are bizarre. Some of them are remarkable and deeply satisfying. You
can never predict its fate. What I write has a particular purpose and use
for me, but I've learned what it means to me isn't what it means to others.

When you publish a book, it's the world's book. The world edits it."
56 Gallagher, p. 18
57 "Too Much Hocus in the Pocus," p. 4

CHAPTER THREE: JOHN FOWLES'S VARIATIONS

Quotations from Fowles's novels and from *The Ebony Tower* are from the following editions: *The Magus: A Revised Version* (Boston: Little, Brown 1977); *The Collector* (London: Jonathan Cape 1963); *The French Lieutenant's Woman* (Boston: Little, Brown 1969); *The Ebony Tower* (Boston: Little, Brown 1974); *Daniel Martin* (Boston: Atlantic-Little, Brown 1977).

1 "A Personal Note," *The Ebony Tower*, p. 117
2 *Islands* (Boston: Little, Brown 1978), p. 83
3 For discussions of the changes Fowles made for the revised edition of *The Magus* see Ronald Binns, "A New Version of *The Magus*," *Critical Quarterly*, 19 (1977), pp. 79-84 and Barry N. Olshen, *John Fowles* (New York: Ungar, 1978), pp. 58-62.
4 Foreword to *The Magus: A Revised Version*, p. 9; Joseph Campbell, "An Interview with John Fowles," *Contemporary Literature*, 17 (1976), pp. 457-8
5 "Making with the Metaphysics" (review of *The Magus*), *Observer* (1 May 1966), p. 27
6 "Interview with Author John Fowles," *Maclean's* (14 November 1977), p. 8
7 Campbell, p. 467
8 "Notes on an Unfinished Novel," in Thomas McCormack, ed., *Afterwords: Novelists on Their Novels* (New York: Harper & Row 1969), p. 170
9 McCormack, p. 165; "My Recollections of Kafka," in R.G. Collins, ed., *The Novel and Its Changing Form* (Winnipeg: University of Manitoba Press 1972), p. 183
10 Quoted in Richard Yallop, "The Reluctant Guru," *Guardian* (9 June 1977), p. 8
11 "John Fowles," interview in Roy Newquist, ed., *Counterpoint* (New York: Simon & Schuster 1964), pp. 220, 222
12 Daniel Halpern, "A Sort of Exile in Lyme Regis," *London Magazine* (March 1971), p. 39
13 *The Aristos*, revised edition (New York: New American Library 1970), p. 193
14 Newquist, pp. 220, 223
15 *Aristos*, pp. 194, 203, 50
16 Halpern, p. 36; *Aristos*, p. 155; Newquist, p. 223; "I Write Therefore I

Am," *Evergreen Review* 8 (1964), p. 17; McCormack, p. 165; "My Recollections of Kafka," p. 185; "I Write Therefore I Am," p. 90

17 Halpern, p. 39; "My Recollections of Kafka," p. 185

18 Campbell, p. 466

19 Halpern, p. 45

20 *Aristos*, p. 27

21 "I Write Therefore I Am," p. 17

22 *Aristos*, p. 42

23 Halpern, p. 35

24 *Aristos*, p. 175

25 McCormack, p. 172

26 *Aristos*, p. 122

27 William J. Palmer, *The Fiction of John Fowles: Tradition, Art and the Loneliness of Selfhood* (Columbia, Missouri: University of Missouri Press 1974), pp. 64–5

28 *Aristos*, p. 53

29 *Aristos*, p. 10

30 "Against Dryness," in Bradbury, ed., *The Novel Today*, p. 31

31 Palmer, p. 78

32 *Aristos*, p. 165

33 McCormack, p. 165; italics omitted

34 "My Recollections of Kafka," p. 188; *Aristos*, p. 157

35 Halpern, p. 43

36 McCormack, p. 169

37 Halpern, p. 46

38 *Maclean's*, p. 8

39 McCormack, p. 170

40 Afterword to Sir Arthur Conan Doyle, *The Hound of the Baskervilles* (London: John Murray and Jonathan Cape 1974), p. 186; foreword to *Poems*, p. vii

41 Halpern, p. 43

42 Newquist, p. 220; Campbell, p. 458; "I Write Therefore I Am," p. 89

43 Yallop, p. 8

44 Afterword to *The Hound of the Baskervilles*, pp. 195–6

45 "Giving the Reader a Choice: A Conversation with John Fowles," *Listener* (31 October 1974), p. 584

46 John Mills, "Fowles' Indeterminacy: An Art of Alternatives," *West Coast Review*, 10 (1975), p. 36

47 This is the definition of *pristine* Fowles supplies in the "Label Words" appendix to the first edition of *The Aristos* (Boston: Little, Brown 1964), p. 239.

48 "The Orgastic Fiction of John Fowles," *Hollins Critic*, 6 (1969), p. 6

49 "Too Much Hocus in the Pocus," p. 4

50 Preface to *The House of the Seven Gables*, vol. 2 of *The Centenary Edition of the Works of Nathaniel Hawthorne* (Columbus, Ohio: Ohio State University Press, 1965), p. 1

51 Afterword to Alain-Fournier, *The Wanderer*, trans. Lowell Bair (New York: New American Library 1971), p. 223

52 "Too Much Hocus in the Pocus," p. 4

53 Preface to *The House of the Seven Gables*, p. 2

54 "I Write Therefore I Am," p. 17

55 Foreword to *Poems*, p. vii

56 Quoted in Donald Fanger, "Solzhenitsyn: Art and Foreign Matter," in John B. Dunlop et al., eds, *Aleksandr Solzhenitsyn: Critical Essays and Documentary Materials* (Belmont, MA: Norland 1973), p. 158

57 Newquist, p. 218

58 "The Achievement of John Fowles," *Encounter*, 35 (1970), p. 64

59 *Aristos*, p. 10

60 "I Write Therefore I Am," p. 17

61 The distinction between *kairos* and *chronos* is Frank Kermode's. See his *The Sense of an Ending: Studies in the Theory of Fiction* (New York: Oxford University Press 1967), pp. 46-7

62 *Maclean's*, p. 4

63 "Hardy and the Hag," in Lance St John Butler, ed., *Thomas Hardy after Fifty Years* (London: Macmillan 1977), p. 35

64 John Fowles and Frank Horvat, *The Tree* (Boston: Little, Brown 1979), [p. 56]

CHAPTER FOUR: V.S. NAIPAUL: CLEAR-SIGHTEDNESS AND SENSIBILITY

Quotations from Naipaul's novels and collections of shorter fiction are from the following editions: *The Mystic Masseur* (London: André Deutsch 1957); *The Suffrage of Elvira* (London: André Deutsch 1958); *Miguel Street* (London: André Deutsch 1959); *A House for Mr Biswas* (London: André Deutsch 1961); *Mr Stone and the Knights Companion* (London: André Deutsch 1963); *The Mimic Men* (London: André Deutsch 1967); *A Flag on the Island* (London: André Deutsch 1967); *In a Free State* (London: André Deutsch 1971); *Guerrillas* (London: André Deutsch 1975); *A Bend in the River* (New York: Knopf 1979).

1 *An Area of Darkness* (London: André Deutsch 1964), pp. 279-80

2 *The Middle Passage* (London: André Deutsch 1962), p. 28; "Terror in Trinidad," *Observer* (26 October 1969), p. 4

3 "The Regional Barrier"; reprinted under the title "London" in *The Over-*

crowded Barracoon and Other Articles (London: André Deutsch 1972), pp. 11, 14

4 "Un Pé Pourrie," *New Yorker* (21 May 1979), p. 141

5 "Without a Place," interview with Ian Hamilton, *TLS* (30 July 1971), p. 36

6 By far the best of the full-length critical studies of Naipaul is Landeg White's *V.S. Naipaul: A Critical Introduction* (London: Macmillan 1975). Robert D. Hamner's *Critical Perspectives on V.S. Naipaul* (Washington, DC: Three Continents Press 1977) contains a full annotated bibliography of books, articles, and reviews by and about Naipaul.

7 "Images," *New Statesman* (24 September 1965), p. 452

8 Gordon Rohlehr, "The Ironic Approach: The Novels of V.S. Naipaul," in Hamner, *Critical Perspectives*, p. 179; William Walsh, *V.S. Naipaul* (Edinburgh: Oliver & Boyd 1973), pp. 30, 42, 43, 71

9 "The Regional Barrier," p. 11

10 "Critics and Criticism," *Bim*, 38 (1964), p. 76

11 "What's Wrong with Being a Snob?," reprinted in Hamner, *Critical Perspectives*, p. 37

12 *V.S. Naipaul: An Introduction to His Work* (London: Heinemann 1972), pp. 130, 7

13 E.H. Gombrich, "Imagery and Art in the Romantic Period," *Meditations on a Hobby Horse and Other Essays on the Theory of Art*, second edition (London: Phaidon 1971), p. 126

14 "Comprehending Borges," *New York Review of Books* (19 October 1972), p. 3

15 *An Area of Darkness*, p. 226

16 "Critics and Criticism," p. 75

17 *India: A Wounded Civilization* (New York: Knopf 1977), pp. 10, 13. In a 1979 interview, Naipaul observed: "In the west, when you write you feel that you write for a certain kind of individual. And you assume that readers can feel themselves to be individuals. This is not an eternal in the world, not a constant. To write a kind of literature that I can find interesting you need to acquire an anxiety about man as an individual, and even in Europe this is a relatively new thing. There are some 'Asiatics' writing, it is true. But they are recording for this outside audience their little tribal rites and they're seen really not as new writers enlarging the sensibilities of readers accustomed to works of real literary value." (Bharati Mukherjee and Robert Boyers, "A Conversation with V.S. Naipaul," *Salmagundi*, 54 [1981], p. 5)

18 Quoted in Elizabeth Hardwick, "Meeting V.S. Naipaul," *New York Times Book Review* (13 May 1979), p. 36

19 "Conrad's Darkness," p. 215; quoted in Hardwick, p. 36

20 "Conrad's Darkness," p. 227
21 "Australia Deserta," *New Statesman* (16 October 1964), p. 513
22 Quoted in Gussow, p. 19
23 "Without a Place," p. 898
24 "Australia Deserta," p. 515
25 "Critics and Criticism," p. 76
26 Quoted in Hardwick, p. 36
27 Quoted in Gussow, p. 22
28 Quoted in Gussow, p. 19
29 "New Novels," *New Statesman* (31 May 1958), p. 705
30 "Australia Deserta," p. 513
31 "The Documentary Heresy," p. 108. John Fowles's opinions on "the documentary approach" are close to Naipaul's: "For me this will always represent a fundamental heresy. A novel is one person's view of life, not a *collage* of documentations" ("I Write Therefore I Am," p. 89).
32 Foreword to *The Middle Passage*, p. 5
33 "New Novels," *New Statesman* (14 March 1959), p. 376
34 "Conrad's Darkness," pp. 220, 222; the last phrase, from Anthony Powell's *The Acceptance World*, is quoted by Naipaul in "The Regional Barrier," p. 10. John Fowles's description of the creative activity of his mind is closely similar: "I know when I am writing well. I am writing with more than the sum of my acquired knowledge, skill and experience; with something from outside myself" ("I Write Therefore I Am," p. 89). To describe this process Fowles also uses the word "magic," which he defines as "one's arrival at some truth or development one could not have logically predicted or expected (*Islands*, p. 30).
35 "Critics and Criticism," p. 77
36 "V.S. Naipaul Tells How Writing Changes a Writer," *Tapia*, 3 (2 December 1973), p. 11
37 These articles were reprinted by Naipaul in *The Return of Eva Perón, with The Killings of Trinidad*.
38 *India: A Wounded Civilization*, pp. 185-6. The phrase "the creative activity of the mind," quoted by Naipaul, is Balzac's.
39 "Speaking of Writing: V.S. Naipaul," *The Times* (2 January 1964), p. 11; Israel Shenker, "V.S. Naipaul: Man without a Society," *New York Times Book Review* (17 October 1971), p. 23
40 "Unfurnished Entrails: The Novelist V.S. Naipaul in Conversation with Jim Douglas Henry," *Listener* (25 November 1971), p. 721; "Writing is Magic," p. 57; "V.S. Naipaul Tells How Writing Changes a Writer," p. 11
41 Quoted in Gussow, p. 22

42 *The Middle Passage*, p. 72

43 "Fresh Winds from the West," *Spectator* (2 May 1958), p. 565

44 *India: A Wounded Civilization*, pp. 12-13

45 *The Pleasures of Exile* (London: Michael Joseph 1960), p. 225

46 Foreword to Seepersad Naipaul, *The Adventures of Gurudeva and Other Stories* (London: André Deutsch 1976), p. 15

47 *The Middle Passage*, p. 70

48 "The Novelist V.S. Naipaul Talks to Nigel Bingham about His Childhood in Trinidad," *Listener* (7 September 1972), p. 306

49 Foreword to *The Adventures of Gurudeva*, p. 17

50 In a discussion of the achievement of *A House for Mr Biswas*, A.J. Gurr ("Third-World Novels: Naipaul and After," *Journal of Commonwealth Literature*, 7 [1972]) suggestively cites George Eliot's famous dictum: "The greatest benefit we owe to the artist is the extension of our sympathies ... a picture of human life such as a great artist can give, surprises even the trivial and the selfish into that attention to what is apart from themselves, which may be called the raw material of moral sentiment" ("The Natural History of German Life," *Essays of George Eliot*, Thomas Pinney, ed. [New York: Columbia University Press 1963], p. 270).

51 *The Middle Passage*, pp. 81-2

52 "Speaking of Writing," p. 11

53 Dan Jacobson, "Self-Help in Hot Places," review of *A House for Mr Biswas*, *New Statesman* (29 September 1961), p. 440

54 "Writing Is Magic," p. 57

55 Introduction to Giuseppe di Lampedusa, *Two Stories and a Memory* (New York: Pantheon 1962), p. 13

56 "Speaking of Writing," p. 11

57 "Climacteric," *New Statesman* (31 May 1963), p. 831

58 "London Again," *New York Review of Books* (19 March 1964), p. 21

59 "Pooter," *The Times* (9 November 1968), p. 23

60 "The Writer," reprinted in Hamner, *Critical Perspectives*, p. 32

61 "Unfurnished Entrails," p. 721

62 In *The Middle Passage* (pp. 103-4) Naipaul describes his reaction to "the sight of exposed food in the midst of [the] dust and mud" of an Amerindian hut in British Guiana: it "had the same effect on me as the screech of chalk on a board ... I felt then that reverence for food – rules for its handling, interdictions – was one of the essentials of civilization."

63 M.M. Mahood, *The Colonial Encounter: A Reading of Six Novels* (London: Rex Collings 1977), pp. 158, 164

64 White, p. 185

65 *The Overcrowded Barracoon*, pp. 250, 253
66 *India: A Wounded Civilization*, p. 150
67 "Without a Place," p. 897
68 "Without a Dog's Chance," *New York Review of Books* (18 May 1972), p. 31
69 "Conrad's Darkness," pp. 207, 216, 219
70 "Unfurnished Entrails," p. 721; quoted in Alex Hamilton, "Living a Life on Approval," *Guardian* (4 October 1971), p. 8
71 "Without a Place," p. 898
72 "The Documentary Heresy," pp. 107-8
73 Quoted in Gussow, p. 22
74 Quoted in Hardwick, p. 36
75 "General Preface to the Novels and Poems [Wessex Edition 1912]," in Harold Orel, ed., *Thomas Hardy's Personal Writings* (Lawrence: University of Kansas Press 1966), p. 49
76 "Without a Dog's Chance," p. 31

CONCLUSION

1 "Fear and Trembling at Yale," *American Scholar*, 46 (1977), p. 467

Index